S0-FBX-677

Propaganda Analysis

A Study of Inferences
Made from Nazi Propaganda in World War II

Alexander L. George

The RAND Corporation

HM
263
G43

ROW, PETERSON AND COMPANY
Evanston, Illinois   White Plains, New York

74645

Copyright © 1959
The RAND Corporation

All rights reserved for all countries, including the right of translation

5606

Library of Congress "cataloguing in
source" information for this book appears at the end of the Index.

Permission to quote from the following books has been granted by Doubleday & Co., Inc.:
    The Goebbels Diaries, translated by Louis P. Lochner. Copyright 1948 by
The Fireside Press, Inc.
    Crusade in Europe, by Dwight D. Eisenhower. Copyright 1948 by Double-
day & Co., Inc.
    Joseph Goebbels, by Curt Riess. Copyright 1948 by Curt Riess.

MANUFACTURED IN THE UNITED STATES OF AMERICA

For My Mother

Preface

During World War II all major powers obtained important information by monitoring the mass communications of opponents, allies, and neutrals.

In the United States the task of monitoring and reporting on the broadcasts of other countries was assigned to the Foreign Broadcast Intelligence Service (FBIS) of the Federal Communications Commission (FCC). Other agencies made arrangements to read and excerpt significant materials from selected newspapers throughout the world.

The mass communications media of other countries provided useful factual information to a number of American agencies concerned in some manner with the conduct of the war. Among these were the Office of War Information, the Office of Strategic Services, the Board of Economic Warfare, and the Departments of War, Navy, and State. Interest in world-wide mass communications was heightened by wartime conditions because the difficulty of obtaining information through other channels made these mass media at times the exclusive source of information about certain areas, notably the Far East.

This material was subjected to propaganda analysis as well as to examination for purely factual information. Propaganda analysis, or the analysis of propaganda communications, has two general purposes: (*a*) the summary, or selective description, of what is being said by the propagandist and (*b*) the interpretation of the intentions, strategy, and calculations behind propaganda communications. These two aspects of propaganda analysis correspond to the distinction, familiar in the theory of content analysis,[1] between *description* of content and *inferences* made from content as to the intentions and calculations behind the propaganda. While both types of propaganda-analysis results—description and inference—were of interest to intelligence specialists and policy-makers, inferences were potentially more valuable and also more difficult for the propaganda analysts to make. Accordingly, this report focuses largely on the problem of making propaganda-analysis inferences.

Insofar as is known, only the United States and Great Britain made efforts to develop systematic techniques of propaganda analysis. In the United States, the Analysis Division of the FBIS was specifically charged with the task of propaganda analysis. Although intelligence and research agencies elsewhere in the government also engaged in this activity, there were some important differences between the propaganda analysis performed by the FCC and that of other agencies. In the first place, the FCC relied almost exclusively on examination of a single source—mass communications; and at first it examined only radio materials, but later used press materials as well. In contrast, other agencies combined analysis of propaganda communications with the use of other types of intelligence materials. A second difference was that only the FCC analysts studied *all* the available radio and press output. In other agencies investigators were more selective in their coverage of propaganda materials, focusing upon excerpts bearing on special subject matters.

The FCC analysts, therefore, studied propaganda exclusively and intensively. Over a period of time they acquired specialized and detailed knowledge of the behavior of individual propaganda sources in issuing communications. They attempted to identify the characteristic patterns of communication of each source in different types of situations in order to apply the knowledge thus obtained in making inferences as to the intentions and calculations of the propagandist.

In their work the FCC analysts were confronted with two difficulties which are also encountered to some extent in the study of other types of manipulative communication. The propaganda analyst cannot exercise much control or influence over what the propagandist says but must work with whatever the propagandist offers him. Then, he must reckon with the possibility of deception, for the propagandist is not unmindful of the need for withholding information of direct interest to the analyst.

After the war considerable interest was expressed in a systematic assessment of the utility of the new propaganda-analysis techniques which had been developed and applied during the war. The value of propaganda analysis as a tool of intelligence and research for policy-making purposes was itself the subject of diverse opinions.[2] While a large number of inferences had been made during the war, the accuracy of all but a few of them was unknown.

The desire for an evaluation of wartime propaganda analysis centered more upon the questions of its accuracy and its potential uses than upon the actual use made of its results during the war. Among the general questions to which answers were sought were the following: Is the propaganda-analysis approach better than less systematic forms of "educated guessing" by informed observers, journalists, etc.? Is propaganda analysis better than other intelligence and research methods for answering certain types of questions?

Questions of this type can be answered conclusively only by rigorous statistical analysis of the results of an appropriate trial or test situation. The author undertook the present study with the realization that in several important respects the propaganda-analysis operation conducted by the FCC during World War II did not constitute an ideal test situation. The decision to appraise its performance was made, nonetheless, for several compelling reasons.

In the first place, it would be difficult to reproduce in a research experiment the great variety of factors that affect propaganda analysis carried out under operational conditions. In any case, since propaganda analysis had received during the war a major operational trial, it seemed advisable to evaluate this experience as fully as possible before undertaking the difficult task of devising more systematic tests.

The author selected the FCC analyses of German propaganda for assessment, rather than its analyses of other countries' propaganda, for several compelling reasons. Vast quantities of captured German war records and numerous interviews with leading German officials were available for documenting the policy intentions and calculations behind the propaganda which the FCC analysts studied. Matching FCC inferences against historical evidence of this type made it possible to determine the accuracy of many, though by no means all, of the inferences. The object of this verification procedure, however, was not so much to pass judgment upon the performance of the FCC analysts as to appraise the general utility of the techniques which they had employed.

In practice it proved difficult to make a wholly adequate statistical analysis of the successes and failures achieved by the FCC analysts. The fact that 81 per cent of the FCC inferences that could be scored proved to be accurate cannot be taken as a conclusive demonstration of the utility of propaganda analysis for a number of reasons, which are discussed at some length in Part IV and in Appendix I.

Nonetheless, the FCC analysts made correct inferences on a wide variety of questions of interest to policy-makers at the time, and they were also able to give, over a period of months, a continually reliable analysis on a given intelligence problem (for example, the private expectations of Nazi leaders regarding a possible attempt by the Allies to establish a second front). This strongly suggests that the propaganda-analysis method is capable of more than isolated, hit-or-miss successes.

Perhaps the most challenging task faced in evaluating the FCC propaganda analysis was that of codifying the procedures employed by the FCC analysts. When the FCC began its operations, there existed no blueprint of procedures for drawing inferences about the intentions and calculations of a propagandist from his communications. The FCC analysts had to develop their own techniques and methods of making inferences. In a typical FCC propaganda analysis, the analyst inferred, for example, that certain contents in Nazi propaganda indicated that a particular propaganda strategy was being implemented, or that a particular political or military policy had been decided upon, or that Nazi leaders were privately expecting reverses or successes, or that there had been changes in the situation confronting them which had not yet been publicly revealed and were not yet known to Allied observers.

The FCC analysts usually gave reasons to support these inferences and, in many cases, to justify rejection of alternative inferences. These reasons were of various kinds. In one instance an FCC analyst might hold that what was now being said in Nazi propaganda was evidence of a change in Nazi intentions because a similar shift in propaganda had occurred on previous occasions when a similar change in policy took place. He might remark on the failure, in another case, of Nazi propagandists to say something that would normally be expected in the situation at hand. In yet another case, he might be impressed by changes in Nazi propaganda strategy on a certain subject, which could be accounted for only by postulating certain events and decisions behind the scenes or by inferring that Nazi expectations about the outcome of the action under discussion had changed.

Even a cursory inspection of the work of the FCC analysts yielded many useful impressions of the way in which they went about making inferences. To codify and generalize their methods of making inferences, however, was a much more difficult task. The reasoning on behalf of the inferences was rarely complete; that is, the logical structure of the inferences was neither fully stated nor readily apparent in the published FCC reports. In some cases the analysts based their inferences upon generalizations and reasoning which were not made explicit; in other cases their inferences did not follow clearly from the evidence in the propaganda or from the incomplete reasoning which they offered in their reports; in still other cases they gave fairly detailed accounts of the reasons for considering one inference plausible but seemed to give little or no attention to alternative hypotheses which might be equally plausible. At times they drew attention to certain features in Nazi propaganda as if to indicate that these constituted the evidence for their hypotheses; but, on closer inspection, their reports and reasoning did not bear this out, and the evidence contained in the propaganda remained ambiguous or unclearly stated.

The procedures and methods of making inferences employed by the FCC analysts were therefore not entirely systematic. The FCC inferences rested to a considerable extent on the intuitive skill and judgment of persons who had become expert in the ways of Nazi propaganda and political behavior but who never fully articulated their expertise.

Yet the fact that so many of the FCC analyses turned out to be correct, when compared with the historical evidence, made it highly desirable that an attempt should be made to codify the procedures they followed in making inferences. The way in which this task was approached, the difficulties encountered, and the results achieved are described at length in the chapters which follow.

In the end, it proved possible to articulate and to codify many aspects of propaganda-analysis procedure. It was also found that the reasons for the success or failure of specific inferences could frequently be identified. It seems, therefore, that propaganda analysis can become a reasonably objective diagnostic tool for making certain kinds of inferences and that its techniques are capable of refinement and improvement.

It would be overly sanguine, however, to expect that all the inferential procedures employed in propaganda analysis have been or can be fully objectified and codified. A distinction needs to be drawn between the procedures followed to infer the *actions* taken by a political elite and its propagandists and those used to infer the speaker's intended *meaning*. ("Actions" in this sense covers both (*a*) the steps taken, by the elite and propagandists, and (*b*) the calculations, or determinants, behind these steps.) As indicated in the preceding paragraph, it proved possible to codify to a considerable extent the methods employed in inferring *action,* but it was somewhat less feasible to characterize the methods of inferring *meaning.* The propaganda analyst's task of inferring the speaker's intended meaning and that of inferring action and the determinants of action are, of course, interrelated. The analyst's first step in many inferences is to estimate the meanings intended by the speaker, that is, the sense in which he uses the words in question. ("Capitalism," for instance, conveys quite different things when used by an American and by a Russian.) The next step, from a formal or logical standpoint, is to infer the speaker's purpose, or propaganda goal. The analyst must find the connection between his inference as to the speaker's meaning and his inference as to the speaker's purpose. In doing this, he links the meaning and action components of the behavior sequence under study, since the speaker's purpose is one of the aspects of the action, as that term is used here. An inference about the speaker's purpose (or propaganda goal), in turn, may lead to inferences about other aspects of the action, such as the political policy or intention which that propaganda goal is designed to promote or the calculations and situational estimates on which that policy and that propaganda strategy are based.

In order to determine the communicator's precise intended meaning the propaganda analyst makes as intensive an assessment as he thinks necessary of the situational and behavioral, as well as the linguistic, contexts of the words in question. It is this aspect of his procedure, often highly interpretive, which it is difficult to objectify and codify. The analyst in this type of qualitative content analysis is willing to utilize an interpretive procedure which is of uncertain reliability because he attaches great importance to securing a valid determination of the speaker's intended meaning. In contrast, in what is known as quantitative[3] content analysis, the investigator often accepts restrictions on taking contextual factors into account in estimating meaning so that he can better insure the reliability of his results.

The most the writer was able to do in the direction of codifying the analyst's assessment of the meanings of words was to specify the elements of situational and behavioral context which the analyst took into account in inferring the speaker's intended meaning. It should also be reiterated that the two processes of inferring the speaker's intended meaning and of inferring his purpose are closely interrelated and that, therefore, this type of analysis of meaning takes place *within* an action context.

In the course of this study the writer encountered general methodological questions common to other fields within the behavioral sciences. The effort to clarify the procedures of inferring meaning and action in propaganda analysis, for instance, is a manifestation of a widespread problem, namely, that of transforming inferential procedures and expert judgments which at the present time are largely in the nature of intuitive art into science. The problem encountered in propaganda analysis has its counterpart in many diagnostic fields —for example, clinical psychology, psychiatry, psychoanalysis, clinical medicine, and the analysis of responses to "open-end" questions in opinion and attitude surveys, that is, questions to which the person interviewed is allowed to reply freely and at length in his own words.

No mechanical or clerical procedure has yet been devised which will replace the skill of the experienced diagnostician. Yet many aspects of a diagnostic technique, such as propaganda analysis, can be made more explicit. By making only *some* of them more explicit, it is true, the expert cannot hope to provide an account of his procedures that will permit other investigators to proceed as he would in all cases.

Nonetheless, by making the bases for his judgments at least somewhat explicit, the propaganda analyst performs a valuable service in several respects. First, he gives other persons—the clients for his findings or other propaganda analysts—at least some grounds for evaluating his inferences. Second, by specifying which types of information and knowledge about the political elite and its propaganda organization are relevant for making specific inferences, the analyst identifies areas for additional research which may in time substantially raise the reliability of inferences. Finally, he contributes to the development of a body of knowledge about his technique and thus to a doctrine of propaganda analysis. However rudimentary it may be, such a doctrine is useful for teaching the skill to qualified and talented students. In time, as inferential procedures continue to be systematized and clarified, it is hoped that better and more accurate results will be achieved. This, at least, has been the rationale for the effort made throughout this study to codify propaganda-analysis procedures.

For purposes of discussion this report treats separately the procedures used in propaganda analysis (*a*) to determine the choice of political and propaganda actions and (*b*) to interpret the propagandist's intended meanings. It is true that, from a formal or logical standpoint, the task of interpreting a speaker's meanings is prior to that of inferring something about the national policies and actions which the propaganda is supposed to implement. Nonetheless, the decision was made to treat "action" before "meaning" in this book because, as indicated in Part I, it is the action framework which is distinctive of propaganda analysis and which sets the problems for the propaganda analyst. Moreover, as will be seen in Part II, it is within an action context that the propaganda analyst approaches the task of interpreting the speaker's intended meanings.

Part II also takes up the limitations of the quantitative variant of content analysis for purposes of propaganda analysis. Next, a non-quantitative variant of content analysis which has been found particularly useful in propaganda analysis is described and explained. Readers without any previous background in content analysis may find it useful to glance at the Introduction and first chapter of Part II before beginning Part I.

Part III outlines a situational approach to propaganda analysis. It illustrates with many concrete examples from the FCC's experience how the propaganda-analysis methods outlined in Part I can be employed to predict an opponent's major actions, to decipher an opponent's propaganda anticipation of action that may be directed at his side, and to make inferences about favorable and unfavorable changes in the opponent's situation.

Part IV reports the results of the statistical appraisal of the successful and unsuccessful inferences made by the FCC analysts.

ALEXANDER L. GEORGE

Santa Monica, California
January, 1959

NOTES

1. On this point see Bernard Berelson, *Content Analysis in Communication Research* (The Free Press, Glencoe, Ill., 1952).

2. For critical appraisals see Leonard W. Doob, *Public Opinion and Propaganda* (Henry Holt and Co., New York, 1948), pp. 195 and 307, and Edward Shils, *The Present State of American Sociology* (The Free Press, Glencoe, Ill., 1948), p. 38. For favorable judgments see Bruce Lockhart, *Comes the Reckoning* (Putnam and Co., Ltd., London, 1947), p. 154; Wallace Carroll, *Persuade Or Perish* (Houghton Mifflin Co., Boston, 1948), pp. 152 ff.; and R. H. S. Crossman, "Psychological Warfare," *Journal of the Royal United Services Institution* (August, 1952), p. 328.

3. For a discussion of other differences between qualitative and quantitative content analyses see Part II, pp. 77–121.

Acknowledgments

This study was prepared as part of the research program under-taken for the U.S. Air Force by The RAND Corporation. The main results of the study were originally reported directly to the Air Force and other interested federal agencies some years ago. Many people have contributed to the study, some by writings of their own from which I have drawn, others by offering helpful criticism of the manuscript.

I am particularly indebted to Hans Speier. During World War II, as Chief of the German Section of the Analysis Division, Foreign Broadcast Intelligence Service, Federal Communications Commission, he prepared or supervised most of the studies of Nazi propaganda analyzed in this book. As a junior member of the staff of the Analysis Division, I was privileged to contribute to some of those studies and to become acquainted at first hand with the difficulties of propaganda analysis. We often wished in those days, when we were attempting so boldly and yet so uncertainly to make infer-ences from Nazi propaganda, that we could lay hold of the direc-tives which inspired certain statements or really know what Goeb-bels' calculations were at various turning points of the war. When records of the Nazi conduct of the war fell into American hands after the defeat of Germany, Hans Speier encouraged me to under-take an examination of them with a view to determining where we had been correct, and where incorrect, in our wartime inferences and, more important and more difficult, why. Such an assessment and analysis, we both thought, might contribute to the development of a *method* of propaganda analysis. During the past several years, as Chief of the Social Science Division of The RAND Corporation, Hans Speier has made it possible for me, as a staff member, to de-vote a considerable amount of time to completing this study and has generously given me the benefit of his judgment of the manuscript in its various stages of development.

Portions of the manuscript and earlier drafts of it were read by Bernard Berelson, Irving L. Janis, Abraham Kaplan, Harold D.

Lasswell, Ithiel de Sola Pool, and Edward A. Shils. Their knowledge and judgment saved me from errors and helped sharpen the focus of the research.

A similar task was performed by several colleagues at The RAND Corporation: Martin Albaum, W. Phillips Davison, Herbert Goldhamer, Joseph M. Goldsen, Victor M. Hunt, Nathan Leites, and Myron Rush. To all of them I want to express my warm appreciation. I am also indebted to Andrew W. Marshall for technical assistance with the statistical analysis in Part IV, and to Eric Willenz for help in the collection and processing of data. Elise F. Kendrick, Sibylle O. Crane, and Emmanuel G. Mesthene provided indispensable editorial services.

I would like to thank Professor Avery Leiserson, presently chairman of the Political Science Department of Vanderbilt University. He was chairman of the thesis committee which accepted this study as a dissertation for the Ph.D. degree at the University of Chicago and was helpful and encouraging throughout.

An earlier version of the material in Part II of the book was presented to the Work Conference on Theory and Technique of Content Analysis, held in February, 1955, at the University of Illinois under the sponsorship of the Committee on Linguistics and Psychology of the Social Science Research Council. I am grateful to Charles E. Osgood, chairman of the Committee, and other participants in the conference for their stimulating discussion and helpful comments.

Appreciation is expressed for permission to quote from works published by E. P. Dutton & Co., Inc.; Doubleday & Co., Inc.; Oxford University Press, Inc.; and the University of Minnesota Press.

The manuscript was completed during 1956–57, while I was a Fellow at the Center for Advanced Study in the Behavioral Sciences. It is a pleasure to express my appreciation to Dr. Ralph W. Tyler, director of the Center, and to his staff for the opportunities and services which they provided, and to colleagues at the Center, especially Dr. David Hamburg, who discussed various aspects of the research with me.

A. L. G.

Table of Contents

Part II: Propaganda Analysis and the Study of Communication

Part III: Methodology and Applications

Part IV: Validation of Inferences

Appendixes

List of Case Studies

Part I

Propaganda Analysis and the Study of Action

Introduction

In recent years specialists in the methodology of social research have become increasingly aware of the need for systematic methods which would be intermediate between the relatively intuitive, impressionistic approaches which still characterize much social and political investigation and the precise procedures of the most advanced sectors of the natural sciences. Increasing attention is being given to the possibility of articulating and codifying such intermediate methodologies.

Among the types of inquiry in which the possibility of systematization is being explored is that which has been called "causal analysis in the single case," that is, the attempt to infer or explain some of the causes (or antecedent conditions) of or reasons for individual instances of behavior or choice of action. In this connection, the authors of a leading casebook on research methodology [1] have recently suggested that efforts be made to codify the actual procedures employed by the historian, the clinical psychologist, the linguist, and others who study problems of behavior without making much use of quantitative research methods. For purposes of illustration the authors of this casebook examine a number of market and social research studies which exemplify what is aptly called "the empirical analysis of action." Common to all of these is the investigator's effort to infer components of purposive behavior which are not usually accessible to direct observation and to account for individual action in situations of choice.

Methodological advances in the empirical analysis of action and in the causal analysis of the single case would be of considerable potential significance for political analysis and for other research of interest to policy-makers, so much of which falls squarely within this area of methodological investigation.

The Study of Propaganda in an Action Framework

Propaganda analysis may in fact be regarded as a specific application of the empirical analysis of action. Moreover, inferences made in propaganda analysis are often causal analyses of the single case.

The specific intentions and calculations of the communicator, and sometimes the situational factors (that is, the actual events and conditions in his environment) which affect his choices of action, are inferred from the character of his propaganda communications. Propaganda analysis focuses upon the use of communication as an instrument of political policy. Propaganda analysis, therefore, cannot separate the study of political communication from its action framework.

In this respect propaganda analysis differs strikingly from those content analyses of political communication which attempt to infer the latent, atemporal political *attitudes* of the communicator,[2] for that type of study usually pays minimum attention to the manipulative and propagandistic aspects of the communication from which the source's attitudes are inferred.

In the past several decades systematic research and theoretical speculation on political communication have had a predominantly scientific orientation. That is, they have been concerned not so much with the problem of causal analysis in the individual case as with the formulation of broad generalizations and, ultimately, of general laws governing political communication.

In propaganda analysis, however, as in historical explanation,[3] the investigator is not interested in scientific inquiry per se. Like the historian, the propaganda analyst seeks to clarify the relationship between individual events. In order to do so, he sometimes decides to treat events as the scientist does, as instances of a type or as members of a class. He may also attempt to investigate relationships between classes of events. But, since the practical object of his inquiry is to infer specific antecedent conditions of individual actions, the propaganda analyst will readily abandon this approach, if it does not succeed, in favor of a method which is less explicitly scientific and closer to forms of inference and explanation utilized in everyday life. He will use available knowledge in drawing his inferences but will do so within the framework of a relatively intuitive logic-of-the-situation approach.

The fact that his inferences are therefore relatively interpretive, however, does not mean that the propaganda analyst dispenses with generalizations about political communication and political behavior. From the standpoint of formal logic, even interpretive inferences about the intentions and calculations of a communicator rest upon generalizations of some sort, though these may be in part trivial and may remain largely implicit.

Generalizations employed in a logic-of-the-situation approach are quite different from those aimed at in efforts to develop a science of political communication based on statistical correlations between content features and either speaker or audience variables. In the former approach the form and content of the generalizations, and the theoretical structures which they imply, are shaped by the historical and action frameworks within which the propaganda analysis is conducted (see Chapter 5).

The study of political communications within an action framework, as in propaganda analysis, has implications for theory which have not been fully investigated. Propaganda analysis is essentially in accord with the rationale of games of strategy, as it is one of the tools which each player in a conflict situation may use in attempting to improve his information about his opponent's intentions, strategy, policy calculations, expectations, and estimates of the situation. It might be desirable to attempt to construct a theory of political communication using games of strategy involving conflict as an analogy. In such an attempt behavioral models would be needed which would focus squarely on factors affecting choice of strategy and action and which, in doing so, would take account of various limits on rational calculation and of the role of information—or intelligence—about the opponent.

Because of its implications for a general theory of political communication, the author feels that propaganda analysis merits the attention not only of those interested in its immediate and pragmatic value as an intelligence technique but also of those concerned with advancing the scientific study of political communication. The author found that, in the course of his attempt to systematize the propaganda analysis conducted by the FCC during World War II and to formalize its methodology, it was necessary for him to embark upon the construction, however tentative and incomplete, of a general theoretical model for the study of propaganda as an instrument of political action. Such a preliminary model appears in Part I of this study; the situational component of it is elaborated in Part III.

Problems and Procedures of Codification

Part I reports in detail the results of the writer's effort to reconstruct and codify the methods which the FCC analysts developed and successfully employed in making inferences. Before the FCC began its propaganda-analysis operations, various efforts had been made to adapt the technique of content analysis so that it could be used to infer the intentions of totalitarian governments. Pioneer work by Harold D. Lasswell and his associates, by Ernst Kris, Hans Speier, and others offered useful suggestions as to how this problem might be approached. Some of this early work is reviewed in Chapter 3.

These early procedures and methods underwent considerable adaptation and revision in the course of the FCC operation. As they were compelled to turn out concrete results of immediate value, the FCC analysts were forced to experiment and to develop procedures that would produce inferences on subjects of interest to their clients. Although there were undoubtedly some advantages in working on a pragmatic task under real-life conditions, the FCC analysts were also laboring under certain disadvantages, such as deadlines and work pressures which would be unusual in a study of such difficult problems in leisurely academic milieus. For example, it was hardly ever possible to repeat a propaganda analysis by employing different investigators, to analyze the same material with different methods simultaneously, to compare systematically the yield of different methods and their value for different purposes, or to engage in painstaking methodological discussions.

As a result, the procedures employed by the FCC analysts were not fully articulated. They had no special terminology for much of what they were doing. Nor did they attempt to formulate rules of inference or criteria for weighing the plausibility of their inferences. In brief, the content analysis performed by the FCC was in many respects a creative, intuitive process without a systematic basis or doctrine, although this is not to say that the FCC analysts were unaware of methodological considerations.

The author used the following procedure in codifying the largely implicit methodology of the FCC's propaganda analysis.

1. The first step in constructing a method of inference for the analysis of a particular kind of action or purposive behavior is to *classify the specific inferences which the investigator wishes to make.* In the present case such a classification, or typology, was derived empirically from an inspection of the inferences which the FCC analysts had actually made. The author identified seven general types of inferences, which included most of the specific infer-

ences made by the FCC. All are inferences as to factors (referred to here as "antecedent conditions") which helped determine the content of the communications. The classification and illustrative inferences are presented in Chapter 1.

2. The next step was to *locate these antecedent conditions within an over-all system of behavior* of which the propaganda content was the end product, or dependent variable. That is, the author had to identify other possible antecedent conditions which the FCC analysts did not attempt to infer but which affected those components of propaganda and political behavior about which they did make inferences. Then, having identified *all* the major antecedent conditions of propaganda communications, the author next had to *depict the general relationships between the various antecedent conditions* comprising this system of behavior. The results of this phase of the study are reported in Chapter 2.

3. The next step was to *identify patterns of reasoning employed in individual inferences* and thereby codify the more general methods which the FCC analysts used to infer the types of antecedent conditions of interest to them. The results of this effort are reported in Chapter 4. Since several steps were involved in the codification of methods of inference, it will be useful to discuss in some detail here the problems which were encountered.

In undertaking to codify propaganda-analysis methodology, it seemed advantageous for the writer to concentrate attention initially on those FCC inferences which had been correct. The fact that they had been correct provided at least some basis for hoping that the methods on which they had presumably been based were valid.

There are in practice various ways of testing or assessing the accuracy of inferences derived by means of propaganda analysis. In the first place, a propaganda-analysis inference can be compared with more direct evidence of the speaker's intention, his strategy, calculations, state of information, etc. Second, inferences from propaganda analysis can be cross-checked with conclusions about the same problems derived from other types of evidence. Third, a propaganda-analysis inference may be assessed by an internal check on the logic and plausibility of the reasoning on which it rests and by evaluating, in turn, the degree of confirmation enjoyed by the generalizations employed, tacitly or explicitly, by the analyst in supporting that specific inference. (One of the results of a fuller codification of propaganda analysis, as attempted in this report, is that it facilitates assessment of individual inferences by means of this internal check.) Finally, in some cases, propaganda-analysis inferences of the speaker's intentions, policies, etc., can be made the basis for predicting something about his subsequent actions. If employed with appropriate caution, the subsequent success or failure of such predictions can be taken sometimes as evidence of the validity of the initial propaganda-analysis prediction.

The first of these methods of assessing inferences was employed in the present evaluation of wartime propaganda analysis. Thus, an attempt was made to validate or verify inferences of Nazi intentions, etc., by comparing them with historical materials on the Nazi conduct of the war to which access was obtained after the war. Of course, the fact that any single propaganda-analysis inference was found to be accurate would not offer much assurance as to the validity of the method used to make that particular inference. An inference can always be right for the wrong reasons. Accordingly, a large number of correct inferences were examined, for, if a common pattern of reasoning could be discerned in a great many successful inferences, it would seem probable that that pattern of reasoning had contributed to the successes achieved and had demonstrated its utility.

The preceding remarks should not be taken as implying that only correct inferences were studied in reconstructing and evaluating the methods employed by the FCC analysts. For, admittedly, much can often be learned from mistakes as well as from successes. Thus, for example, one test of the general methods reconstructed from successful FCC inferences was to see whether they enabled one to make a satisfactory critical diagnosis of inferences which had turned out to be incorrect or were in other ways faulty. Incorrect and ambiguous FCC inferences were analyzed from this standpoint, and the codified methods did help to pinpoint deficiencies in procedure or reasoning which seemed to account, in many cases, for their having been incorrect or faulty (see also p. 140).

In their reports the FCC analysts usually gave some of the evidence and reasoning on which their inferences were based, as a means of indicating how plausible they considered various inferences to be. But this reasoning was usually incomplete and often even sketchy. The first task in codification, therefore, was to make explicit, reconstruct, and fill in the reasoning which could logically be presumed to support each inference. This procedure is usually referred to in the literature of logical analysis as "rational reconstruction."

In practice, efforts at rational reconstruction are not always success-ful. In the present study, however, they were facilitated by the fact that at least some of the FCC inferences were models of relatively complete and explicit reasoning. The detailed structure of these in-ferences was helpful in guiding efforts to identify the missing portions in the reasoning of other inferences. Then, too, the writer benefited by having had experience as a propaganda analyst in the FCC operation under review as well as in a joint British-American propaganda-analysis unit.

This reconstruction of individual inferences was undertaken as a preliminary to the codifying of general "methods of inference," a term used to refer to the patterns or logical structures of reasoning employed in deriving certain types of conclusions from certain types of premises. There was, of course, no guarantee that any patterns would be discovered in the work of the FCC analysts. Only recon-struction and comparison of a large number of individual inferences would make it possible, in time, to decide whether any general pat-terns of reasoning could be identified.

Because so much of the reasoning for many individual inferences was implicit, initial efforts at articulation often proved unsatisfactory; in some cases, the problem had to be reconsidered a number of times. Tentative reconstructions periodically led the writer to jump to pre-liminary (and often sketchy and erroneous) codifications of gen-eral methods of inference. An attempt was then made to utilize these tentative codifications, in turn, as guides to the reconstruction of in-dividual inferences. In practice, therefore, there was a reciprocal re-lationship between the two tasks. The writer was forced many times to turn from one task to the other, to retrace his steps, and to abandon or refine individual reconstructions as well as preliminary codifica-tions. Tentative reconstructions of individual inferences were tested against tentative formulations of general methods of inference and vice versa. As a result, both reconstructions and formulations were progressively sharpened and brought into consonance with one an-other.

At an early stage in the study it was decided that interviews with the former FCC analysts would not provide a short cut or a more re-liable basis for filling in the incomplete reasoning in their inferences or for codifying the general methods of inference implicit in their work. Only intensive and repeated interviews might have offered useful results. Since this procedure was not feasible, no interviews of this type were undertaken. It should be noted, however, that Hans

Speier, who had been chief of the section which produced the German propaganda analyses, reviewed earlier versions of all the case studies presented in this volume. His comments frequently required the writer to reconsider tentative reconstructions of inferences.

Possible Uses and Limitations of the Codification of Propaganda-Analysis Methodology

In the end, two general and rather different methods of inference were identified in the work of the FCC analysts. These are referred to in this report as the "direct" and the "indirect" methods and are described in detail in Chapter 4. Of these two approaches, the indirect method is the more complex and is perhaps less familiar to students of methodology. It derives particular interest from the fact that it was developed in an operational situation and proved useful in making inferences from highly instrumental communications (communications primarily aimed at manipulating audiences rather than at conveying information or expressing the real thoughts and emotions of the communicator)—a task at which methods based on simple statistical correlations between content features and communicator variables had been unsuccessful.

At the same time, the essential features of the indirect method are not novel. It closely resembles what has been termed above the "logic-of-the-situation approach," which is the approach used in everyday life to infer another person's state of mind and is the method followed by historians, political analysts, and other investigators concerned with the analysis of different types of action. The indirect method and the logic-of-the-situation approach appear to have a certain resemblance, too, to what, in psychology and psychiatry, is often referred to as "clinical judgment."

Although commonly used, the logic-of-the-situation approach is, as a rule, methodologically undeveloped. It is generally employed in a relatively intuitive, or interpretive, fashion. What is novel about the logic-of-the-situation approach as it appears in the indirect method of propaganda analysis, then, is the extent to which it has been made explicit and codified. In this study an attempt has been made to articulate the major components, or inferential steps, of a logic-of-the-situation judgment and to indicate the kinds of generalizations logically required to support each step in a logic-of-the-situation assessment.

For this reason the model, or action schema, for propaganda analysis presented in Chapter 2 (p. 25) and the detailed codification of the indirect method presented in Chapter 4 may prove suggestive for other applications of the logic-of-the-situation approach, especially for investigators who attempt to infer invisible components of purposive behavior and action from a speaker's instrumental communications.

Research into political behavior often utilizes analysis of communication materials. The purposes and techniques of this analysis may vary substantially, however, from those which characterize the type of propaganda analysis studied here. It is important to recognize that the methods developed and employed by the FCC analysts in making their inferences were largely determined by the types of inferences which were of potential value to policy-makers and intelligence specialists.

It is obvious enough that the FCC analysts would have confined their inferences to matters of intelligence interest at the time. It may be less evident, however, that the seven types of antecedent conditions of interest to policy-makers necessarily constituted the starting point for FCC efforts to develop appropriate methods of inference and that somewhat different methods would probably have evolved had different antecedent conditions been the object of interest. Of course, it was not possible in this investigation to develop methods of inference for all possible and worthy uses of communication analysis; but, in codifying the FCC's propaganda-analysis methods, the author has attempted to place the problems encountered in a context sufficiently broad to relate them to the more general problem of developing theories and methodologies for the study of political behavior and political action. He hopes thereby to have lessened the risk of intellectual and scientific parochialism involved in studying concrete problems of political policy, which are inevitably of a somewhat transient character.

NOTES

1. Paul F. Lazarsfeld and Morris Rosenberg (eds.), *The Language of Social Research* (The Free Press, Glencoe, Ill., 1955); see especially p. 7 and Section V, "The Empirical Analysis of Action."

2. See, for example, the various Project RADIR content-analysis studies published by the Stanford University Press, Stanford, Calif., in 1951 and 1952 under the auspices of the Hoover Institute as "Hoover Institute Studies," Series C: *Symbols*.

3. Among historians, it is particularly the Idealists who have made the concept of action central. From the definition of history as being properly concerned with human thoughts and experiences, however, they have drawn conclusions about the historian's methodological apparatus which are often both obscure and dubious. It has been left to others to clarify the nature and logical structure of historical explanation. For this purpose, they have had to go beyond formal statements on the distinctive method of history to an empirical analysis of what historians actually do when they attempt to explain. The most detailed effort of this type appears to be that by Patrick Gardiner, *The Nature of Historical Explanation* (Oxford University Press, London, 1952). An illuminating and balanced appraisal from a Positivist standpoint is provided by Carl G. Hempel, "The Function of General Laws in History," in H. Feigl and W. Sellars (eds.), *Readings in Philosophical Analysis* (Appleton-Century-Crofts, New York, 1949), pp. 459–71.

ONE

A Classification of Propaganda-Analysis Inferences

As a preliminary to the attempt to codify propaganda-analysis methodology, the methods of inference used by the FCC analysts had to be reconstructed. The first step in this process was to recognize what types of inference they were interested in making. The FCC analysts did not employ a systematic terminology to characterize their inferences. The writer was therefore faced with the problem of classifying these inferences or, more specifically, the antecedent conditions about which the inferences were made. The terms used in this classification are somewhat arbitrary; the important task was to make an effective distinction between the various conditions inferred.

The following categories of antecedent conditions include practically all of the specific inferences made by the FCC analysts.

1. *Propaganda Directives*. It is well known that large-scale propaganda operations, such as that of the Nazi regime, require a direction and co-ordination which are formalized to a considerable extent. The numerous writers and speakers comprising a large propaganda organization are guided by means of explicit directives, which specify either in general terms or in specific detail the lines, themes, omissions, emphases, minimizations, etc., to be introduced into propaganda aimed at various audiences. Many FCC inferences constituted efforts to reconstruct the directives according to which the propaganda under analysis was formulated.

EXAMPLE:

Directives apparently forbid (a) further heroization of [German] defeat [at Stalingrad]; (b) exultation in current successes; and (c) predictions of future victories (*CEA* #11, March 26, 1943, p. C-1).[1]

2. *Propaganda Goals.* The term "propaganda goal" is used here for the specific objective of a given propaganda message. The FCC analysts frequently attempted to infer what the propagandist was attempting to accomplish by a particular message or by a particular line, theme, emphasis, or omission within that message. The term "propaganda strategy" is used in this study to refer to a number of interrelated propaganda goals or to the relation of specific goals to broader ones.

EXAMPLES:

[On Nazi propaganda treatment of Allied air raids on Germany:] No doubt Goebbels wants to give the impression of utter frankness. He wants foreign audiences to believe that Germany is suffering (*CEA* #9, March 12, 1943, p. C-5).

[Goebbels' denial that he is "trying to stick out peace feelers" was explained by the analyst as having been intended to combat one of the weaknesses of propaganda stressing the "Red Menace," namely, the possibility of interpreting it as an admission of German weakness (*ibid.*, p. D-1)].

3. *Propaganda Techniques.* This term refers to the way in which a propaganda goal is implemented, i.e., to the way in which specific communication devices are employed in an effort to achieve the propaganda goal.

EXAMPLE:

[On propaganda treatment of recent Allied air raids on Germany:] This technique of minimizing the importance and damage of raids by ignoring them is a standard Nazi practice (*CEA* #8, March 5, 1943, p. C-5).

In discussing propaganda techniques the FCC analysts sometimes attempted to point out the technical problems faced by the Nazi propagandists.

EXAMPLES:

Nazi radio spokesmen in their treatment of the fighting in the East during the current week exhibit once more an appreciable measure of embarrassment, confusion and doubt as to what form of presentation will be most effective for their purposes (*ibid.*, p. C-1).

Apparently Dr. Goebbels is afraid that too much talk about this measure [dissolution of various subsidiary Nazi Party organizations] might be publicly interpreted as an official acknowledgment that criticism of Party shirking has been correct (*CEA* #11, March 26, 1943, p. B-4).

4. *Situational Factors*. This rather inadequate term refers to a variety of events and conditions in the communicator's environment, such as the actual condition of public morale, the state of food reserves, the relative position and strength of opposing forces on a battlefront, the outcome of military engagements, or the position of neutral states toward the belligerents. It should be emphasized that "situational factors" (a possible synonym would be "objective conditions") in this discussion of the FCC inferences refers to the state of affairs as they actually were rather than to the estimates of these conditions held by Nazi leaders.

EXAMPLES:

[On the Russian front:] Another Front Report of February 27 tends to confirm the view that the Wehrmacht may be suffering from a genuine shortage of manpower . . . (*CEA* #8, March 5, 1943, p. C-2).

[On German morale:] There can be little doubt that anxiety and despondency are widespread (*ibid.*, p. B-2).

5. *Nazi Elite Estimates of Situational Factors*. From the standpoint of policy-makers for whom propaganda analysis was undertaken, it was often just as important—if not more so—to know whether Nazi leaders were aware of certain objective facts as to know what these facts were; it was important to know what estimate of the situation they had come to. For example, how did Nazi leaders interpret Allied preparations to invade Europe? How did they evaluate the effects on morale of Allied air raids on Germany? How did they evaluate the course of the antisubmarine campaign waged by Allied naval forces? What were the Nazi estimates of Allied capabilities and intentions?

EXAMPLE:

[On the military situation on the Russian front:] Indication of a growing sense of security on the part of the Nazi elite is the fact that the German public is being enabled by wording of the communiqué to use their maps in following the battles in the East [in other words, the propagandists were then revealing the names of battle sites] (*CEA* #9, March 12, 1943, p. A-2).

6. *Nazi Elite Expectations*. The term "expectations" is here used to

refer to the variety of forecasts and predictions which enter into and influence policy-making. The expectations may concern future events completely outside the control of the policy-maker, or they may concern events and developments which he may in varying degrees be able to influence; and the "events" may be those occurring in the immediate or in the more distant future. They may concern the expected consequences of alternative policies under consideration or policies and actions which an opponent or neutral may undertake. They may be related to military, political, diplomatic, economic, psychological, or propaganda events and developments. They may be in the nature of conditional predictions. Finally, expectations may be held with any of considerably varying degrees of certainty.

EXAMPLES:

Such pervading caution [in propaganda] probably reflects a cautious [Nazi elite] evaluation of Axis prospects in Tunisia, now that the Allies have started their offensive on two fronts (*CEA* #11, March 26, 1943, p. C-6).

[On Allied air raids on Germany:] Obviously, the [Nazi] belief is dwindling that such losses [of planes], however large, may discourage the raiders from a renewal of their efforts (*CEA* #10, March 19, 1943, p. C-9).

[On rumors that Finland would make a separate peace:] Goebbels desires to keep such rumors alive, since they promote disunity among the United Nations. *He has no fear that they will have any result so far as Finland's continued participation in the war is concerned,* nor does he need to buttress Finland's will to fight (*ibid.*, p. B-11; italics supplied).

7. Nazi Elite Policies, Intentions, and Actions. National policies were established by the Nazi regime to govern the use of military, economic, diplomatic, political, and propaganda instruments of power for the purpose of reaching certain objectives, domestic and foreign. The specific moves undertaken in order to further these objectives are referred to here as "actions." The term "intentions" is employed in this study to indicate both future actions which the regime decided upon and the objectives behind current actions.

EXAMPLES:

Since Goebbels is extremely cautious in making predictions and since he knows that Goering laid himself wide open by making a number of risky promises he could not keep, it seems safe to assume that Germany is going to introduce new weapons into the air war over Germany (*CEA* #11, March 26, 1943, p. A-1).

As for new Axis military plans, Tunisia, Spain and Turkey will bear watching, since no significant mention is made of these areas in the Axis comments on the anti-Casablanca meeting [i.e., Ribbentrop visit to Rome] (*CEA* #8, March 25, 1943, p. D-11).

The FCC analysts occasionally attempted to make inferences about types of antecedent conditions other than these seven—e.g., the psychological state of the Nazi leaders and propagandists, the extent to which a propagandist was informed about a classified matter or development by the Nazi leaders into whose sphere it fell, or the possibility of conflicts and rivalries within the leadership group. But since the bulk of the FCC inferences were about the seven types of antecedent conditions listed,[2] it is probably unnecessary to expand the classification.

It should be noted that some of the general antecedent conditions listed above could be refined into more specific categories. Such an elaboration, however, is not essential to the purpose of this study.

NOTES

1. The abbreviation *CEA* will be used in referring to and quoting from the *Central European Analysis* produced by the German Section, Analysis Division, Foreign Broadcast Intelligence Service, Federal Communications Commission.

2. For example, of a total of 729 inferences made from Nazi propaganda during one two-month sample period (March–April, 1943), 446 referred to aspects of Nazi propaganda goals, techniques, and directives; 122 to situational factors or events affecting Nazi elite behavior and propaganda strategy; and 161 to aspects of Nazi elite behavior (estimates, expectations, and intentions). None referred to antecedent conditions other than the seven listed here.

TWO

A General Action Schema for Propaganda Analysis

Once the types of antecedent conditions about which inferences were made had been classified, the second step in reconstructing the FCC methods of inference was twofold; it consisted of (*a*) locating the types of antecedent conditions of interest within the over-all system of behavior of which the available propaganda communications are the end product (or dependent variable) and (*b*) depicting the general relationships between the conditions (or variables) comprising the system in question.[1]

In this chapter an attempt is made to formulate a model of action not only for the FCC operation but also for more general use in propaganda analysis. The model indicates some of the points in the behavioral sequence at which critical choices must be made which will determine the content of the propaganda finally issued.[2] The term "action schema" is employed for this model to avoid the connotations created by current uses of the word "model." The concept (and even the term) "action schema," moreover, is not unfamiliar in the literature of social research.[3]

In the formulation of an action schema, the investigator must bear in mind that the interests of the propaganda analyst are selective. The antecedent conditions the propaganda analyst wishes to infer from propaganda are unlikely to comprise all the possible antecedent conditions, or major variables, of the system which produced the propaganda. It could not be assumed—indeed, it was obviously not true—

that the seven types of inferences attempted by the FCC analysts comprised all the variables affecting Nazi communication behavior. And these seven types of antecedent conditions were so interrelated with other conditions or variables that the latter could not be ignored in developing methods of inference.

What was required, therefore, was a general analysis of the over-all system of behavior implicit in the political-communication process studied by the FCC analysts. For this purpose a general familiarity with modern political regimes and elites, especially those of a totalitarian character, was necessary.

It will be useful to begin this inquiry by characterizing more precisely the nature of the political communications which formed the raw materials available for the FCC propaganda analysis.

This Nazi propaganda was, in the first place, public (rather than private) communication from an elite. It was mass communication in the sense of being channeled through mass media (radio and press), but it was *not* mass communication in the sense of being intended exclusively for a homogeneous, undifferentiated mass audience.

Next, it was entirely one-way communication, from speaker to audience, and was mostly of an impersonal character, in that speaker and audience were not in a face-to-face situation. In this type of political discourse there is a lack of interaction between communicator and audience *in the course of* individual acts of communication.[4] There is no concurrent reaction from the audience which permits the speaker to see, as he proceeds, where his intended meanings need clarification—to alter message and technique on the spot in order better to achieve intended effects. Rather, interaction and reaction, to the extent that they occur, take place *after* individual acts of communication have been completed. Subsequent acts of communication may be influenced, of course, by intelligence reports and other indications of audience response. This has important implications in making inferences and was taken into account by the FCC personnel, particularly in trend analyses, where they related changes in propaganda line to situational changes assumed to have come to the attention of the propagandist.

Another characteristic of the communications available for analysis was that they consisted largely of material which had been prepared with some deliberation and put into final shape prior to being made available to the intended audience. For the most part the FCC analysts were not dealing with a flow of communication produced relatively spontaneously at the moment of transmission to an audience.

These general characteristics of Nazi propaganda communications serve to underline the organized, *institutional* features of the process by means of which they were prepared. Therefore, even a general knowledge of this process is useful in helping to construct an action schema and in developing methods of inference. Similarly useful is detailed knowledge about the propaganda organization—its structure and functioning—which are discussed in Part II, pp. 111 ff., and especially in Chapter 7.

The feature of Nazi propaganda most important in developing a method of inference was the fact that it was part of a totalitarian political system. From this fact a number of assumptions having important methodological implications could safely be made.[5] These assumptions were that:

1. Mass communications (directed to both domestic and foreign audiences) were being used by the Nazi elite as an *instrument of policy,* in a highly purposeful and deliberative fashion, in order to implement goals of domestic and foreign policy.

2. The selection of goals and strategies for these communication channels was *closely co-ordinated* with the policy calculations, estimates, expectations, and intentions of the Nazi leaders.

3. All channels of mass communication and their contents were subject to *centralized control* through the Propaganda Ministry and other co-ordinating bodies.

It is also of interest to note that the antecedent conditions of propaganda inferred by the FCC analysts recall the major steps in the process of producing propaganda. In making inferences about propaganda goals, techniques, and directives, the FCC analysts were, in a sense, reconstructing some of the major steps in the production of these propaganda communications, as will be discussed later in this chapter.

Two conclusions emerge from the preceding discussion: (*a*) that the communications available for propaganda analysis were the product of two interrelated behavioral systems, the *political decision-making (or policy-calculating) system* and the *propaganda decision-making system,* and (*b*) that the latter stood generally in a secondary, auxiliary relationship to the former.[6] In other words, the propaganda materials analyzed were the end product of communication behavior, which was one of several instruments of purposive political behavior.

These two interrelated behavioral systems had to be encompassed in the proposed action schema. Provision also had to be made for the relevant situational factors, or objective conditions in the environment of these behavioral systems. It was noted in the preceding chapter that among the types of antecedent conditions which the FCC analysts attempted to infer were situational factors. Actually, the FCC analysts could not have ignored these factors in inferring other types of antecedent conditions even if they had not been expected to infer them. For developments in the war and other situational factors had a direct impact on those aspects of Nazi political and propaganda behavior of interest to the FCC analysts and were one of the important determinants of this behavior.

It would be necessary, if the action schema were to be more detailed, to distinguish between situational factors which particularly affect the calculation and determination of policies by the elite and those which affect choices of propaganda strategy. Such developments in the environment as audience reactions to past propaganda, changing audience attitudes, morale trends, etc., may not be important enough to warrant the attention or consideration of top policy-makers but may yet be significant in the determination and implementation of propaganda strategy.

On the other hand, the fact that certain situational factors are important enough to concern top policy-makers does not mean that the propagandist has no responsibility with regard to them. Whether the impact of such factors upon the estimates and calculations of top policy-makers is immediate, cumulative, or delayed, the propagandist often feels constrained to take immediate note of them. He is virtually compelled to say something about important events which are already public knowledge or may soon become so. For every propagandist is often *forced* to talk when he would prefer to say nothing. Propagandists of different countries differ in this respect only in degree.

Accordingly, the propagandist is continually engaged in making public responses to a variety of events. These events, of course, may be verbal (speeches, broadcasts, etc.) or nonverbal (military actions, political appointments, etc.). In either case, they may be known to one audience and not to another, or they may be known as yet only privately (to a few), so that publicity given them is in the nature of a

74645

disclosure. To respond to events in a responsible, effective manner, the propagandist must (*a*) estimate the meaning and significance of these developments for all of his audiences whom these events concern, (*b*) appraise the probable impact of these events on the policy calculations and expectations of his own and other governments, and (*c*) anticipate possible future adjustments in policies and actions of his own and other governments as a result of these changes in the situation.

The significance and implications for policy of some events can be interpreted more easily than others. Although the propagandist may obtain guidance and background information for this purpose from persons and offices closer to top policy-makers than he himself is, occasionally he has to talk about events without benefit of an authoritative estimate of their significance. He may then discuss them in a noncommittal, temporizing manner, at least until their significance is more fully assessed within the government, but discuss them he probably must.

Situational factors, therefore, are one of the important determinants of Nazi propaganda behavior.

The preceding discussion has identified some of the major variables or components of the system of behavior which produced Nazi propaganda. The major variables discussed thus far parallel the seven types of antecedent conditions which formed the subject of the FCC inferences. But an action schema of what determined Nazi propaganda behavior would be incomplete if it stopped here. Obviously, there were various other types of determinants of Nazi political and communication behavior, which will be indicated briefly below.

If the part of the action schema dealing with the political decision-making of the Nazi elite were to be more fully elaborated, a number of important variables would have to be specified. However, such a systematic extension of the schema would require more intensive analysis than is necessary here. Any such elaboration would benefit from a study of simple models of rational behavior for policy-making in conflict situations.[7] It would have to take into consideration the *value system* of the political elite, that is, the set of values and value priorities which determine the objectives which the elite pursues and its choice of a course of action from among the alternatives open to it. It would take into account what has been called the *"operational code,"* [8] or general rules of political strategy and conduct which the elite favors. It would also refer to the elite's *image of its opponent* in the conflict situation, that is, the degree of rationality attributed to the opponent; the value system attributed to the opponent; assumptions as to the way in which the opponent makes use of information, formulates estimates and expectations, considers alternative choices of action, and makes risk calculations; the operational code attributed to the opponent, etc.

A number of additional variables in propaganda behavior would also have to be specified if the action schema were to be more fully elaborated. The rational calculation and employment of propaganda are directly affected by what the propagandist believes *the capabilities and limitations of propaganda* are as an instrument of policy. They are also affected by the propagandist's general *image of the audiences* to which communications are being addressed, that is, by what the propagandist understands to be the values and aspirations of these audiences, their position in the political structure, and their ability to influence various types of decisions and actions, their politically relevant attitudes and expectations, etc. The calculation and employment of propaganda are influenced, too, by the political intelligence available to the propagandist and his concept and use of it, that is, by the kind of information about different audiences which the propagandist deems relevant to his task, the quality of the intelligence obtained, and the ways in which it is utilized in his propaganda operations.

Finally, the calculation and employment of propaganda may be affected to an important degree by the *personal characteristics of the propagandist* and by the *organizational controls* imposed upon him. A propaganda technician needs a certain autonomy in the conduct of propaganda operations in order to be successful. Even the good propagandist may find it difficult to function rationally and efficiently if the exercise of his technical competence is subjected to thwarting influences from the larger political and bureaucratic environment. The net effect of such external pressures may be to heighten the individual propagandist's concern with personal considerations, such as income, security, and safety, to the point that it interferes substantially with the exercise of his best technical judgment in propaganda matters. The propagandist is inefficient or unskillful in his output if he disregards what he knows about the audience and applies directives automatically and inflexibly. He may be inefficient because he is afraid to deviate from directives in his concern over safety. He is unskillful, rather than inefficient, when his personal allegiance to official beliefs or to the authorities leaves him incapable of a detached, flexible assessment of the factors on which the success of his propaganda depends. Thus, he may feel intensely that the official line, whatever it is, is correct and may regard following it in his output as more important than applying it intelligently with a view to his knowledge of audience predispositions.

In addition to these variables, *cultural* and *ideological factors* influence both political and propaganda behavior and would have to be specified in a more elaborate action schema. These factors, present as dispositions in the political elite and the propagandists, are significant in understanding the meaning and style of Nazi communications and drawing successful inferences about Nazi policy calculations and propaganda strategy. Although ideological and cultural determinants may be expected to change in time, under the impact of events, they are relatively *stable* in comparison with situational factors, which, particularly in wartime, change so rapidly. It is thus safe to assume that *variations in the content of Nazi propaganda were more likely to reflect changes in situational factors and in Nazi policy calculations than changes in the basic ideological and cultural determinants of behavior.*

This assumption, implicit in the work of the FCC analysts, has important methodological implications for the problem of making inferences. It suffices to note here that any over-all explanation of the characteristics of Nazi propaganda would indeed have required reference to ideological and cultural factors. Certainly *some* characteristics of Nazi propaganda would probably have to be explained largely in terms of ideological or cultural determinants. But, as these characteristics of Nazi propaganda were not likely to reflect the antecedent conditions of interest at the time—namely, situational factors, calculations of the Nazi elite, and propaganda behavior—the FCC propaganda analysts were justified in directing their attention to features in Nazi propaganda more likely to serve their purpose.

It so happens that the seven types of antecedent conditions about which the FCC analysts attempted to make inferences comprised the major *unstable* variables in the system of behavior which produced the propaganda. Available knowledge of (or hypotheses about) the relatively *stable* determinants of Nazi behavior—cultural and ideological dispositions of the Nazi leaders, their value system, their operational code, their image of their opponents, etc.—was used by the

FCC analysts as an aid in inferring the precise character of unstable variables in specific situations.

For present purposes, the preceding observations may be summarized by depicting schematically the general interrelationships among (only) the major unstable variables in the system which produced the propaganda. These are the variables which are likely to vary from one inferential problem to another and which will, therefore, demand explicit and systematic attention from the propaganda analyst in each case. The analyst will also take into account the other, more stable variables which have been mentioned, but to include these in the action schema would complicate it unduly.

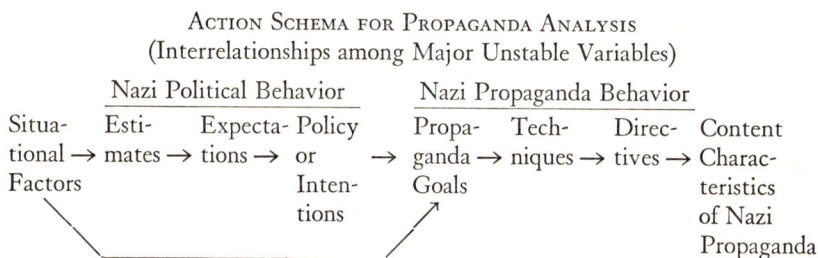

ACTION SCHEMA FOR PROPAGANDA ANALYSIS
(Interrelationships among Major Unstable Variables)

Nazi Political Behavior				Nazi Propaganda Behavior			
Situational Factors	Esti- mates	Expecta- tions	Policy or Inten- tions	Propa- ganda Goals	Tech- niques	Direc- tives	Content Charac- teristics of Nazi Propaganda

Situational Factors → Estimates → Expectations → Policy or Intentions → Propaganda Goals → Techniques → Directives → Content Characteristics of Nazi Propaganda

The purpose of drawing up an action schema for propaganda analysis has been to clarify problems of methodology in making inferences in the particular application of content analysis under study. The action schema outlined here focuses on the purposive, calculating aspects of political behavior and the related communication process because, for the most part, the inferences attempted by the FCC emphasized these aspects. But this does not imply that nonpurposive, noncalculating factors, such as the structure of control [9] within the propaganda organization whose output is being analyzed, are never of importance in determining the content characteristics of propaganda. ("Content characteristics" are any characteristics of the content itself as distinguished from characteristics of the speaker or audience.) As a matter of fact, these factors must frequently be taken into account in attempting to use content characteristics of propaganda as indicators of purposive antecedent conditions. For example, as will be indicated in Chapter 7, errors in making inferences can sometimes be traced to faulty information or assumptions about the structure of control within the propaganda organization. But to include nonpurposive factors in the action schema would have greatly complicated, and perhaps lessened the graphic value of, the diagram.

The general action schema for propaganda analysis presented in this chapter has another important limitation (in addition to the omission of nonpurposive variables), to which attention was drawn in the Introduction. While the schema portrays an important part of the process of producing political communications, it is not sufficiently detailed to make it appropriate for inferring types of antecedent conditions other than the seven of interest to the FCC propaganda analysts. Other applications of content analysis might well require somewhat different action schemata.

For example, if the objective of the research were to infer an elite's image of its opponent, the investigator would have to ask himself which types of political communications produced by that elite were likely to be most useful as raw material for inferring its private image of an opponent. He might decide that this research question could be answered more reliably by an analysis of the content, not of that elite's mass propaganda, but rather of its indoctrination materials for party cadres. Or, if it were necessary to rely upon an analysis of mass communications for this purpose, a competent investigator would realize that the methodological problem of inferring an elite's true image of its opponent from propaganda materials like these is rather different from, and more challenging than, that of inferring its propaganda strategy.

If the research were to be aimed at inferring relatively *stable* determinants of an elite's political and propaganda behavior, additional methodological problems would be raised. Content analysis can be and has been used for this purpose, however.[10] The observation made earlier that the ideological dispositions of Nazi leaders and spokesmen could be considered to be relatively stable of course does not exclude the possibility that some were weaker in their allegiance to Nazi ideology than others, or that the ideological allegiance of some weakened as the fortunes of war turned against Germany. Propaganda analysts can be asked to investigate such hypotheses. (Inferences in this area were occasionally attempted by the FCC analysts, but no attempt has been made to reconstruct the methods of inference they may have employed for this purpose.) Analysts would find the task of obtaining reliable evidence of ideological dispositions in propaganda complicated by the need to take into account the possibility that what they considered to be indicators of the speaker's private ideological dispositions were in fact, to a greater or lesser extent, reflections of his propaganda strategy and techniques. In other words, it might be difficult to find content indicators (that is, content characteristics which indicated the existence) of the speaker's ideological attitudes which were not contaminated by the propaganda strategies he happened to be pursuing. The task, therefore, would be either (*a*) to find content indicators of private attitudes which were independent of the speaker's use of propaganda communications as an instrument of policy, that is, indicators which revealed his private attitudes without his knowing it, or (*b*) to attempt to infer the speaker's private attitudes indirectly, by taking into account how his attempt to use propaganda for political purposes might have affected his public references or allusions.[11]

Similarly, a reconsideration of the action schema, of the appropriateness of available political communications, and of methodological problems of drawing inferences would be necessary if the research problem were to infer policy conflicts and power rivalries within a political elite. This problem is important in political analysis. The FCC analysts did occasionally attempt inferences of this type, but no effort has been made here to reconstruct or improve upon whatever methodology they may have employed for this purpose. Many contemporary analysts also attempt to make reliable inferences in this field partly or wholly by means of some form of content analysis of the publicly available political communications of the elite they are studying. Few such analysts, however, have attempted to set down in detail what method they employ for this purpose or to justify it from any rigorous standpoint.[12]

NOTES

1. Recently, "accounting scheme" has been proposed as a general methodological term to designate the set of antecedent conditions which the investigator proposes to take into account in any systematic empirical analysis of a specific type of action (in Paul F. Lazarsfeld and Morris Rosenberg [eds.], *The Language of Social Research* [The Free Press, Glencoe, Ill., 1955], pp. 338 and 390). The list of seven antecedent conditions in the previous chapter can be regarded as an accounting scheme in this sense. However, as will be noted, the present chapter goes beyond a mere listing of the causal factors to be taken into account and attempts to depict the general relationships between these causal factors (or antecedent conditions) and their position within an over-all system of behavior which includes other causal factors as well.

2. While psychological models of action which have been proposed by various investigators (for example, Edward C. Tolman's "A Psychological Model," Part 3 of Talcott Parsons and Edward Shils [eds.], *Toward a General Theory of Action* [Harvard University Press,

Cambridge, Mass., 1952]) were often suggestive, they were not directly useful for purposes of the present study. More pertinent for the purpose were general models, however simple, of rational behavior in conflict situations, such as that in Herbert A. Simon, "Some Strategic Considerations in the Construction of Social Science Models," in Paul F. Lazarsfeld (ed.), *Mathematical Thinking in the Social Sciences* (The Free Press, Glencoe, Ill., 1954), pp. 388–415.

3. See the discussion of "An Action Schema" in A. Kornhauser and Paul F. Lazarsfeld, "The Analysis of Consumer Actions," in Lazarsfeld and Rosenberg, *op. cit.*, pp. 393–96.

4. This is not true, of course, of those propaganda speeches which were given before a live audience and either broadcast simultaneously or reprinted in the press as actually spoken. It is known, for example, that some Nazi leaders, including Hitler, departed from their texts or notes on such occasions, influenced partly by on-the-spot impressions of audience response.

5. A refinement and qualification of these assumptions during the course of propaganda-analysis operations would be essential and would enable the propaganda analyst to make better inferences. This task is not undertaken here. Qualification of these assumptions would be particularly important if the analyst were interested in making inferences about policy conflicts and frictions among members of the elite.

6. To imply, as this formulation does, that propaganda is dependent upon political policy is somewhat misleading. Actually, the relationship is to some extent reciprocal. Technical calculations entering into the determination of propaganda may be important enough on occasion to exercise an influence on political decision-making. Moreover, leading propagandists may seek (as Goebbels did on occasion) to utilize their control over communications as an instrument to further their own political ambitions or the policies favored by the clique to which they belong.

7. See Simon, *op. cit.*, pp. 388–415.

8. See Nathan Leites, *A Study of Bolshevism* (The Free Press, Glencoe, Ill., 1953), pp. 15–26 and *passim*.

9. By structure of control, or control structure, is meant, briefly, (*a*) the manner in which propaganda is co-ordinated with political policy, (*b*) the manner in which propaganda policy is formulated and implemented, (*c*) the allocation of specialized propaganda roles or functions to different media, media units, speakers, and writers, and (*d*) the character of the internal working relationship within the propaganda organization between those who decide propaganda policy and those who implement it. (For a fuller discussion see Chapter 7.)

10. See the derivation of the Bolsheviks' operational code from certain of the writings of Lenin and Stalin by Leites, *op. cit.*, and the content analysis of esoteric and exoteric communist communications by Gabriel Almond, in *The Appeals of Communism* (Princeton University Press, Princeton, N.J., 1954).

11. The two alternative general approaches to making inferences suggested here are further developed in Chapter 4.

12. The most disciplined and imaginative content-analysis research on contemporary political problems of this type known to the writer is the work of my colleague, Myron Rush. See his *The Rise of Khrushchev* (Public Affairs Press, Washington, D.C., 1958). Also interesting, though far less rigorous, is Franz Borkenau's "Getting at the Facts behind the Soviet Façade: An Expert Explains His 'Content Analysis' Method," *Commentary* (April, 1954), pp. 393–400.

For an attempt to infer the relative power status of members of the Politburo, which contains a relatively explicit, though incomplete, account of the methodological problems encountered, see Nathan Leites, Elsa Bernaut, and Raymond Garthoff, "Politburo Images of Stalin," *World Politics* (April, 1951), pp. 317–39.

THREE

Two Early Approaches to Methods of Inference

Once the types of inferences which the FCC propaganda analysts wished to make had been classified and an action schema depicting the general interrelationships among the antecedent conditions of propaganda of interest to them had been constructed, the next step in the attempt to codify propaganda-analysis methodology was to identify the patterns of reasoning employed in individual FCC inferences. Before the results of this third and final step in codification are reported (in Chapter 4), it may be useful to digress now by reviewing the early history and development of efforts to adapt content analysis for purposes of making specific inferences about Nazi intentions and policy calculations.

Two methodological approaches can be identified in these early efforts. Neither proved very satisfactory when tried under operational conditions. In time, working without explicit attention to methodology, the FCC propaganda analysts developed a different approach (the indirect method), which was more successful.

The two earlier methods of making inferences owed their origin and character to the fact that content analysis was initially developed, some years before World War II, as a tool for the *scientific* study of political communication. Those who pioneered with Harold D. Lasswell in its development were interested in acquiring scientific knowledge about political communication. Accordingly, content analysis was originally defined and developed in order to list and measure the frequency of occurrence of certain characteristics of the political communication under study and to classify them under general terms, or content categories, which were suggested by a tentative theory of political communication.[1] The objective of the research in this original content-analysis approach was to make general inferences, or scientific generalizations, in the form of one-to-one regularities or correlations between some content indicator (or class of indicators) and some state or characteristic of the communicator or his environment.[2]

It should be evident, therefore, that the original purpose which attended the development of content analysis was quite different from the purpose of the type of propaganda analysis under survey here, which was distinguished by its interest in making specific inferences about individual, concrete events. In this type of research, scientific knowledge about political communication is useful only where it helps make the specific, concrete inferences of interest to policymakers.

The question of methods of inferring the specific intent and related calculations of the communicator in any given situation from what he said did not receive much attention until the war. Certain methods of making specific inferences were, of course, implicit in the effort to study political communication from a scientific point of view. It is only natural that these implicit methods and the scientific orientation described above should have provided the starting point when scholars turned their attention to the interesting possibility of adapting the content-analysis technique to making concrete inferences about Nazi intentions.

Thus, early considerations of the problem generally took it for granted that inferring the communicator's intention would require discovery of a *regular* pattern in the communicator's past behavior, which would serve as a rule of inference in new instances. The logic of this approach was briefly indicated by Harold D. Lasswell in an early memorandum on the subject:

In general we should like to predict from R [content of propaganda], the intended initiative of certain persons or groups, the facts of indulgent or deprivational changes in their environment, and their future responses to specified E's [events]. More specifically: Do the Nazi leaders *regularly* mask an intended initiative by projecting a plan of the intended type upon their enemies? Do the Nazi leaders *regularly* understate victories during the early phases of military success?[3]

In early efforts to use content analysis to predict actions of the opponent, the two approaches which have been mentioned sought a pattern or regularity in the opponent's past behavior. The first approach attempted to discover a relationship between the opponent's intention of initiating a certain type of action and a certain *content characteristic* of his propaganda; the second tried to discover a relationship between the opponent's intention of initiating a certain type of action and a certain *propaganda strategy* pursued by him prior to his initiative.

In order to use either of these approaches for purposes of prediction it was necessary, of course, to formulate empirical generalizations about Nazi behavior based on regular recurrence of one pattern or the other. But observation of past Nazi behavior from this standpoint did not seem to disclose regularly recurring relationships of either type. A general content characteristic common to Nazi propaganda preceding previous Nazi military initiatives could not be found. Nor could one propaganda strategy be pinpointed as preceding each initiative.

In both cases, the danger of ex post facto explanations of the relationship of propaganda to intent soon became evident. It was always easier *after* a Nazi initiative to point to content indicators or to a propaganda strategy which seemed to have foreshadowed the action. But the rule of inference (or generalization) thus "discovered" never seemed to hold reliably for other Nazi initiatives.

In fact, inspection of German propaganda prior to several major Nazi military initiatives seemed to show that the same propaganda strategy had *not* been followed in each case. German propaganda seemed to have prepared for its invasion of Norway by accusing the Allies of aggressive designs on that country, i.e., by use of the propaganda technique known as "projection," which consists of attributing intentions similar to your own to an opponent who does not have such intentions.[4] Its technique before the invasion of the Low Countries and France, however, was to divert attention to another area, the Balkans, which it accused the Allies of getting ready to attack. Thus, the simple technique of projection in the case of Norway seemed to be followed by a combination of projection-diversion in the case of the invasion of the Low Countries and France.[5] And an entirely different propaganda pattern had preceded the invasion of Poland and Yugoslavia and the incorporation of Czechoslovakia (March, 1939); these countries had been accused of terrorizing German nationals, conducting anti-German politics, harboring aggressive military intentions toward Germany, and of being unable to check internal disorders and chaotic economic and social conditions.[6] Finally, none of these earlier patterns of preparation was followed in the case of the German invasion of Russia, when nothing at all was said about the U.S.S.R. prior to the German attack, and Goebbels made an elaborate attempt to create the impression that the Germans were about to invade the British Isles.

It was thus impossible to find a regular, fixed relationship between major Nazi military initiatives and accompanying propaganda strategies. Yet successful predictions of Nazi initiatives were occasionally made during the course of the war by content analysts as well as journalists. Were these successes to be attributed merely to chance? This seemed likely, since they certainly were not based on any rule or generalization relating initiatives to propaganda patterns or strategy. Thus, one postwar appraisal of the value of content analysis for predicting enemy initiatives stated:

> During the early years of World War II, journalists frequently anticipated German military action on the basis of Nazi propaganda, and similar inferences were made by both governmental and nongovernmental analysts. Since almost all possible military actions were anticipated at one time or another, some predictions and estimates of current situations were bound to be correct. But whether content analysis produced results significantly better than chance . . . the evidence is by no means clear at the present time.
>
> . . . It is difficult to see, on the basis of such *inconsistent propaganda patterns,* how either event [German invasion of Norway and of the Low Countries and France] could have been predicted with any reliability. At the very least, how was the analyst to know at the time whether the technique of projection or of diversion was being used?[7]

Other writers, though not so pessimistic in their conclusions, could not explain very precisely how content analysis could be used to predict an opponent's intentions:

> In discussing the part played by anticipation of action in German propaganda, we deal with propaganda campaigns of various types; some short, concentrated, and of great intensity, others of low intensity spread over long periods. *The techniques vary considerably, and few devices are indiscriminately repeated.* Through study of these techniques, one learns to read between the lines of German propaganda.[8]

The difficulties encountered in these early approaches to the problem of drawing inferences have been briefly indicated. The major observation to be made in a critical evaluation of them is that they were based on an inadequate conception of the behavioral system of which Nazi propaganda was a part; that is, the (implicit) methods used in these approaches to drawing inferences were not appropriate to the nature of the system in question. The two approaches, though they were based upon a search for empirical regularities (and perhaps an implicit reliance upon probability theory), were both inappropriate, but for rather different reasons.

The *first* approach, it will be recalled, rested upon attempts to find regular relationships (in past behavior) between types of elite intentions (e.g., plans for military aggression) and types of content characteristics in that elite's propaganda (e.g., accusations that the opponent had aggressive intentions). Such regularities, if observed in past instances, could be used as a basis for predicting Nazi intentions in similar cases in the future. Presumably the same methodological approach could be generalized for purposes of inferring different types of Nazi intentions, if regularities could be observed between other intentions and other propaganda characteristics in the past. The schema in applying this method would in every case be in accord with the accompanying diagram. The same schema would apply if the regular-

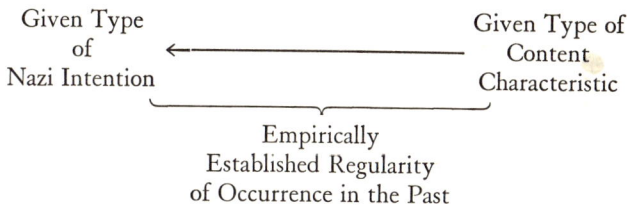

Given Type
of
Nazi Intention
←————————————
Given Type of
Content
Characteristic

Empirically
Established Regularity
of Occurrence in the Past

ity had been observed in only some part of the cases in the past (rather than in every case).

This schema takes no cognizance of the element of strategy in Nazi behavior. That is, it ignores or regards as irrelevant the fact that political elites use communications under their control in various ways to prepare for forthcoming actions and policies. Thus, for example, when surprise is considered important to the success of an action, propaganda may be used to deceive or mislead the opponent as to the elite's intentions. In other cases propaganda may be used to lead given audiences to expect a forthcoming action or policy in order to heighten its psychological impact or to reduce undesired effects. In all such cases, of course, the content of the propaganda will necessarily reflect in some way the specific propaganda strategy being pursued in connection with the forthcoming action or policy. But it should be clear that for any one type of action or policy (for example, a major military initiative) the specific strategy of preparatory propaganda may vary from one concrete instance to another. Therefore, it is unlikely that content characteristics which directly reflect propaganda strategy will also *regularly* reflect the type of intention behind the strategy.

Accordingly, the task of finding regularly recurring relationships between types of content characteristics and types of elite intentions is more complicated than it appears at first glance. The fact that propaganda strategy is an *unstable,* fluctuating variable which often intervenes between elite intentions and content characteristics makes it difficult to obtain one-to-one correlations between them.

So far as is known, in early efforts to use content analysis to infer intentions, no attempt was made to cope with the difficulties caused by eliminating considerations of propaganda strategy. This approach, when examined more carefully, evidently makes the assumption that it is possible to find types of content characteristics that are *independent* of any propaganda strategy used to implement a certain type of elite intention but that regularly occur whenever that type of intention is present. (In the next chapter this approach is more fully formulated, under the term "direct method of inference.")

The *second* of the two early approaches, on the other hand, did not bypass the propaganda-strategy variable. Rather, it attempted to find a regularly recurring relationship between a type of propaganda strategy and a type of elite intention. Such a relationship, if established on the basis of observation of past Nazi behavior, would then serve as a rule for making inferences in new cases.

One of the difficulties encountered in this approach lay in its oversimplification of the role of strategy in the Nazi system. Although propaganda, as was noted above, may be used to further an intended elite initiative in a variety of ways, the second of the two early approaches concerned itself with only one type of propaganda goal, that of *masking* a forthcoming initiative. Apparently the assumption was that, if the propagandist's technique of masking an initiative could be deciphered, the key to successful prediction would be obtained.[9]

When such an assumption is linked with a search for regularities, it overlooks the fact that the propagandist, in conflict situations, is well aware that his present behavior (verbal and nonverbal) is being closely observed for clues to his intentions and calculations. In view of what is known about the Nazi system, it seems overly hopeful to have expected that a certain type of elite intention (or forthcoming initiative) would regularly be accompanied by a certain type of propaganda strategy. There was always the likelihood that the communicator would deliberately vary the pattern for masking initiatives in order to maximize deception.

Another shortcoming of this early approach was that, in their preoccupation with but one type of preparatory propaganda goal, the proponents of this approach were perhaps slow in recognizing that preparatory propaganda can be and is used to further the success of an intended initiative in other ways. In time, analysts did realize that the psychological preparation by the Nazis for their major military initiatives involved more than the masking goal.[10] This opened the way for developing a new method of making inferences. However, its implications for the problem of predicting Nazi initiatives were not systematically developed by wartime analysts. (An effort to do this is made in the next chapter.)

In sum, it may be observed that both of the early efforts to develop methods for inferring Nazi initiatives failed because they oversimplified, in different ways, the system of political and propaganda behavior to which they were supposed to be applicable. (See Chapter 2, pp. 20–25, for a fuller analysis of this system.) Attempts to infer Nazi initiatives continued to be made in specific situations at various times during the war. But, perhaps because of disillusionment over the failure of the two earlier approaches, no further efforts were made to formulate systematic methods of making such inferences.

NOTES

1. For bibliographical references see Bernard Berelson, *Content Analysis in Communication Research* (The Free Press, Glencoe, Ill., 1952), esp. pp. 23–25, 199–200, 213.

2. The early "scientific" approach to content analysis described here, it should be noted, made use of the *simplest* type of inferential model, namely, one resting upon the possibility of a one-to-one correlation between some type of content feature and some state or characteristic of the communicator or his environment. A more complex inferential model is employed in the "indirect method," discussed later. This point is further discussed on p. 46.

3. Harold D. Lasswell, "Specimen Hypotheses about the Focus of Attention in World Politics" (The Experimental Division for the Study of War Time Communications, Library of Congress, unpublished memorandum, February, 1942), p. 4; italics supplied.

4. Following the Nazi invasion of Norway in April, 1940, content analysts generally as-

sumed that Nazi propaganda had employed this technique in masking the invasion. Actually, however, there is some reason to doubt whether the simple technique of projection was used by the Nazis in this case. Evidence at the Nuremberg Trial indicates, rather, that the Nazi leaders actually feared that the Western Allies were planning to invade Norway themselves (see Raeder's testimony and the Tribunal's judgment: I.M.T. [International Military Tribunal], *Trial of the Major War Criminals* [Nuremberg, 1948], Vol. XIV, pp. 85–100, 187–93; Vol. I, pp. 204–9). That the Allies indeed had such plans is revealed in Winston S. Churchill, *The Gathering Storm* (Vol. I of *The Second World War;* Houghton Mifflin Co., Boston, 1948), esp. pp. 543–44, 559–61, and 579. See also Kingston Derry, *The Campaign in Norway* (United Kingdom Military Series, History of the Second World War; H.M.S.O., London, 1952), and F. H. Hinsley, *Hitler's Strategy* (Cambridge University Press, London, 1951), pp. 50–52.

5. For a somewhat different interpretation see Philip E. Jacob, "The Theory and Strategy of Nazi Short-Wave Propaganda," esp. pp. 99–100, in Harwood L. Childs and John B. Whitton (eds.), *Propaganda by Short-Wave* (Princeton University Press, Princeton, N.J., 1942), pp. 49–108.

6. For an authoritative Nazi description of how some of these aggressions were prepared propagandistically see the affidavit submitted by Fritzsche to the Nuremberg Tribunal, Document No. 3469–PS in *Nazi Conspiracy and Aggression* (U.S. Government Printing Office, Washington, 1946), Vol. VI, pp. 184–90 (translation); summarized *ibid.*, Vol. II, pp. 1041–46.

7. Berelson, *op. cit.,* pp. 84, 85–86; italics supplied.

8. Ernst Kris and Hans Speier, *German Radio Propaganda* (Oxford University Press, London, 1944), p. 291; italics supplied. These authors asserted that "propaganda analysis has in the past been helpful in detecting the enemies' intentions." Since the case studies they present (*ibid.,* pp. 292–325) were made after the event, they do not document this assertion but suggest that prediction is possible if reliable rules of making inferences can be discovered. It should be noted, indeed, that the work of the Project on Totalitarian Communications (Kris and Speier) was not focused upon making inferences for intelligence purposes but was aimed, rather, at discovering propositions about Nazi propaganda behavior.

9. Such a point of view appears to have been implicit in the work of the Experimental Division for the Study of War Time Communications, Library of Congress. Thus in Lasswell, *op. cit.,* pp. 10–14, five techniques of masking initiatives were identified: avowal, denial, ignoral, projection, and diversion.

10. Thus, Kris and Speier (*op. cit.,* pp. 289–91) recognized (only) three possible propaganda aims that might enter into the preparation campaign preceding an initiative: (*a*) "campaigns of justification to prepare the German people for a new danger of war," (*b*) "to instigate hate against the future enemy," and (*c*) "to confuse or to intimidate opponents and potential opponents." (The last is actually two separate aims, of which masking the initiative is one and intimidation is the other; thus, actually, four aims were identified.)

FOUR

The Direct and Indirect Methods
of Inference

In the Introduction reference was made to the special problems and procedures encountered in attempting a rational reconstruction of the reasoning in individual FCC inferences and a codification of general patterns of reasoning, or methods of inference, common to a great many individual inferences. This chapter will present the results of the codification—the formulation of what are here called the "direct" and "indirect" methods of inference.

The Two Methods Contrasted

The *direct method* is merely a more complete formulation of the first of the two earlier approaches; it, too, bypasses propaganda-behavior variables and attempts to infer elite calculations or situational factors directly from content indicators. The *indirect method,* on the other hand, considers propaganda strategy an intermediate step between elite intentions and content characteristics.

Two major differences between the direct and indirect methods are singled out for discussion here, namely, the difference with respect to the *type of content feature employed as an indicator* in making inferences as to antecedent conditions, and the difference with respect to the *type of generalization* required to support inferences in the two methods.

The direct method requires that content characteristics be found in propaganda which occur *regularly* and *only* when a certain type of elite intention occurs (or elite expectation or estimate, or situational factor, if one of these is being inferred).

Here an important distinction between the direct and indirect methods may be noted. The types of regularities which the direct method requires as a basis for inferences are *correlations* of a non-causal character; that is, the regularity does not imply a causal relation between the condition inferred and the content indicator. In employing the direct method, the propaganda analyst does not make causal imputations; he does when utilizing the indirect method.

The limitations of the direct method in this respect are rather self-evident. As in any use of statistical correlations as a basis for prediction, there can be no assurance that regularities observed in the past will recur. This limitation is particularly serious when, as in propaganda analysis, the regularities needed to support inferences are usually postulated from observation of relatively few past cases. Such correlations or observed regularities are of dubious validity as rules of inference. Yet, unless he is to postpone efforts at making inferences on current problems, the propaganda analyst employing the direct method finds himself with no recourse but to work with such dubious postulations.

Another limitation of the direct method is that a very great variety of correlations of this type is required. Each observed regularity is capable of supporting only a particular kind of inference. Since the analyst wishes to make many different kinds of inference, he is confronted with the necessity of discovering many different regularities. But the a priori assumption that such regularities do indeed exist and need only to be discovered seems dubious, and a great deal of research would be necessary to establish whether or not it is valid.

It is important to recognize that in seeking such regularities, or noncausal correlations, for the direct method, types of content characteristics must be sought which are *insensitive to* or *independent of* possible variations in propaganda strategy. Because propaganda strategy is an intervening, unstable variable between elite political behavior and propaganda contents, it may happen that a regularity observed in a small number of past cases is, in a manner as yet unrecognized by the analyst, dependent on the simultaneous and recurring presence in these cases of a certain propaganda strategy. A change in propaganda strategy in subsequent cases, then, may eliminate the assumed regularity. Therefore, since most postulations of regularities are based on relatively few cases, the analyst is likely to lose confidence in any postulation which falls short of perfect correlation.

This emphasizes the importance for the direct method of content characteristics which are insensitive to and independent of propaganda strategy. The direct method is on firm ground only when it employs as content indicators those features of content over which the propagandist does not exercise control or of whose correlation with a type of elite intention (and, therefore, of whose possible information-giving value to the investigator) he remains unaware. Such content features are likely to be *symptomatic* and nonconscious features of a propagandist's effort to implement elite policies and intentions rather than a direct reflection of the propaganda strategy he employs for this purpose.[1]

An example of the use of such content features in a direct inference occurs in Case Study No. 12.2,* Inference 4, p. 197, in Part III, in which the FCC analyst inferred the Nazis' relative degree of confidence in repulsing an Allied invasion at various possible points. The inference rested upon the generalization that the more frequently and specifically defensive capabilities in an area are mentioned, the greater is the propagandist's confidence in his side's ability to meet an opponent's initiative in that area.

In practice it is often difficult to justify the assumption that content indicators employed for purposes of a direct inference are insensitive to variations in propaganda strategy. Many attempts at direct inference can be challenged on this score. It often happens that, when the propaganda analyst is ostensibly relying upon the direct method, he is also using elements of the indirect method. Closer examination of his reasoning may reveal that the inference he is making is not based solely on the assumed regularity between a content characteristic and a type of elite intention but is being supplemented by more or less tacit speculations about propaganda strategy. It may be preferable in such cases to drop the formal adherence to the direct method and to explore more explicitly and systematically the indirect approach.

The fact that the direct and indirect methods sometimes are blurred in practice does not invalidate the distinction between them. It is true that even an analyst who, unlike the FCC investigators, is conscious of the distinction between the two methods may have difficulty deciding whether to regard given content characteristics as be-

* I.e., Case Study No. 2 in Chapter 12.

ing sensitive to or independent of propaganda strategy. In such cases, the analyst may make either an indirect or a direct inference, but he will be wise to consider carefully the reasons for regarding the content characteristics either as sensitive to or independent of propaganda strategy. And he will do well to consider how the inference might vary depending on his decision as to the relationship between the content characteristics and the propaganda strategy.

The *indirect method* recognizes that the behavior of the propagandist, in selecting communication goals and strategies and in implementing them, constitutes an intermediate step between elite intentions and propaganda content. It expects, therefore, that the content of communication used to support a given elite intention or policy will directly reflect the propaganda strategy adopted for this purpose by the propagandist.

In contrast to the direct method, therefore, the indirect method requires the propaganda analyst to identify content characteristics in propaganda which are *sensitive to* and *dependent upon* propaganda strategy. From a logical standpoint, the first step in the indirect method is always to establish the propaganda goal or strategy underlying the specified content.

Hence, from a logical standpoint, the indirect method is comprised of *a series of interconnected inferences,* or causal imputations. Whereas an inference from content to a certain type of elite behavior (or to a situational factor) is made as a *single* step in the direct method, such an inference is broken up into a number of smaller steps in the indirect method. The analyst attempts to identify the intermediate events linking the content to the elite behavior (or situational factor), which together comprise parts of a causal chain.[2] Each individual step, or causal imputation, in the series of interconnected inferences is then capable of being supported by appropriate reasoning and evidence.

The difference between the direct and indirect methods in this respect can be depicted diagrammatically (see page 41).

The inferential diagram for the indirect method is somewhat simplified. Certain propaganda-behavior variables discussed in Chapter 2 are left out here, and alternative patterns of inference are not indicated. The close resemblance between this diagram and the action schema developed in Chapter 2 is not surprising, since essentially the indirect method attempts, in making inferences, to exploit the analyst's knowledge of the general interrelationships among the major unstable components of the system of behavior.

DIRECT METHOD:

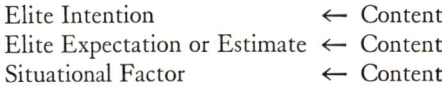

Elite Intention	← Content
Elite Expectation or Estimate	← Content
Situational Factor	← Content

INDIRECT METHOD:

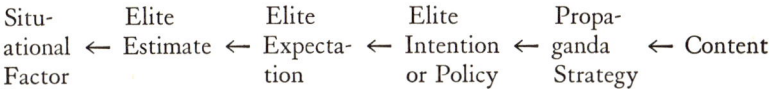

Situ- ational ← Estimate	Elite	← Expecta-	Elite	← Intention	Elite	← ganda	Propa-	← Content

Situ-   Elite   Elite   Elite   Propa-
ational ← Estimate ← Expecta- ← Intention ← ganda   ← Content
Factor   tion   or Policy   Strategy

It should be noted that the direct and indirect methods as defined here, like the action schema of Chapter 2, are presented as being appropriate for inferring only those seven antecedent conditions that were of interest to the FCC analysts. These two methods were developed empirically and logically in terms of what specifically takes place and is needed to infer *these* seven types of antecedent conditions.

However, it may be worth while to compare these two methods with alternative methods for making the same types of inferences or with methods for inferring other types of antecedent conditions. Thus, an alternative to the indirect method would be to infer an elite intention by making a preliminary inference *not* about propaganda strategy but rather about nonpurposive aspects of the propaganda production process:

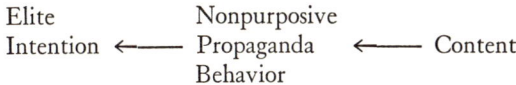

Elite   Nonpurposive
Intention ←——— Propaganda   ←——— Content
                   Behavior

A method different from *both* of the two FCC methods would be one, for example, which inferred elite ideological dispositions or values from content without making any intermediate inferences:

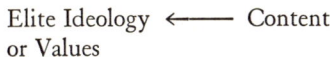

Elite Ideology ←——— Content
or Values

Each of these new methods would require a set of distinctive empirical generalizations to serve as reasoning in support of specific inferences, and this reasoning would differ from that appropriate for supporting the FCC inferences. Thus both are clearly not identical with the direct or indirect methods.

The Relationship between the Two Methods

The preceding section has emphasized the logical and procedural distinctions between the direct and indirect methods. The fact that the propaganda analyst is often forced to interpret content evidence from the standpoint of both methods does not warrant the conclusion that the two methods are being merged, that they overlap, or that the distinction between them is an artificial one. For, as has been noted, the two methods use radically different types of supporting generalizations and reasoning.

Certain predispositions on the part of the investigator may determine which approach he uses. Analysts who favor a systematic approach are likely to rely upon the direct method in the *early* stages of a propaganda-analysis operation, as long as they know relatively little about the peculiarities of the political and propaganda system in question. On the other hand, investigators who are generally skeptical of a scientific approach are less likely to begin their work in propaganda analysis by trying to use the direct method; they are more likely to begin with an intuitive, common-sense version of the indirect method, based on what they feel to be the logic of the situation in individual instances.

The direct method is also more likely to be favored by specialists in communication research, whose background knowledge and skill is largely confined to the techniques of communication research, than by political analysts and area specialists, who have a more sophisticated and detailed knowledge of the political elite, its political and propaganda behavior, and the specialized political vocabulary which it employs.

As a matter of fact, if the distinct character and requirements of the two methods are clearly grasped by an investigator, it may be possible for him to use them in a supplementary fashion. The possible relationship between the two approaches may take the following form. In the preliminary phases of a propaganda-analysis problem, when the investigator is engaged in scanning large bodies of communication material in order to formulate inferential hunches, the one-to-one correlations which form the working tools of the direct approach may have a certain utility, uncertain and tentative though they may be. That is, the generalizations of the direct method may be useful in *hypothesis formation*. If the analyst is familiar with a large number of possible one-to-one correlations, he may be more alert to the presence, in propaganda material, of possible content indicators of those aspects of the communicator's state of mind and of his situational milieu which he is interested in inferring. Realizing the uncertain validity of the regularities postulated in these one-to-one correlations, however, the analyst knows that he cannot rely upon them to support a specific inference in any single case. Therefore, any inferential hypothesis suggested to him by the content terms of a direct one-to-one generalization must be examined carefully. In order to do this, the analyst engages in an intensive analysis of the particular case at hand, taking into account all the additional variables and contextual considerations which might affect the applicability of the direct generalization. In particular, as suggested in the preceding section, the analyst must consider carefully the matter of the communicator's *goal or strategy,* an important intervening variable which is not taken into account in the direct method.

Transitions from an initial use of noncausal correlations (as in the direct method) to causal imputation of middle steps in a chain of reasoning are not unusual in efforts to explain and predict in everyday life and in social research. The initial observation and use of a possible noncausal statistical correlation between two types of events is often preliminary to a more refined investigation of causal chains and networks.

The recommended relationship in using the two methods can now be stated quite simply. It is, first, that the direct approach be utilized in *hypothesis formation* for whatever it is worth (which depends upon the number and quality of the tentative, incompletely confirmed one-to-one correlations that are available) and that the indirect method be utilized in the *assessment,* or testing, of the inferential hunches derived from the direct approach. Second, it is recommended that such transitions from the direct to the indirect approach be made quite deliberately, in full awareness that the indirect method requires logic-of-the-situation reasoning and the use of generalizations other than the one-to-one type of correlation between a content indicator and an aspect of the elite's political behavior or situational milieu.[3]

The use of the indirect method for refining, elaborating, and assessing inferential hunches, as recommended here, appears to have an analogue in certain areas of historical explanation. The one-to-one correlations of the direct method in propaganda analysis resemble in certain respects what Patrick Gardiner calls the "loose" and "porous" generalizations available to the historian for explanation of the single case. The inadequacy of these historical generalizations for the purpose evidently forces the historian to operate with criteria and procedures of explanation which are different from those used in more advanced forms of scientific explanation.

"Generalizations of the kind in question," Gardiner suggests, merely

provide indications, and rough ones at that, of the sorts of factors which, *under certain circumstances,* we expect to find correlated with other sorts of factors; but . . . they leave open to historical investigation and analysis the task of eliciting the specific nature of those factors *on a particular occasion,* and the precise manner in which the factors are causally connected with one another.[4]

In other words, because of the "loose" and "porous" nature of available generalizations—a characterization which may be fairly applied also to the highly tentative one-to-one correlations of the direct method—the risk in moving from the general hypothesis or law to the particular case at hand is very much greater in history than in most forms of scientific procedure. Accordingly, historians rightly do not expect to derive any considerable support for their explanations of particular events from laws or broad historical generalizations and often regard it as necessary to support (or supplement) a broad explanatory hypothesis with a lengthy and detailed analysis of the individual historical case at hand. In this respect, once more, the problems and procedures of the propaganda analyst are closely analogous to those of the historian.

NOTES

1. On the difference between interpretation of "intent" and "symptoms" in the analysis of communication see P. Kecskemeti, *Meaning, Communication, and Value* (University of Chicago Press, Chicago, 1952), pp. 60–61.

2. Note the resemblance of the logical structure of indirect inferences to the historian's practice described by Hempel as filling in an "explanation sketch." On this point see Carl G. Hempel, "The Function of General Laws in History," in H. Feigl and W. Sellars (eds.), *Readings in Philosophical Analysis* (Appleton-Century-Crofts, New York, 1949), pp. 465–66; Patrick Gardiner, *The Nature of Historical Explanation* (Oxford University Press, London, 1952), pp. 91–97; W. H. Walsh, *An Introduction to the Philosophy of History* (Hutchinson House, London, 1951), pp. 23–24, 59–64; J. W. N. Watkins, "Ideal Types and Historical Explanation," in H. Feigl and M. Brodbeck (eds.), *Readings in the Philosophy of Science* (Appleton-Century-Crofts, New York, 1953), pp. 723–43, *passim.*

3. For additional discussion and illustrative material on the use of the tentative correlations of the direct method in hypothesis formation see Part III, pp. 229 ff.

4. Gardiner, *op. cit.,* pp. 93, 96–97; italics supplied.

FIVE

Generalizations Appropriate to the Indirect Method

It has been noted that the indirect method in propaganda analysis is similar to the logic-of-the-situation approach employed in everyday life and in certain forms of historical explanation. Though often utilized in an intuitive fashion, the logic-of-the-situation approach is nonetheless based upon certain types of supporting generalizations. This fact is sometimes overlooked or minimized because the generalizations underlying logic-of-the-situation assessments often remain implicit and may be rather universally accepted as laws of human nature or psychology. Or their status as generalizations may be overlooked because they are applied only to single individuals and specific groups rather than to people as a whole.

It is the objective of this chapter to characterize explicitly the various types of generalizations employed in the indirect method and to show at what points they are used to support various steps in indirect inferences. Chapter 6 will then describe in greater detail how these generalizations are employed within the logic-of-the-situation framework.

The generalizations employed in making inferences via the indirect method are quite different from the type of regularity, or correlation, between a content feature and some aspect of political behavior or of the situation which is required by the direct method. In order of increasing specificity, the types of generalization used in the indirect method are:

45

1. General knowledge of the character of the interrelationships among the variables comprising the system of behavior.
2. Knowledge of how *people in general* behave when engaged in the type of activity of interest (i.e., in the behavior, political and propaganda, which constitutes the system of behavior).
3. Knowledge of how *particular individuals* (the political elite and its propagandists, both as a group and as individuals) behave when engaged in the type of activity of interest.
   a) Generalizations about the preferred solutions and habitual behavior of the elite and propagandists in question when confronted with different types of action problems.
   b) Generalizations about the manner in which the elite and propagandists in question behave under conditions which make a rational choice of the best means for achieving a desired end difficult.

Of these three types of knowledge, the first was examined in some detail in Chapter 2, where a general action schema was outlined. General knowledge of the interrelationships and interdependencies among the several variables comprising the system of behavior may in fact be regarded as among the *general laws* of propaganda analysis. Knowledge of these general interrelationships provides the investigator with an inferential model which is appreciably more complex than the simple one which underlies most forms of rigorous content analysis, i.e., the effort to discover a one-to-one correlation between some content indicator (or class of indicators) and some state or characteristic of the communicator or of his environment. As was indicated in Chapter 3, the historical development of propaganda-analysis methodology has been marked by a breakdown of initial efforts to employ the simple one-to-one inferential model and by its replacement with the more complex inferential schema which constitutes the indirect method.

As far as the second of the listed types of generalizations goes, it suffices to note that such general knowledge is not enough to support the concrete inferences of interest in propaganda analysis. Knowledge about human nature, knowledge of how people in general behave in certain situations, is of substantial value to the propaganda analyst, especially in providing a first tentative inference when he is faced with a specific problem concerning a specific actor. But this knowledge must be supplemented by more specific knowledge of the habitual modes of behavior of the principal groups and individuals whose actions in concrete situations the propaganda analyst is trying to understand.[1]

The third type of knowledge, however, which is of particular relevance for the indirect method, may profitably be discussed in detail at this point. In the following paragraphs consideration is given to each of the two types of generalizations (3, *a* and *b,* above) which may be made about the principal actors whose actions are of interest to the propaganda analyst. In the following chapter an attempt is made to describe the manner in which these generalizations enter into the analyst's mode of reasoning and to characterize that mode of reasoning in greater detail.

Generalizations about the Actor's Preferred Solutions and Habitual Behavior

In many cases, generalizations about the actor's preferred solutions and habitual behavior are the major component in the analyst's reasoning. Examples of their use are frequent in the case studies presented in Part III. Yet it should be noted at the outset that, however useful the analyst may find them, such generalizations cannot be relied upon exclusively in making inferences.

The indirect method, it was pointed out above, consists of a series of interconnected inferences, a series of steps linking the content to propaganda and elite political behavior or situational factors. This method was diagrammed as:

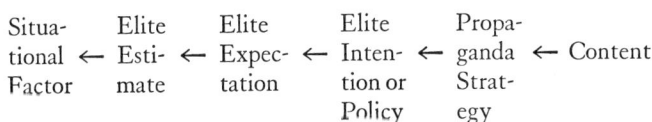

Situa-	Elite	Elite	Elite	Propa-	
tional ←	Esti- ←	Expec- ←	Inten- ←	ganda ←	Content
Factor	mate	tation	tion or	Strat-	
			Policy	egy	

Each step in this diagram, each causal imputation, requires adequate supporting reasoning, and the reasoning will often include generalizations about some aspect of the actor's habitual mode of behavior and his preferred solutions. A generalization is relevant, however, only if it covers precisely the segment of action or behavior encompassed in the particular step the analyst is taking. It is thus logical to classify and discuss these generalizations according to the steps in the series of inferences to which they apply. For this purpose, four major steps may be considered to comprise the structure of an indirect inference: (1) from content to propaganda goal or strategy,

(2) from propaganda strategy to elite intention or policy, (3) from elite intention or policy to elite expectation and/or estimate, and (4) from elite estimate to situational factor. (The two steps from elite intention or policy to elite expectation, and from the latter to elite estimate, are combined into one simply because in practice they are so closely associated that it would be difficult to consider them separately.) Granted that this analysis of the major steps in inferences and of the reasoning underlying them is neither complete nor fully satisfactory—for the inferential process is a highly complex one; yet it is useful for purposes of discussing the generalizations of the indirect method.

INFERENCE FROM CONTENT TO PROPAGANDA GOAL (OR STRATEGY)

The propagandist may be viewed as making a series of choices and decisions when he translates a given propaganda strategy into specific communication content. Not all of these decisions will be made consciously; nonetheless, many of them will reflect the communicator's judgment as to how he can make the communication most effective in the circumstances in which he judges it to be taking place. The sequence of choices may be depicted, schematically, as follows: selection of specific propaganda *goal* or goals to implement a propaganda strategy → selection of communication (or propaganda) *devices and techniques* to further a given propaganda goal → selection of *meanings* to be included in the message, and selection of appropriate *words* by means of which the intended meanings are to be conveyed to the audience addressed. This sequence, in abbreviated terms, is as follows:

Speaker's Purpose → Techniques → Semantical Behavior [2]

When a propaganda analyst uses the indirect method to make an inference from content to propaganda goal or strategy (speaker's purpose), it is therefore obvious that he must take into account that aspect of the communicator's behavior referred to above as selection of communication (or propaganda) devices and techniques. (The subject of the speaker's semantical behavior is discussed in detail in Part II, Chapter 10.) The analyst asks himself such questions as: What is the range of propaganda techniques with which the communicator is familiar? How skillful is he in selecting from among alternative propaganda techniques those which are most appropriate for the task at hand?

This is to say that the propaganda analyst employing the indirect method requires knowledge about the *technical expertise and skill-fulness* of the propaganda system under scrutiny and that of individual propagandists employed therein. He needs to know how certain propaganda goals are characteristically implemented by the propaganda organization in question. He also needs some appreciation of the organization's degree of skillfulness in assessing technical propaganda questions, of the range and quality of its information about audience predispositions and its sensitivity to such considerations, and of the efficiency and faithfulness with which propaganda directives are translated into propaganda content by operational personnel.

INFERENCE FROM PROPAGANDA STRATEGY TO ELITE INTENTION OR POLICY

Every political elite develops in time a set of preferred solutions for the more or less standardized types of problems that arise in employing propaganda as an instrument of policy. These preferred solutions reflect its accumulated experience and judgment and serve as guides to decision and action in day-to-day operations when new situations arise.

Every political elite also has a set of operating beliefs as to which types of propaganda goals and objectives (i.e., strategy) to pursue in order best to support different types of national policies and interests in different types of situations. This set of beliefs, or *operational propaganda theory,* reflects the regime's evaluation of the capabilities and limitations of propaganda as an instrument of policy and its estimate of the prerequisites for successful propaganda.

An elite's operational propaganda theory should be distinguished from its formal propaganda doctrine, that is, the authoritative theoretical writings or classics it has produced on the subject of propaganda. Although the propaganda analyst may find it rewarding to study these because they may be influential in determining the regime's propaganda practices, knowledge of the regime's operational theory must be derived empirically from a study of its actual propaganda behavior.

The propaganda analyst makes the basic assumption that propaganda is co-ordinated with elite policies and policy calculations; but if he is to make inferences from propaganda strategy to elite intention or policy, he needs more concrete knowledge, which he can obtain only from a set of empirically derived generalizations about an elite's operational propaganda theory.

An elite's decision to follow a certain propaganda strategy depends not merely on its policies and intentions but also on some of the estimates and expectations which have helped to determine these policies and intentions. For example, the policy which a regime has decided to pursue may be considered risky in certain respects or likely to entail certain negative consequences. Accordingly, the propaganda strategy which the regime selects to support that policy may be designed to make these risks less likely to occur or to minimize the expected negative consequences. On the other hand, a propaganda strategy may be designed to enhance expected gains or to achieve additional gains. In attempting to infer whether policy considerations like these have influenced selection of a propaganda strategy, the analyst makes use of what he knows about the regime's operational propaganda theory.

Inference from Elite Intention or Policy to Elite Expectation and/or Estimate

An elite's estimates and expectations may influence policy and action without directly affecting propaganda strategy. In order to infer these estimates and expectations, the analyst must know something about the elite's *operational code,* that is, the general rules of political strategy and tactics on which the elite bases its decisions and behavior in specific instances, consciously or unconsciously. An operational code reflects the way an elite views the game of politics and the arena where it is played.

Research into the operational code of the elite whose propaganda is to be analyzed is not usually considered to be a task of propaganda analysis itself. Rather, it is assumed that propaganda analysts already have some knowledge of the ways of the political elite in question or can obtain such knowledge by consulting analyses of the composition, ideology, and past behavior of the elite prepared by specialists in such matters. Nevertheless, what is meant by an elite's operational code may be clarified by a brief discussion of the ways in which knowledge of it may be obtained. Either of two research procedures may be employed by the investigator. He may study those writings of the elite which contain serious discussions of the problem of correct strategy and tactics in order to learn what rules of strategy and tactics—or habitual ways of thinking and acting—the elite favors. Or he may deduce these rules from a systematic study of a large number of the actions of the elite.[3]

An operational code which is derived by the investigator solely from statements by the elite about questions of strategy and tactics has certain obvious limitations. For example, the elite may use the code more to rationalize and justify its decisions and actions than to determine policy calculations. Yet, even such a code may have an indirect and partial effect on policy calculations by delimiting the range of behavior which can be readily justified.

It is preferable, nonetheless, to formulate an elite's operational code empirically from a study of its actions. The two research approaches, of course, may be usefully combined by testing and refining formulations of the code derived initially from an analysis of the elite's writings against an empirical analysis of the elite's actions.

A formulation in general terms of an elite's operational code may offer considerable assistance to the analyst who attempts to infer its estimates and expectations in particular situations. The operational code, however, cannot be safely used alone to predict or explain the actions of an elite. For one thing, an elite may revise its general view of correct strategy and tactics on the basis of new experience and a subsequent re-evaluation of past events. Moreover, the rules comprising a code may be ambiguous, inconsistent, or incomplete; and the conditions under which any particular rule is applied may be difficult to identify.

Nonetheless, the code may be useful to the analyst because it provides a frame of reference which suggests ways of interpreting available clues, often of a fragmentary character, as to the calculations behind current policies and actions. The generalizations comprising the code help the analyst formulate alternative hypotheses or inferences against which to weigh available evidence on current policy calculations. At the least, the code may enable the analyst to delimit the range of types of behavior which that elite is likely to display in a certain situation.

Although knowledge of an elite's operational code obviously does not permit the analyst to dispense with an intensive study of the case at hand in all its individuality and complexity, it should facilitate the task of reconstructing some of the hidden policy calculations.

INFERENCE FROM ELITE ESTIMATE TO SITUATIONAL FACTOR

The amount and quality of information about current developments at home and abroad available to an elite and its intelligence specialists determine, of course, the caliber of its official estimates of new situations and events. But a variety of other factors may color these estimates more subtly: the elite's basic political values, its image of an opponent, its operational code, the ideology and theory of historical development to which it subscribes, the criteria it employs to assess the power of participants in world politics, and the policies and policy calculations to which it happens to be currently committed.

It was noted earlier that an elite's estimate of situational factors often influences its selection of propaganda strategy. It may therefore be possible for an analyst to infer the estimates which seem logically to underlie the adoption of a particular propaganda strategy or to infer that a change in these situational estimates may be responsible for a change in propaganda strategy when one has taken place. In addition, the analyst may be able to go beyond the elite estimates which he has inferred and to deduce something about the true character of the situations and events to which these estimates refer. Such a deduction, in the form of an inference, is especially useful when the situational factors are not directly observable by an outsider. In order to make the inference, the analyst must know something about the *patterns of perception and estimation* which are characteristic for the elite in question. What are the general characteristics of the information-seeking and information-evaluating activities of the elite in question? In what ways may its estimates be subtly colored by its political values, its image of opponents, its own operational code, the criteria by means of which it assesses the relative power of participants in world politics, the policies and policy calculations to which it is currently committed?

Knowledge of what these patterns are (or even hypotheses about them) will enable the investigator to assess in what circumstances and for what types of problems an elite is likely to make realistic or distorted estimates of certain types of situational factors. For example, is the incidence of poor domestic morale likely to be exaggerated or minimized in elite estimates? Are the regime's estimates of internal opposition, of its vulnerability to psychological warfare, etc., likely to be realistic or distorted?

The ways in which the four types of generalizations identified above are used to support different steps in the indirect method are indicated schematically in the accompanying diagram. The arrows indicate various logical paths of inference. The logical function of each of the four types of generalizations is indicated by a brace show-

USE OF GENERALIZATIONS ABOUT THE ACTOR'S HABITUAL BEHAVIOR IN THE INDIRECT METHOD

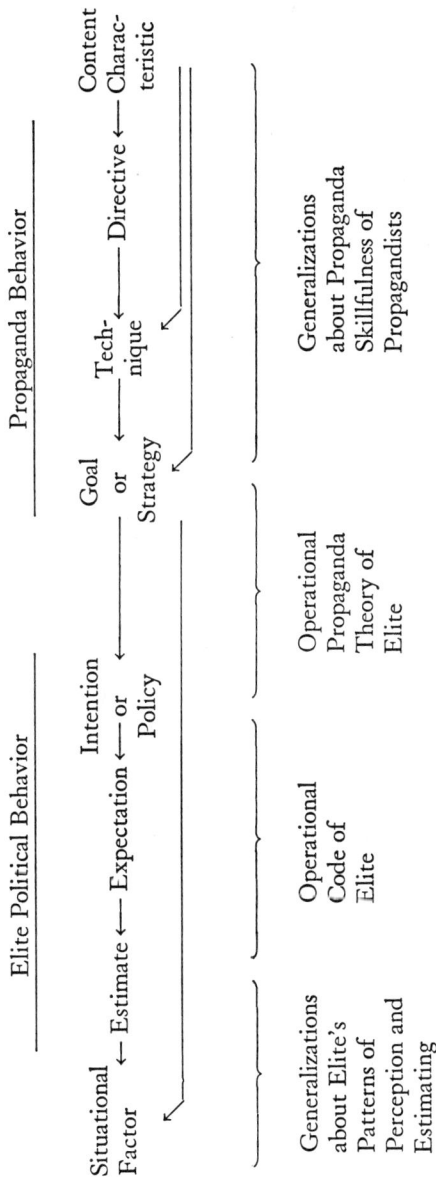

Elite Political Behavior

Situational Factor ← Estimate ← Expectation ← Intention or Policy

Propaganda Behavior

Goal or Strategy ← Technique ← Directive ← Content Characteristic

Generalizations about Elite's Patterns of Perception and Estimating

Operational Code of Elite

Operational Propaganda Theory of Elite

Generalizations about Propaganda Skillfulness of Propagandists

ing which step in inference that type of generalization can support. It should be noted that the diagram does not attempt to depict how these generalizations are used in the context of the logic-of-the-situation type of explanation (see below, pp. 58–63), which is central to the indirect method of inference.

Generalizations about the Actor's Behavior under Conditions Which Make a Rational Choice Difficult

Although generalizations about the propagandist's preferred solutions and habitual behavior may be very helpful to the analyst, he cannot usually expect to make an inference simply by attempting to discover which habitual pattern of behavior has been repeated. Various factors limit the usefulness of such a procedure.

For one thing, many situations which confront political elites and their propagandists are not standardized. The choice of action in such situations is not routine or automatic but requires fresh calculation of the relationships between means and ends and of the possible gains and losses which would result from the alternative ways of acting open to the decision-maker. The final choice of action decided upon by the actor may resemble one of his preferred solutions or a previously adopted response pattern, but it is also likely to contain special features which reflect unusual aspects of the present situation as assessed by the actor. Accordingly, it is risky for the analyst to interpret a new propaganda communication in terms exclusively of a habitual mode of response to a given type of situation or problem, even when a first inspection suggests to him that a previously noted pattern has been repeated. Rather, he must consider whether the present case embodies unique aspects which have affected the choice of action by the elite and its propagandists.

The problem of making inferences in such cases is further complicated by the fact that content characteristics of propaganda taken by themselves may be unreliable indicators of the actor's total response to a situation. Propaganda statements which are similar in content may, in different instances, be parts of different total response patterns. For example, virtually the same propaganda statement may be made in one instance when the elite is intent on taking a certain action and in another instance when it is only bluffing.[4] Thus, the situational and behavioral implications of a statement—as against its communicative or manifest semantical meaning—depend upon the *context* in which it occurs.[5]

And finally, the possibility that language may be used for deception should make the propaganda analyst cautious in seizing upon a familiar pattern as an indication that the present instance is another occurrence of a preferred solution or of habitual action.

Since, then, the propaganda analyst recognizes that present behavior is not necessarily exactly like or even close to habitual behavior, he is prepared to qualify his knowledge of how an actor generally behaves in a given situation if an appraisal of the individual and unique aspects of the case in question suggests that the actor may have had reason to behave differently this time.

A basic assumption made by the propaganda analyst is that the behavior under examination is purposive, that is, that the elite and the propagandist are trying to achieve something they want. He assumes, further, that to some extent they employ rational calculation for this purpose.

At this point the analyst finds useful the second of the two types of generalizations about how particular individuals behave when engaged in specific activities (generalization 3, *b*, on p. 46).

An elite and its propagandists are frequently faced with conditions which make it difficult for them to make a rational choice of the best means of achieving a desired end. The analyst's knowledge of how they generally behave under such conditions, hypothetical though this knowledge will necessarily be, is particularly important when the unusual aspects of a given case are under assessment.

In the most general sense, a rational choice is one which leads to the most preferred set of consequences. But success in rational calculation, in its simplest form, requires (*a*) the presentation to the decision-maker of a set of alternative courses of action for choice; (*b*) knowledge and information that permit him to predict the consequences of choosing any given alternative; and (*c*) a criterion for determining which set of estimated consequences he prefers (and, therefore, which course of action he should choose).[6]

It is well known that in politics it is difficult to meet the three requirements just noted and that, therefore, the problem of making rational choices is highly complex and difficult. Different elites may be expected to have somewhat different ways of coping with the conditions which make rational choices difficult. While it is hardly correct to suggest that elites have been systematically studied and compared from this standpoint, nonetheless every political and propaganda analyst inevitably makes some assumptions, whether conscious or not, about how the political elite whose actions he is studying attempts to deal with the uncertainties of political prognostication and planning.[7] A more systematic statement and assessment of such assumptions, or hypotheses, would be desirable. It will suffice here to suggest some of the points around which a more explicit and systematic treatment of the problem could be centered.

In the first place, for an actor to choose rationally among alternative courses of action, it is necessary that he be able to judge each possible outcome to be "better," "the same," or "worse" than any other possible outcome. This can be the case, however, only if the decision-maker possesses a span of attention wide enough to enable him to consider the probable consequences, both immediate and long range, of all alternative courses of action. This can be the case, too, only if he possesses a single, consistent system of values which can be applied simultaneously to the whole range of action. But, in practice, few decision-makers always demonstrate such a wide span of attention. And, moreover, the decision-maker's preferences, or values, may be manifold, conflicting, and unstable; it may be difficult for him to find one criterion by which to measure all of them, or to establish a clear system of priorities among them for purposes of deciding which possible outcome is best for him.

Next, as many students of politics have pointed out, it is difficult to forecast the consequences of alternative courses of action in politics. There are usually significant limits to the amount of essential knowledge and information which is available to the decision-maker or, for that matter, to anyone else. It is also difficult to plan foreign policy or to select medium- and long-range strategies because other political elites and natural events play a role in determining what will happen. These limitations upon the possibility of predicting the outcome of alternative courses of action affect the time perspective which an elite displays in its policy calculations and the theory underlying the range, multiplicity, and specificity of objectives which it pursues. Elites may be expected to differ, too, in the extent to which (and the circumstances under which) they prefer to defer choice of action in order to obtain more information.

In the third place, it may not be possible in any situation to identify or consider sufficiently all the available alternative courses of action before a choice of policy or action is made. Policy-making and decision processes may not favor the development of considered judgments and carefully weighed decisions. Thorough consideration of available alternatives may be impossible for a number of reasons; for example, in some situations it may be necessary to act very quickly, or some alternative courses of action are emotionally distasteful while others are attractive for sentimental reasons or because of irrelevant considerations. Also, where the power of decision is shared, policy decisions may reflect a compromise of different viewpoints or the realities of brute power rather than the best possible wisdom.

NOTES

1. A similar point is made by J. W. N. Watkins, "Ideal Types and Historical Explanation," in H. Feigl and M. Brodbeck (eds.), *Readings in the Philosophy of Science* (Appleton-Century-Crofts, New York, 1953), pp. 734–43, in distinguishing between different types of historical explanation. What he calls "explanation in principle" relies upon typical dispositions and disregards personal differences. In contrast, the premises of an "explanation in detail" must be the specific dispositions, beliefs, and relationships of actual people. He comments, further, that explanation in principle is the field par excellence for ideal types, whereas for purposes of explanation in detail ideal types are mostly constructed *ad hoc* and rendered increasingly realistic until they become empirical reconstructions. Similar distinctions can be made for different forms of economic analysis.

2. It will be recognized that, in considering only the semantic choices made by the speaker, this discussion has been considerably oversimplified. A fuller treatment would also consider the nonlexical features of the communication, such as size of print, position on the page, pauses and errors in speech, etc.

3. For a statement of what is meant by an elite's operational code and how a formulation of such a code may be used to explain and predict that elite's actions see the Introduction to Nathan Leites, *A Study of Bolshevism* (The Free Press, Glencoe, Ill., 1953). The following paragraphs condense Leites' treatment of the problem and elaborate it in several respects.

4. A parallel problem is encountered in the practice of clinical psychiatry. As Paul E. Meehl observes: "The complicated kinds of mutual interaction between internal variables and external events which characterizes human clinical material result in a situation in which a response having a specified topography, emitted in a specified stimulus field, may indicate different states of internal variables depending upon all well-confirmed hypotheses about the individual. In ordinary life, we recognize this when we say that the behavior will suggest, in the extreme case, even opposite interpretations when the behavior occurs in two individuals concerning whose personality structure we have already considerable knowledge." From Paul E. Meehl, *Clinical* vs. *Statistical Prediction: A Theoretical Analysis and a Review of the Evidence*, p. 52. Copyright, 1954, by the University of Minnesota Press. Reprinted by permission of the publisher.

5. On this point see P. Kecskemeti, *Meaning, Communication, and Value* (University of Chicago Press, Chicago, 1952), pp. 25–61. See also below, Part II, Chapter 10.

6. These requirements are noted by Herbert A. Simon, "Some Strategic Considerations in the Construction of Social Science Models," in Paul F. Lazarsfeld (ed.), *Mathematical Thinking in the Social Sciences* (The Free Press, Glencoe, Ill., 1954), p. 391. Particularly useful for the purposes of this study is Simon's discussion (pp. 393–94) of the conditions which "bound" or limit rational behavior.

7. A number of interesting hypotheses concerning historical and national differences among elites in this respect are advanced by Hans Speier in "Psychological Warfare Reconsidered," in his *Social Order and the Risks of War* (George W. Stewart, New York, 1952), pp. 433–55.

SIX

The Logic-of-the-Situation Approach as Applied in the Indirect Method

In the *direct* method, it will be recalled, an inference about an elite intention is made by means of a simple deduction. For this purpose the analyst requires only (*a*) an empirical generalization which postulates a regularity, or high statistical correlation, between a type of content characteristic and the type of elite intention in question, and (*b*) a factual observation as to whether this type of content characteristic is present or not present in the body of communication under examination. These two items serve, respectively, as the major and minor premises for the deduction.

In breaking up the broad noncausal inference which is characteristic of the direct method into a series of smaller causal imputations, the indirect method introduces a mode of reasoning which is far more complex than that described in the preceding paragraph.

The mode of reasoning required by the indirect method appears to be a special application of the procedure of causal imputation in historical explanation.[1] In this type of explanation the investigator attempts to approximate the logic of experiment by means of a mental rehearsal of hypothetical outcomes. Changes in the value of one or more variables are postulated by the investigator in order to appraise the consequences, if any, for other variables. By means of such imaginative rehearsals the investigator reaches a conclusion as to what the nonobservable factors were which determined the action or behavior in question. Just as the historian applies this procedure to infer the subjective side of particular actions, the propaganda analyst utilizes a similar approach in attempting to reconstruct some aspect of the calculations and situational determinants behind specific, individual propaganda messages.[2]

More particularly, the indirect method of inference bears a close resemblance to what Karl Popper has aptly called the "logic-of-the-situation approach." [3] The actor is assumed to choose among alternative courses of action on the basis of his assessment of the logic of the situation which confronts him. His choice of action is based upon the set of conditions (termed "initial conditions" in some technical formulations of the method) with which he is operating at the time. These initial conditions include the actor's values and his aims, the information available to him about relevant aspects of the situation, and the knowledge available to him for estimating future developments and the probable consequences of each of the alternative courses of action open to him.

In employing the logic-of-the-situation method to analyze and explain the action in question, the investigator attempts to reconstruct the specific initial conditions to which the actor responded in that instance. Now, what the logic-of-the-situation approach assumes as a kind of first approximation is the trivial general law that sane persons as a rule act more or less rationally. In other words, faced with the same situation and bound by the same initial conditions, different persons (for example, the actor and the analyst) will arrive at the same conclusion as to which course of action is preferable. The analyst's task, then, is the following: knowing what course of action the actor did select, the analyst attempts to reconstruct the initial conditions to which that choice of action would have been a rational response. That is, he tries to assess whether available evidence on the initial conditions is adequate for his purpose; if not, he searches for additional evidence on the initial conditions; to the extent necessary, he hypothesizes the correct version of any initial condition on which available evidence seems inadequate, inaccurate, or is missing altogether.

Some accounts of the logic-of-the-situation approach go no further, or not much further, than the preceding description.[4] They therefore give a deceptively simple picture of the operation of the logic-of-the-situation approach and underestimate the problems encountered should the analyst attempt to test, or demonstrate the plausibility of, the insights and hunches which the method yields. For the analytical value of the general assumption that all persons tend to act rationally is, in practice, frequently rather modest. As already noted, many choices of political action take place under conditions which make it difficult for the actor to decide which alternative will be most advantageous to him. In such instances the general assumption that all sane persons tend to act rationally is not nearly so helpful to the analyst as various generalizations about the actor's habitual ways of acting and about his behavior under conditions which make a rational choice difficult.

The propaganda analyst's task in a specific inferential problem may now be specified more fully. It is to infer, by means of the procedure of causal imputation—that is, by a mental rehearsal of hypothetical outcomes—the value of one or more of the unstable variables in the system of behavior under study. The analyst already knows (or can assume with a high degree of confidence) the value of some of these unstable variables, and he knows the *general* interrelationship among the variables. In many cases, for example, he knows the general nature of the situation, if not the concrete situational factors themselves, to which the actor is presumably responding in some fashion. In such cases, the analyst asks himself: How would the actor be expected to behave in that situation? In trying to answer this question, he uses available knowledge (generalizations) about the ways in which the actor has acted in past situations of this type. He also attempts to decide what is novel about the present situation and about the initial conditions of the situation which determined the actor's view of the logic of that situation. This in turn allows the analyst to decide how—or if—the generalizations as to how the actor usually behaves must be qualified.

The propaganda analyst examines the available behavioral data (in this case, the propaganda communications) in order to identify content features which may be the *consequences* of a particular choice of action in that situation. The scanning of propaganda communications for this purpose proceeds in intimate conjunction with the rehearsal in the analyst's mind of alternative inferences as to antecedent conditions.[5] During the course of this mental rehearsal various content features of the propaganda may be tentatively regarded as indicators of various possible action responses. In many cases, content characteristics which "indicate" (permit the analyst to infer) the propagandist's goal or strategy can be readily spotted. The task then becomes to infer other unstable components, or antecedent conditions, of the action.

The analyst feels that he has made a correct reconstruction of the action when he can (*a*) isolate a content feature and one or more of its antecedent conditions and (*b*) join them together by a strand of reasoning which he considers most plausible in accounting for the action response.

The analyst's reasoning takes the form of filling in, or assigning a value to, each of the major unstable variables which are not already known, and supporting this reconstruction both by generalizations and by logic-of-the-situation assessments. This type of inferential reasoning may be likened to an effort to reconstruct the missing pieces in a mosaic. Certain parts of the mosaic are given or readily assumed. Other pieces in the mosaic, however (including the conditions which the analyst particularly wants to clarify), are missing. In effect, therefore, the analyst rehearses in his mind the different possible versions of each particular missing variable which he wants to infer, trying to decide which version is the most plausible, given the known value of the content variable and the known or postulated values of other antecedent conditions.

Trend Analysis in a Cross-Sectional Context

While the objective of the propaganda analyst is to make specific inferences about the state of the system of behavior at any given time, his method of doing so is a form of sequential or trend analysis. In order to characterize the essential features of this mode of analysis, we make some initial simplifying assumptions. Thus, it is assumed that the propaganda analyst is concerned exclusively with but one inferential problem and that he limits his attention to those propaganda statements which bear directly on the topic or subject matter in question: e.g., the fighting on the Russian front, measures for total mobilization of resources, etc.

In sequential or trend analysis the investigator observes closely any changes in the propaganda treatment of the topic of interest to him. The problem of inference is that of determining whether the noted changes in propaganda content reflect important changes in any of the interrelated unstable variables which comprise the political-propaganda system of behavior described earlier. Thus, do the changes in propaganda content reflect changes in propaganda behavior, i.e., a change in propaganda directives, techniques and/or strategy concerning the topic in question? Do these content changes reflect changes only in propaganda behavior or in related elite behavior and/or situational factors as well?

It should be noted that the *absence* of change in propaganda treatment of a topic also may have inferential significance at times. The propaganda analyst often has independent knowledge of changes in the situational environment which may be expected to have some impact on the political and propaganda behavior of the opponent. In such cases he may be able to make interesting inferences from the apparent nonresponsiveness of propaganda to changes in the situation (see, for example, Case Study 13.6, pp. 237–40).

The analyst's problem in interpreting the significance of changes in propaganda content may now be stated in somewhat greater detail.

Some changes in propaganda content may reflect merely *adjustments of propaganda technique or themes to new situational factors,* while other unstable variables, such as the propaganda goal or strategy, remain constant. For example, as a result of new information about audience predispositions or about audience reactions to earlier propaganda, or because of a reassessment of old information of this character, the propagandist may decide that a different communication approach (technique) is more likely to secure the propaganda goal he has been aiming at.

In other cases, however, changes in propaganda content can be plausibly explained only by postulating *the adoption of a new propaganda goal or strategy* or the dropping of one which was previously being pursued. The analyst must then consider whether the new propaganda goal is designed to implement a standing elite policy or a new elite policy (either decided upon or under consideration). He must also consider whether other reasons lie behind the adoption of the new goal: Is it a response to situational changes? To new elite estimates or expectations? To a new elite intention or action?

Any exploration of the reasons for the adoption of a new propaganda objective or strategy involves going one or more steps beyond propaganda behavior in explaining the presence of certain content characteristics in propaganda. This additional step in causal imputation is an important one, because, if it can be taken successfully, propaganda analysis can be used to infer not merely matters of *propaganda* strategy but also *elite* policies, intentions, and calculations. In other words, propaganda analysis at this point becomes a tool for inferring aspects of the opponent's political behavior and changes in his situation which are not always available to direct observation, and its potential value as an intelligence technique to policy-makers is thereby considerably increased.

It is obvious that if a propaganda analyst is to explore the reasons for the adoption of a certain propaganda goal, he must be able to deduce precisely how propaganda behavior is co-ordinated with political policy—precisely how propaganda is being used in the instance under consideration to further elite actions and policies. It would be very useful to him for this purpose to have at his disposal a list of all the possible ways in which an elite intention, action, or policy can be implemented propagandistically. This would facilitate a systematic consideration of alternatives in any particular inferential problem. Such a list would comprise *a catalogue of all the types of propaganda goals which might conceivably be pursued in each of the major types of action situations which arise repeatedly in international conflict situations.*

In order to be of the greatest use, the list not only should be as exhaustive as possible; it should also describe the types of propaganda objectives in sufficiently *general* terms that it would apply to all or many of the specific inferential problems likely to arise. This task is undertaken in Part III.

In the preceding account of the sequential or trend mode of analysis, the task of the propaganda analyst was deliberately oversimplified for presentational purposes. Contrary to the assumption made for this purpose, the propaganda analyst cannot afford to ignore everything in the propaganda which does not bear directly upon the subject matter of interest to him. As a matter of fact, the *totality* of propaganda at any given moment must also be examined by him in attempting to make inferences from a trend in propaganda treatment of a specific subject matter.

The political propagandist we are concerned with, it must be remembered, pursues a number of objectives simultaneously in talking about a variety of subject matters. Any experienced director of national propaganda attempts to co-ordinate and harmonize the selection and implementation of propaganda goals. The set of current propaganda goals and propaganda lines must be mutually compatible; if not actually supporting and reinforcing one another, certainly they ought at least not conflict with one another. Moreover, a higher priority will often be assigned to the achievement of one propaganda objective than to others; accordingly, the propaganda treatment of matters of lesser interest to the propagandist may be partly determined by considerations of over-all strategy.

The interrelationship between propaganda treatment of different topics may take various forms. If, for example, the war on the Russian front was going badly for the Germans, Goebbels might compensate by playing up the "successes" being achieved by German U-boats against Allied shipping. The propaganda analyst who was making a study of German propaganda on the war at sea would therefore have to consider not merely the sequential development of Goebbels' propaganda line on the war at sea and the possibility that Goebbels was giving increased propaganda emphasis to German U-boat successes because of actual or expected changes in the situation which influenced the German view of the course and prospects of the war at sea; he would also have to consider the totality of German propaganda and possible shifts in Goebbels' over-all propaganda strategy. As a result, the analyst might then consider an alternative explanation for the increased propaganda emphasis on German U-boat successes, namely, that it was required by Goebbels' over-all propaganda strategy or by a desire on his part to distract attention from, or to compensate for, the German defeats on the Russian front.

One of the case studies drawn from the FCC experience provides a particularly good example of the way in which a dominating propaganda objective may influence the propaganda treatment of related subjects. In this case, Goebbels deliberately underplayed for awhile important defensive successes achieved by the German army on the Russian front. He did so because the improvement in the military situation removed one of the major props of his anti-Bolshevik propaganda campaign, to which he gave highest priority at the time (see Case Study No. 13.6, pp. 237–40).

The preceding discussion may be summarized by noting that one of the requirements of sequential or trend analysis is that any one component of the propagandist's behavior be viewed in the context of the rest of the propagandist's behavior. The analyst is likely to misinterpret the significance of changes in the propaganda treatment of any single topic if he isolates the study of that topic from a consideration of the propagandist's over-all strategy. Propaganda behavior has a unitary character as well as a developmental dimension; the separate strands of propaganda development must be viewed as interrelated parts of a whole. Therefore, propaganda analysis must combine *linear analysis of individual trends* in propaganda with *cross-sectional or structural analysis of the entire propaganda behavior* at any given time. This fact has some important implications for the organization of propaganda-analysis operations. Provision must be made for examining all of the output of a propaganda system and for evaluating its over-all propaganda strategy. Any division of labor which divorces trend analysis of individual subjects from cross-sectional analyses of the entirety of propaganda and propaganda strategy may result in incorrect or misleading interpretations of specific trends.

NOTES

1. For an explicit general account of causal imputation in historical explanation and its relation to the logic of empirical proof see the commentary on Max Weber's contributions to this field in Talcott Parsons, *The Structure of Social Action* (2d ed.; The Free Press, Glencoe, Ill., 1949), pp. 610 ff.

2. Such an interest in the particulars of a specific action again brings the propaganda analyst in some respects close to the clinical psychologist. Both are very much concerned with the relation of lawfulness and uniqueness in efforts to explain and predict in the individual case. Certain parallels can be detected between the propaganda analyst's use of the indirect method and the clinician's effort to infer some of the antecedent conditions of a communication produced by a patient by postulating hypotheses concerning his personality and other internal variables.

The propaganda analyst shares with the clinician an interest in evaluating the significance of small segments of behavior in the larger context in which they occur. In attempting to make precise explanations of the individual case, both train themselves to notice what is *unusual* about the case at hand, to identify and weigh those aspects of behavior which may provide a basis for inference perhaps just because they occur only *rarely* in cases of this kind. This point is developed further in Part II of this study. For an account of the logic of clinical activity see Paul E. Meehl, *Clinical* vs. *Statistical Prediction: A Theoretical Analysis and a Review of the Evidence* (University of Minnesota Press, Minneapolis, 1954), esp. Chapters 4 and 6.

3. Karl R. Popper, *The Open Society and Its Enemies* (2d rev. ed.; Routledge and K. Paul, London, 1952), Vol. II, pp. 96–97, 265.

It may be noted that Patrick Gardiner (in *The Nature of Historical Explanation* [Oxford University Press, London, 1952], pp. 49–50, 113–39) regards the logic-of-the-situation approach as one of two types of historical explanation. He apparently considers it to be a form of "motivational" explanation which is noncausal and nonscientific. (The other type of historical explanation of action is in terms of "general laws of human response to specified types of situation.")

Gardiner's distinction between these two types of historical explanation of action seems to correspond to the distinction between "explanation in principle" and "explanation in detail" proposed by J. W. N. Watkins, "Ideal Types and Historical Explanation," in H. Feigl and M. Brodbeck (eds.), *Readings in the Philosophy of Science* (Appleton-Century-Crofts, New York, 1953), pp. 734–43. Watkins, however, is more impressed than is Gardiner with the parallels of explanation in detail to scientific explanation. In this respect his position is closer to that taken by Carl G. Hempel and Paul Oppenheim in "Studies in the Logic of Explanation," *Philosophy of Science* (April, 1948), pp. 325–31, on the possibility of placing motivational explanations, at least in principle, within the framework of scientific explanation.

4. For example, Hans Morgenthau writes as follows on the method for analyzing foreign

policy: "It is elementary that the character of a foreign policy can be ascertained only through the examination of the political acts performed and of the foreseeable consequences of these acts. Thus we can find out what statesmen have actually done, and from the foreseeable consequences of their acts we can surmise what their objectives might have been. Yet examination of the facts is not enough. To give meaning to the factual raw material of history, we must approach historical reality with a kind of rational outline, a map which suggests to us the possible meanings of history. In other words, we put ourselves in the position of a statesman who must meet a certain problem of foreign policy under certain circumstances and ask ourselves, what are the rational alternatives from which a statesman may choose who must meet this problem under these circumstances, presuming always that he acts in a rational manner, and which of these rational alternatives was this particular statesman, acting under these circumstances, likely to choose? It is the testing of this rational hypothesis against the actual facts and their consequences which gives meaning to the facts of history and makes the scientific writing of political history possible" ("Another 'Great Debate': The National Interest of the United States," *American Political Science Review* [December, 1952], pp. 965–66).

5. "Antecedent conditions" differ from "initial conditions" in including the changes in the system of behavior (changes in the values of some of the variables) which take place as the actor responds to the situational change or to new information. Initial conditions are limited to the values of the variables *before* the actor responds.

SEVEN

Propaganda Analysis and the Control Structure of the Propaganda Organization

At a number of places throughout the study it is pointed out that the accuracy of inferences made by propaganda analysts depends upon the accuracy of their knowledge of, and the assumptions they make about, the control structure of the propaganda organization whose output is being studied. The term "control structure" is employed here to refer to the manner in which propaganda policy is formulated and implemented within a large-scale propaganda organization. The FCC analysts recognized the importance of knowing the control structure of the Nazi organization, and the findings of the present study strongly support their view.

Among the many aspects of control structure which might be studied, several, of particular importance, are singled out here: (*a*) the manner in which propaganda is co-ordinated with political policy; (*b*) the manner in which propaganda policy is formulated and implemented and control of output is maintained; (*c*) the allocation of specialized propaganda roles or functions to different media, media units, speakers, and writers; (*d*) the character of the internal working relationship within the propaganda organization between propaganda planners and propaganda producers, or between those who decide propaganda policy and those who implement it.

The more detailed and specific the investigator's knowledge of these features of control structure, the more discriminating and accurate his inferences are likely to be. This chapter attempts to outline the specific types of information about control structure which are useful in propaganda analysis and to illustrate in a few instances how this information is utilized in making inferences. Information on matters of control structure can be obtained from official publications, informants, defectors, and, to some extent, careful observation over a period of time of the behavior of the different propaganda sources utilized by the regime in question.

Co-ordination of Propaganda with Political Policy

The accuracy of propaganda-analysis inferences often rests upon a correct assessment of the position which the top propagandist occupies in the political decision-making process. To what extent does the top propagandist participate, formally or informally, in the formation of various national policies? How influential is he, and in what respects, in policy formation?

To what extent is the top propagandist familiar with the flow of intelligence, advice, policy research, and planning that precede different types of decisions which the regime makes? To what extent is he informed in advance of basic policy decisions and the basis for them?

To what extent do leading propagandists exercise initiative in planning propaganda strategy? To what extent do they attempt to play an independent political role, using their control over communications channels to advance their own policy preferences or those of a political clique to which they may belong? To what extent, on the other hand, do leading propagandists attempt to remain neutral in higher-level policy disagreements?

The analysis of German wartime propaganda conducted in the FCC and elsewhere rested on the assumption, generally correct, that Goebbels operated at a very high level within the Nazi leadership hierarchy. He was known to be close to Hitler and other leaders and well informed on intelligence matters and on the calculations governing German policies.

Several FCC inferences turned out to be incorrect because the propaganda analysts did not anticipate that Goebbels would use his propaganda machine to further personal policy views in behind-the-scenes conflicts with other Nazi elite members. One such example must suffice.

Goebbels, who had originated the idea of a total mobilization of

German resources in the winter of 1942–43, was disappointed when Hitler gave the responsibility for drafting the appropriate mobilization measures to a committee of three (Bormann, Keitel, and Lammers) and restricted Goebbels to an advisory role. In a short while Goebbels expressed sharp disappointment that the committee of three did not proceed as quickly and as ruthlessly as he thought necessary.

According to Rudolf Semmler, one of Goebbels' personal aides in the Propaganda Ministry, Goebbels conceived a daring plan to put pressure on Hitler himself in the matter of total mobilization by championing radical demands in a public speech at the Sport Palast. "In this way he may be able," Semmler noted in his diary, "to force Hitler to put an end to half-measures. If his demands are not met then the Government will be compromised. The Fuehrer could not afford that at the moment."[1]

The Sport Palast meeting was carefully staged by Goebbels; it was packed with enough of his supporters to provide him with an effective claque. Goebbels' speech at this meeting was highlighted by a cleverly contrived on-the-spot plebiscite on the issue of total war. Goebbels asked his audience a series of questions regarding their willingness to undertake further sacrifices in order to win the war. To every question, the audience replied with a thunderous "*Ja.*" This climax to the speech was powerful and was aptly labeled by the FCC as one of Goebbels' greatest propaganda stunts.

In this speech, Semmler noted, "Goebbels went much further than Hitler had agreed. He [Goebbels] now hopes to get control of total war measures. Then he would have achieved his ambition."[2] The FCC analyst, however, misinterpreted the calculations behind Goebbels' speech. He thought that the demands for total mobilization which Goebbels made on this occasion were *already* decided upon by the regime and that Goebbels was merely attempting to whip up popular enthusiasm for them. The FCC analysis read as follows:

In dealing with the new German mobilization of labor, Goebbels succeeds, by putting the crowd into the proper mood, in his effort to get them to *demand,* right there and then in the Sport Palast, what the new Nazi decrees actually *impose* on them.[3]

On this occasion the FCC analyst evidently failed to consider that Goebbels might use his position as Propaganda Minister to promote personal views on top policy matters and to advance his personal political ambitions.[4]

Propaganda Organization and Control

Propaganda analysis also requires information or informed hunches as to the manner in which policy formulation and implementation take place in the propaganda operation under scrutiny.

To what extent is control over propaganda policy and operations effectively unified and co-ordinated? In the absence of thoroughly unified control, which individuals and offices operate independently within the fields of public information and propaganda and psychological warfare? What are their particular spheres of activity, the degree of co-ordination between them, the possibilities for conflicting propaganda policies, their individual characteristics as propagandists? Which publicity organs and outlets are used as personal vehicles of public communication by various members and subgroups of the elite?

Information obtained after World War II revealed that the control structure of Nazi propaganda was less unified and co-ordinated than had been thought by well-informed Allied observers. The detailed picture of divided control and jurisdictional conflicts that emerged after the war need not be recapitulated here.[5]

Many useful inferences made by the FCC rested upon knowledge of the special position which a source or speaker occupied within the Nazi propaganda organization as a whole. A number of FCC inferences turned out to be incorrect, however, because of faulty assumptions of unified control within the Nazi propaganda apparatus.

Observed differences between the Nazi radio and press treatment of an issue or event were usually explained by FCC analysts in terms of differentiated propaganda roles allocated to these media by the Propaganda Ministry. Information subsequently available, however, indicates that some of these observed differences may have been due, rather, to occasional lack of co-ordination between the two media resulting from conflicting propaganda policies pursued independently by Goebbels and Reich Press Chief Otto Dietrich. The latter was nominally a subordinate of Goebbels but operated independently as deputy for press policy under Hitler's aegis. Goebbels' directives to the German press were often useless because of the greater prestige of those issued by Dietrich from the Führer's headquarters, where Dietrich was usually stationed.

Similarly, conflicts between Goebbels and Ribbentrop, the German foreign minister, and between Goebbels and the German Army

(OKW) Propaganda Department may have created pitfalls for the unwary propaganda analyst who was bent on interpreting an observed content difference between foreign and domestic propaganda channels in terms of a calculated, integrated policy laid down by a single propaganda authority.

The following evaluation of an incorrect FCC inference on the Allied landing at Salerno, Italy, illustrates this point.

FCC	GOEBBELS
The analyst noted that the German *domestic* media portrayed German successes in the Salerno battle differently than did the German wireless service for the *foreign* press.	*Goebbels Diary,** entry for September 18, 1943, p. 334, shows that the divergence in propaganda treatment (noted correctly by the FCC analyst) had a different explanation.
He explained this as an example of propaganda differentiation: "Because of the greater boomerang dangers, the Nazis are not so extravagant in exploiting the battle on the domestic radio and press," which avoid "extreme claims of a decisive blow" and do not predict "an imminent Allied embarkation."	Goebbels was furious with the OKW public-relations section for having thrown caution to the winds in making premature boasts of complete victory at Salerno. The favorable military situation for the Germans at Salerno was gradually reversed, and German propaganda to foreign audiences found itself out on a limb.
On the other hand, "such extravagant propaganda appears especially in press dispatches to Europe." The analyst's explanation was that this extravagant propaganda was motivated by an attempt "to demonstrate to readers throughout the continent that German power is still dominant" (*CEA #36*, September 16, 1943, p. A-9).*	As a result of this incident, Goebbels later obtained assurances from the Führer that the OKW would be forced to give up its independent functioning in the sphere of news and propaganda (*ibid.,* September 23, 1943, pp. 475–76).

* As noted above (Chapter 1, n. 1), the abbreviation *CEA* is used in this book to refer to the *Central European Analysis* produced by the German Section, Analysis Division, Foreign Broadcast Intelligence Service, Federal Communications Commission, beginning in 1943. The term *"Goebbels Diary"* refers to the volume edited by Louis P. Lochner, *The Goeb-*

Comment. The analyst's error lay in the fact that he assumed unified control—or co-ordination—of the domestic and foreign propaganda sources under investigation. As a matter of fact, *dual* control existed without adequate co-ordination. Because of an incorrect (though plausible) assumption, the analyst mistook it as a case of propaganda differentiation for different audiences.

Allocation of Specialized Roles to Media, Speakers, and Writers

In promoting the objectives of its psychological warfare and domestic propaganda, every political elite allocates special roles and functions to the communications sources and speakers under its control. Precise knowledge of these roles is invaluable to the propaganda analyst for making discriminating inferences.

This problem is considered in some detail in Part II (pp. 111–15). One example will suffice, therefore, to illustrate the manner in which specific information of this type can be used for purposes of inference. As a result of his quarrel with Dietrich over control of the press, Goebbels decided to intensify the political use of radio, which was more thoroughly under his control. The important midday broadcast on the domestic German radio, the "Political Review," was given by a different speaker each day of the week. Goebbels decided to enhance the timeliness and significance of this broadcast by requiring the speaker to attend the morning conference at which he presented the latest propaganda directives and the most recent background information on war developments. These were then to be utilized by the speaker in preparing the "Political Review" broadcast, which followed shortly after the termination of Goebbels' morning conference.

Information of this type is of considerable value for purposes of propaganda analysis. As a matter of fact, some Allied propaganda analysts learned of or guessed the arrangements which Goebbels had made to enhance the importance of the "Political Review," either through intelligence channels or as a result of their analysis of the

---

bels Diaries, 1942–1943 (Doubleday & Co., Inc., Garden City, N.Y., 1948). The term "Microfilm Goebbels diary" refers to portions of Goebbels' diary not published in Lochner's book but available in microfilm at the Hoover War Library, Stanford University, Stanford, California. Translations in this book from the microfilm were made by Eric Willenz of the RAND Social Science Division.

broadcast. Accordingly, they paid particular attention to this daily broadcast for indications of the latest and most authoritative German estimates of the situation and propaganda strategy.

Relation of Propaganda Planners to Operational Propagandists

Information about the relationship of top propaganda planners (and top elite members) to propaganda personnel at the operational level may also be useful in making inferences.

To what extent are operations personnel in the propaganda apparatus taken into the confidence of leaders of the regime and those who decide national policies in political, diplomatic, economic, military, and propaganda spheres? More specifically, to what extent are operations personnel informed as to (*a*) the *objectives* to be achieved by means of the propaganda directives laid down and (*b*) the *policy calculations*—that is, the intentions, expectations, and estimates— which lie behind the choice of the propaganda strategies which operational personnel are asked to implement?

To what extent are operational propagandists given access to the best intelligence available to the regime on the various events and situations which they are asked to talk about publicly? To what extent are they deliberately or inadvertently misled about the true situation by propaganda planners and members of the top elite?

Material which became available after the war [6] indicates that Goebbels did not take subordinates into his confidence in important matters but, often, systematically misled them in the expectation that their propaganda performance would be improved thereby.

He was often as concerned with the morale of sub-elites (Party and governmental officials, bureaucratic personnel, military leaders, etc.) as with the morale of the masses. For he was acutely aware that efficient political control by the regime rested largely upon the leadership qualities of the middle strata of officials through which the top elite was obliged to work. Accordingly, he considered it important to manipulate the body of factual information available to his subordinates in an effort to direct their attitudes and morale.

The assumption which apparently guided Goebbels in dealing with his subordinates in the Propaganda Ministry seems to have been that they would perform their functions as manipulators of public opinion better if they themselves were not too detached from the masses but shared the opinions and attitudes which they were prescribing for the masses.

To this end, Goebbels gave his key subordinates appropriate assurances as to the policy aims of the Nazi leadership. He attempted to boost their morale with calculated pep talks and did not hesitate to dissimulate regarding the true military and political situation. At times he withheld information from his subordinates, fabricated it, or slanted it—all with the aim of establishing a climate of opinion among his subordinates which would improve their performance as propagandists.

Goebbels also recognized that his subordinates would sometimes experience crises of conscience regarding Nazi Germany's moral position. He attempted in several ways to alleviate such moral conflicts, adapting his technique and arguments to the psychology of his associates. He had the Propaganda Ministry systematically check all enemy atrocity charges leveled against Germany and obtained official denials or explanations from the appropriate Reich office. These official denials were circulated throughout other government offices as well as within the Propaganda Ministry and apparently served to allay doubts as to German culpability.

NOTES

1. Rudolf Semmler, *Goebbels: The Man Next to Hitler* (Westhouse, London, 1947), p. 68.

2. *Ibid.*, p. 69.

3. FCC, FBIS, Analysis Division, Special Report #53, *Goebbels Speech of February 18, 1943*, p. 2; italics in original.

4. It was not until after the abortive July 20, 1944, attempt upon Hitler's life that Goebbels was given control over total mobilization. For additional materials on Goebbels' use of propaganda channels to further personal viewpoints or ambitions see Semmler, *op. cit.*, p. 77; Curt Riess, *Joseph Goebbels* (Doubleday & Co., Inc., Garden City, N.Y., 1948), pp. 161–62, 188, 263, 313; Fritzsche's testimony in I.M.T., *Trial of the Major War Criminals* (Nuremberg, 1948), Vol. XVII, p. 190.

5. On wartime knowledge of divided control over propaganda matters within the Nazi elite see D. Sington and A. Weidenfeld, *The Goebbels Experiment* (Yale University Press, New Haven, Conn., 1943), *passim;* Ernst Kris and Hans Speier, *German Radio Propaganda* (Oxford University Press, London, 1944), pp. 24, 53, 144, 470–71.

For the picture which emerged after the war see relevant portions of Louis P. Lochner (ed.), *The Goebbels Diaries, 1942–1943* (Doubleday & Co., Inc., Garden City, N.Y., 1948) (in this study referred to as "*Goebbels Diary*"); the microfilm version of the Goebbels diary (available at the Hoover War Library, Stanford University, Stanford, Calif.; in this study referred to as "Microfilm Goebbels diary"), entries for March 14 and April 9, 1943; Semmler, *op. cit.*, pp. 74, 111–13; Riess, *op. cit.*, pp. 114, 158, 174, 189–90; and testimony by Fritzsche and von Schirmeister (Goebbels' personal aide), in I.M.T., *op. cit.*, Vol. XVII, pp. 146, 154, 165–66, 198, 199, 239–40, 254.

6. See the testimony by Fritzsche and von Schirmeister at the Nuremberg trial in I.M.T., *op. cit.*, Vol. XVII, pp. 153–54, 158, 159, 164, 172–73, 174–75, 186, 243, 250–51, 252. See also Riess, *op. cit.*, p. 237, and the *Goebbels Diary, passim.*

Part II

Propaganda Analysis and the Study
of Communication

Introduction

In Part I of this report, propaganda analysis has been considered from an *action* standpoint. That is, its use as a diagnostic technique for inferring actions taken by a political elite that are usually not open to direct observation has been described in some detail. ("Actions" in this sense, as was noted in the Preface, covers the steps taken by an elite and its propagandists and the calculations leading up to these steps.)

Nonetheless, since it is the actor's verbal behavior from which inferences are made in propaganda analysis, propaganda analysis is, in the first instance, a form of comunication analysis. An inference as to the speaker's *intended meaning* often precedes inferences as to actions. After this first step in the analysis comes an inference as to the speaker's *purpose,* the objective which he hopes to implement by conveying certain meanings to certain audiences. The next step may be an attempt to infer the reasons for the selection of a certain propaganda strategy or to infer the political and military policies and the calculations and estimates of the situation which lie behind the choice of a certain propaganda strategy.

Though propaganda analysis involves the analysis of communication, as does content analysis, it differs in important respects from content analysis, which is usually defined as a quantitative or statistical technique for obtaining data on content features of communication. Propaganda analysis often uses such quantitative procedures; but, at least as applied by the FCC, it also makes considerable use of procedures not encompassed by what is usually meant by content analysis, and it is this aspect of propaganda analysis that is singled out for discussion here.

The respective merits and uses of the quantitative and qualitative approaches to content analysis have long been debated by researchers. Technical and theoretical discussions of content analysis, however, generally have given little attention to the qualitative approach. In fact, there is no one generally accepted meaning for the term "qualitative" in this context. A standard treatise on content analysis (H. D. Lasswell, Nathan Leites, and Associates, *Language of*

Politics, George W. Stewart, Inc., New York, 1949), for example, does not explicitly differentiate between the quantitative and qualitative approaches and discusses only the former.

Bernard Berelson's *Content Analysis in Communication Research* (The Free Press, Glencoe, Ill., 1952), on the other hand, identifies some of the main characteristics of the qualitative approach. His discussion, however, is insufficiently elaborated and leaves it somewhat uncertain whether there is a qualitative method which differs fundamentally from the quantitative approach.

As a matter of fact, most writers on content analysis have defined it as essentially a quantitative technique, thus in effect excluding the qualitative approach as being something other than content analysis. Exceptions to this are Ernst Kris and Hans Speier, who, in *German Radio Propaganda,*[1] offer no explicit definition of content analysis and seem to imply that the technique need not be quantitative. Other writers who favor or have employed the qualitative approach are noted in Berelson (*op. cit.,* pp. 114–34); Berelson considers various definitions of quantitative content analysis on pages 14–18 of his *Content Analysis.*

Quantitative content analysis is basically, as noted above, a statistical technique for getting descriptive data about a content characteristic, or variable. It tabulates the frequency with which a content characteristic occurs in the material under analysis. Its value lies in the fact that it offers the possibility of obtaining relatively precise, objective, and reliable observations about the frequency with which given content characteristics occur singly or in conjunction with one another. In other words, it substitutes controlled observation and systematic counting for impressionistic ways of observing frequencies of occurrence.[2]

The term "qualitative" has been used to refer to a number of different aspects of research procedure, which are often blurred in discussions of the respective merits and shortcomings of the quantitative and qualitative approaches to content analysis. It is desirable at the outset, therefore, to distinguish between these aspects. The term "qualitative" has been used to designate the following:

1. The preliminary reading of   *vs.*   The systematic analyzing of content in order to test hypotheses
   communication materials in
   order to form hypotheses and
   discover new relationships

2. An impressionistic procedure *vs.* A systematic procedure for obtaining precise, objective, and reliable data on content variables
for making observations about content characteristics

3. A flexible[3] procedure for making descriptive observations about content, or coding judgments *vs.* A rigid[3] procedure for doing the same

4. Dichotomous attributes (that is, meaning or nonmeaning characteristics which can be predicated only as belonging or not belonging to a given unit of the communication material)[4] *vs.* Attributes which permit exact measurement (that is, the true quantitative variable)[4] or rank ordering (that is, the serial)

In addition to these four important distinctions, another seems necessary in this report in order to explain propaganda analysis fully. Although the term "qualitative" is sometimes used here too, it seems preferable not to resort to a term so open to misinterpretation, and for that reason the term "nonfrequency" will be introduced here. Quantitative content analysis is by definition concerned with the frequency of occurrence of given content characteristics. However, inferences are not necessarily based on frequency of occurrence. An inferential hypothesis may be based on the mere presence or absence of a given content characteristic or content syndrome[5] within a designated body of communication. Such inferences involve a type of nonstatistical content analysis which this report proposes hereafter to term "nonfrequency analysis," or the "nonfrequency approach." It is, of course, to be contrasted with frequency or quantitative analysis, in which inferences are based, not on whether or not a content characteristic is present within a body of communication, but on *how often* it is present there.

The fact that the nonfrequency approach has been found to be important in the use of propaganda analysis for intelligence purposes does not mean, of course, that this approach will be equally useful or necessary in other applications of communication analysis. Nor should the attention given here to the nonfrequency approach be taken as implying that quantitative techniques have not and cannot be fruitfully applied in the intelligence use of propaganda analysis. The nonfrequency approach is singled out in this discussion for several other reasons.

First, the rationale behind the frequency approach is much better known than the rationale behind the nonfrequency approach. Even though quantitative content analysis is often applied crudely, its basic doctrine is well established. Better training and more adequate supervision of young content analysts by competent investigators may be expected to reduce the likelihood of its misapplication. In any case, though it is both desirable and possible to improve the caliber and utility of quantitative studies in propaganda analysis, this study is not addressed, except occasionally by implication, to this problem.

Second, the use of the nonfrequency approach creates many opportunities for making inferences which would be lost if investigators confined themselves to the frequency approach.

Third, an explanation of the rationale for the nonfrequency approach in propaganda analysis may suggest applications in other fields of communication research as well.

It should be noted that the nonfrequency approach is really an older and more conventional way of analyzing communication than the quantitative approach. Its resemblance to traditional textual analysis is immediately obvious. What is novel, perhaps, in this discussion of nonfrequency analysis is the effort to subject it to methodological analysis and, for this purpose, to employ some of the same general methodological canons that are applied to quantitative content analysis.

To recapitulate, "qualitative" and "quantitative" are used in two different senses in the field of communication research: (a) to distinguish between two different over-all approaches or methods in content analysis and (b) to distinguish between four (or five) specific aspects of an over-all approach to content analysis. The use of these terms in sense (a) is misleading because it conveys the erroneous notion that there are only two types of content analysis. But, actually, the four or five aspects may be combined in a number of ways. Not all of the aspects to which the term "quantitative" is applied always go together.

Nonfrequency analysis is distinguished from many versions of content analysis by the unusual emphasis it places upon obtaining valid estimates of the speaker's intended meaning in each particular instance of communication. To this end the propaganda analyst pays particularly close attention to the contexts—communication, behavioral, and situational—in which the speaker's words appear. Yet the emphasis on valid estimates in this type of analysis does not eliminate the problem of reliability of the content description, even though the investigator may give little formal attention to it. This is the problem of whether different investigators (or the same investigator at different times) would make the same judgments in coding the same material.

The first of the following three chapters considers some of the more important conditions and considerations which often deter propaganda analysts from utilizing the systematic quantitative type of content analysis. The second takes up in some detail and illustrates the difference between the frequency and nonfrequency approaches to content analysis. The third attempts to show how various contextual factors are taken into account in inferring a speaker's intended meaning and his purpose.

NOTES

1. Oxford University Press, London, 1944.

2. For a brief exposition of quantitative content analysis and some of its uses in the study of political communication see H. D. Lasswell, Daniel Lerner, and Ithiel de Sola Pool, *The Comparative Study of Symbols* ("Hoover Institute Studies," Series C: *Symbols*, No. 1; Stanford University Press, Stanford, Calif., 1952). Particularly useful is these authors' sober assessment of the difficulty of satisfying various prerequisites of statistical content analysis.

3. "Flexible" and "rigid" are not opposites, but the extreme points of a continuum. A highly flexible procedure prescribes which content categories are to be coded, but it does not specify the actual words or word clusters which are to be regarded as individual occurrences of these content categories. Thus coders are permitted considerable latitude in deciding when an instance of any content category occurs in the raw material they are reading. At the other extreme, a rigid procedure attempts to specify explicitly and completely the bases on which coding decisions are to be made, leaving the individual coder no room for the exercise of independent judgment. In practice, of course, there are various intermediate degrees of flexibility and rigidity in coding procedures.

4. See pp. 96–97 for illustration of these terms.

5. A syndrome is a set of content characteristics which tend to occur together or which have a certain significance if they occur together.

EIGHT

Nonquantitative Procedures in Propaganda Analysis

In the early stages of the FCC propaganda-analysis operation considerable importance was attached to the quantitative approach. A number of the FCC analysts had had considerable experience with quantitative research techniques; they expected these techniques to prove useful in the attempt to apply content analysis to intelligence problems. Initially a large part of their efforts was devoted to systematic quantitative studies. While some useful results were achieved, in time the FCC analysts came to rely increasingly upon relatively impressionistic and qualitative methods. They did not abandon quantitative studies but undertook them more selectively. The "fishing-expedition" type of quantitative study—that undertaken without specific inferential hypotheses in mind but in the hope of discovering some—they found to be generally unproductive and wasteful. They obtained better results with quantitative studies which were hypothesis-oriented, that is, with studies where they had a relatively clear notion of the type of quantitative content evidence required to support an explicit and concrete inferential hypothesis and where they looked for such evidence.

Details of the FCC's experience with quantitative content analysis will not be reported here. Rather, this chapter will contain a discussion of some of the more important considerations which often deterred propaganda analysts from utilizing systematic quantitative content analysis.

Discovery and Testing of Inferential Hypotheses

Any research may be aimed at discovering possible new relationships or may be designed to test hypothesized relationships. It is important to keep this distinction between *discovery* and *verification* of hypotheses[1] in mind in undertaking research on practical problems, such as those which propaganda analysis attempts to solve, as well as in attacking basic scientific problems.

In the analysis of communication, an impressionistic reading of the materials is often the best way to formulate interesting hypotheses. This preliminary reading of communication materials in order to form hypotheses is often referred to as the qualitative phase of research, as distinguished from the testing of hypotheses, for which more systematic procedures are required. While systematic quantitative content analysis is sometimes employed to discover possible new relationships, its more familiar role is that of testing hypothesized relationships.

What distinguishes propaganda analysis used for intelligence purposes[2] from other applications of content analysis is that a relatively large proportion of the research effort is expended in attempting to achieve new insights into possible relationships and to formulate new inferential hypotheses. At the same time, correspondingly less effort is expended in testing hypotheses by means of systematic quantitative procedures. There are a number of reasons for the relative deemphasis of rigorous quantitative procedures in propaganda analysis; as the FCC found, it is often *difficult,* sometimes *imprudent,* and sometimes *unnecessary* to utilize systematic quantitative procedures.

1. A review of the quantitative content analyses performed by the FCC analysts indicates that many of them were inconclusive as tests of inferential hypotheses. Lack of sophistication in handling quantitative techniques was doubtless partly responsible. But a more basic cause for the relatively disappointing results was probably the rudimentary state of knowledge about political communication, which made it difficult to devise adequate systematic tests of inferential hypotheses. This difficulty contributed to the willingness of the FCC analysts to rely upon less rigorous means of assessing the plausibility of their inferences.

2. It also proved imprudent, in the FCC's experience, to invest heavily in systematic quantitative content analyses. As noted above, the fishing-expedition type of quantitative study was found to be

particularly unproductive and wasteful as a means of discovering possible new relationships and useful inferential hypotheses. More importantly, systematic studies to test inferential hypotheses were often impractical. Given the continuous flow of relevant propaganda materials and the nature of the problems under investigation, inferential hypotheses were subject to repeated revision. Accordingly, the investigator was often more interested in revising and refining an inference on the basis of new material and fresh external information than in making a heavy research investment in a systematic study designed to test a hypothesis which might have to be discarded or revised midway through the analysis. Finally, operational pressures (work-loads, deadlines, etc.) limited the number of quantitative studies—which were relatively expensive—that could be undertaken.

3. Quantitative content descriptions were often unnecessary in attempts to test inferential hypotheses because many FCC propaganda-analysis inferences were nonquantitative in nature. That is, they were based on nonfrequency rather than frequency content indicators, a distinction discussed at length in the next chapter. Here it suffices to note that propaganda analysts often base a specific inference not on how frequently certain words, themes, stereotypes, slogans, etc., are employed but on the fact that such statements do (or do not) occur at all in the communication or in a particular segment of it.

One aspect of a systematic test for any inference is an attempt to ascertain whether the content evidence required for that inference is actually present in the communication being examined. This *content-descriptive* aspect of the test can be handled systematically for inferential hypotheses based on nonfrequency indicators as well as for those based on frequency indicators. In the case of nonfrequency indicators the task is usually a relatively simple one, since it consists in establishing the presence or absence of a given content feature or theme in a designated body of communication. In the case of frequency indicators the task is to establish the frequency of occurrence of the relevant content features in a designated body of communication, which may require an elaborate quantitative content description with a detailed coding scheme and rules for applying it.

Because the task of establishing frequency of occurrence is often relatively difficult, the relationship between description of content and inference, and between the forming and testing of hypotheses, is less intimate in frequency analysis than in nonfrequency analysis. In frequency investigations the forming and refinement of hypotheses tends to stop, at least temporarily, while a systematic test for the hypothesis is organized and carried out. Moreover, in systematic counts of frequency indicators it is often necessary for the investigator to employ a method of successive codings, though the desirability of doing so is not always recognized and carried out. The results of a first coding of the material are examined to see what may have been overlooked, a new code may be developed to take account of subtleties that were missed, and the material is coded again. The process may be repeated several times to insure a proper testing of the initial hypothesis or of the more refined hypotheses subsequently formulated.

Characteristics of Propaganda Communications

Several characteristics of propaganda communications lead investigators to allocate a considerable proportion of their research effort to discovering new hypotheses or refining old ones and to exercise caution in attempting to use systematic quantitative analysis for purposes of testing inferential hypotheses. Because of these characteristics, propaganda analysts find the nonfrequency approach more attractive and productive in many cases than the quantitative type of content analysis.

THE EXISTENCE OF IRRELEVANT CONTENT

As was noted in Chapter 2 of Part I, propaganda communications are highly instrumental. A *number* of goals and strategies are pursued in the stream of propaganda communications which comprise the raw materials for inferences. The propaganda analyst, it must be remembered, is interested in making specific inferences about certain matters of intelligence interest. Accordingly, he must exercise great care in considering which passages in the stream of communication are relevant to each of the goals or strategies of the communicator which he wants to infer.

The difficulty of arriving at such judgments of relevance, and the considerable sensitivity and discrimination which are required for this purpose, are often important reasons for not undertaking elaborate quantitative fishing expeditions of any sizable body of propaganda communications. For the advantages of arriving at a convenient and orderly summary of content and possibly deriving new hypotheses from the data through such fishing expeditions are outweighed for the propaganda analyst by a risk which is implicit in this procedure. This is the danger that content features of the original communication relevant to *different* inferential problems might be recorded as instances of the *same* content category. That is, not all the individual items tabulated under any given content category in such a study may be relevant to the specific inference about the speaker's state of mind which the analyst would like to make.

One of the important requirements of statistical content analysis is that it be "systematic" in the sense that *"all* of the relevant content . . . be analyzed in terms of *all* of the relevant categories, for the problem at hand." [3] But the obverse of this requirement—that none of the *irrelevant* content be analyzed—is equally important. The task of determining the relevant content (or sample) that must be analyzed for a given inferential problem is often more difficult than it appears to be. If too large a body of communication is coded, the danger arises that more data will be obtained under the content categories employed than are pertinent to the specific inferential problem.

In some cases the inclusion of irrelevant content in the analysis may be no more than a waste of manpower. But in other cases it may rule out the possibility of making a useful inference or lead to wholly mistaken inferences. In any case, these difficulties are usually traceable directly to the fact that the quantitative content analysis is planned without very specific hypotheses in mind. The problem may become particularly acute when the investigator engaged in a fishing expedition of this sort deliberately selects broad content categories in order to insure large enough frequencies for purposes of subsequent statistical analysis. [4]

The danger of coding irrelevant content is minimized, on the other hand, when research is designed to test clear-cut hypotheses. For the hypotheses usually indicate or imply the realm of relevant content or the appropriate sample to be coded and thus guide the design of the research.

CHANGES IN THE SPEAKER'S STRATEGY

In the stream of propaganda communications being analyzed, the speaker's strategy on any *single* subject may change abruptly at any time. In attempting inferences about the speaker's state of mind on any subject matter, the propaganda analyst cannot easily draw up a set of content categories that will be appropriate for all possible shifts in the communicator's strategy. He will hesitate to commit himself to a systematic quantitative content description because he fears that *the speaker's strategy may change while the count is being made.*

When such a change takes place and is unnoticed by the analyst, the quantitative content results may lose their value for purposes of making inferences. That is, the content data might well become ambiguous.

In propaganda analysis the instrumental use to which communication is put by the speaker is regarded as a highly unstable variable which intervenes between various other antecedent conditions of communication (e.g., elite policies and calculations) and the content variable. In this respect, propaganda analysis has much in common with the analysis of a patient's communication in a psychotherapy situation. Both the propaganda analyst and the psychotherapist are sensitive to the possibility that the communication goal and strategy of the speaker can change frequently during the course of their effort to make a systematic count of the content features of what he says. For this reason, except when there is reason to believe that the content features selected as indicators are independent of, and insensitive to, variations in the speaker's strategy, frequency counts may be inappropriate as a means of inferring the calculations and conditions which have influenced the choice of a propaganda goal or strategy. To guard against this danger, the significance of content features as possible indicators of the speaker's state of mind should be weighed as much as possible with regard to the individual linguistic, situational, and behavioral contexts in which the features occur and with reference to what has occurred previously in the course of the communication process.[5]

THE EXPANDING UNIVERSE OF RELEVANT COMMUNICATIONS

When employing propaganda analysis as a tool for making inferences about contemporary matters, the investigator is often confronted with the fact that the universe of propaganda communications relevant to his problem may be expanding even while he is attempting to draw inferences from them.

In other words, the propaganda analyst often finds it difficult to keep up with the flow of communications which have some relevance to his inferential problem. His position is that of an investigator who has to formulate alternative inferential hypotheses and to select appropriate content categories before he has seen all the communications that may have to be analyzed. As new communications on the topic are issued by the speaker, the propaganda analyst frequently has to revise the alternative hypotheses he is considering and the content categories he is using. And, because he must meet deadlines, the propaganda analyst frequently states inferences which are necessarily in the nature of interim reports, based upon arbitrary and incomplete segments of relevant data.

These circumstances frequently rule out use of the systematic variant of quantitative content description. It is a familiar prerequisite of quantitative content analysis that the investigator know what he is looking for before beginning to count. The propaganda analyst cannot very well satisfy this requirement of quantitative content analysis when he must continually reconsider his hypotheses and categories as new statements from the source become available. The propaganda analyst cannot be confident that the ordered data on the content variable provided by a quantitative content description of currently available communications will still be adequate for purposes of making inferences when new statements on the topic are received from the source. For the most recent communications may throw new light on the inferential problem, and, on the basis of these new insights, the propaganda analyst may have to reread and reinterpret the earlier propaganda communications which were transformed into ordered data.

A similar problem arises when information not contained in the propaganda communications but bearing upon the inferential problem comes to the attention of the propaganda analyst *after* he has received and analyzed the relevant communications. This information may permit the analyst retrospectively to formulate and assess more discriminating hypotheses about the inferential significance of the propaganda, and, for this purpose, it may be necessary for him to go back to the original propaganda communications.

The circumstances mentioned above, of course, do not rule out systematic quantitative content analysis in principle. A method of successive codings, to which reference has already been made (p. 85, above), is often employed in other types of communication analysis. Sophisticated quantitative investigators recognize that, even in carefully planned studies, the initial processing of raw communication material is likely to yield data inadequate in essential respects.

The method of successive codings, which is essential to studies that begin as fishing expeditions, is therefore often necessary also in hypothesis-oriented research.

The necessity for returning to the original materials in order to read and reread them, therefore, is itself by no means unique to propaganda analysis. Nor is the method of successive codings unknown in propaganda analysis. But the aforementioned concern over coding only the relevant content and the necessity for coping with an expanding universe of relevant communication make the propaganda analyst reluctant to undertake time-consuming quantitative descriptions. These same considerations partly account for his willingness in many cases to settle for a relatively impressionistic estimate of the frequency of relevant content features.

The Importance of Structural Characteristics of Instrumental Communications

Propaganda-analysis procedures are much influenced, finally, by the necessity for taking into account the *structural* characteristics of propaganda communications. The structure of various individual communications encountered in the heterogeneous flow of propaganda available for analysis is naturally not the same. An article by Goebbels appearing in *Das Reich,* for example, was structurally different from a speech by Hitler; and both, certainly, were structurally different from German radio news broadcasts.

Not only must the propaganda analyst avoid clumsy comparisons of content between propaganda communications which are structurally dissimilar, but he must also take structural characteristics into account in analyzing any *single* communication (speech, article, news item, editorial, commentary, etc.). The propaganda intention of an individual communication (and its effect, as well) often depends not merely on the explicit content of its individual statements or propositions but also upon the structural interrelationship of these statements within the communication. It is well known that effective persuasion may depend on more or less subtle manipulation of order, context, and sequence.[6]

This "whole-part" problem (the need for considering the relationship of the parts of a communication to each other and to the whole) [7] has several important implications for procedure in content analysis. It may affect the analyst's choice of units and categories as well as his decision regarding which content-descriptive procedure (statistical or nonstatistical) to employ.

Awareness of the whole-part problem often leads the propaganda analyst to be critical of an important implicit assumption of quantitative content analysis, namely, that each individual item counted as falling under a designated content category is of equal significance for purposes of making inferences.[8] Similarly, the propaganda analyst is often critical of the assumption that the precise frequency of occurrence of explicit propositions, themes, or statements determines their significance in making inferences. He may instead find that explicit propositions are significant in ascertaining the strategy of the propagandist because they occur at all or because they occur in a certain relationship to each other within the communication.[9]

This does not mean that all frequency counts are useless for purposes of propaganda analysis. Frequency tabulations of words, clichés, stereotypes, and slogans may provide an indication not only of propaganda emphasis and techniques but of the communicator's goals and strategy. But such tabulations in themselves give no clue as to the meaning of the content in question. Their chief value, therefore, occurs when the investigator has prior or independent knowledge of their meaning, role, and significance in the system of language habits under study.[10] The significance of explicit propositions (statements, themes, assertions, etc.) for purposes of inferring a speaker's goal is not necessarily dependent upon how often they are repeated by the speaker but may rest on the fact that he makes (or does not make) such statements at all, and on how the statements are structurally and hierarchically interrelated.

In propaganda analysis, then, the usual type of frequency count associated with quantitative content analysis is often quite inappropriate. The procedure employed in ascertaining what propositions are contained in a propaganda communication and in weighing the structural interrelationships of parts undoubtedly is often less systematic than in quantitative content analysis, in which coding judgments are closely prescribed. But in principle the reliability of these observations, too, is subject to investigation.

Close Relation between Description of Content and Inferential Reasoning

Note has been taken in this chapter of several characteristics of propaganda communications and of the conditions under which they are analyzed which account for the investigator's reluctance at times to undertake systematic counts of content features. These same characteristics and conditions often cause content-descriptive and inferential procedures to be unusually closely intertwined in propaganda analysis. That is, inferences as to *what* the propagandist is trying to say and *why* he is trying to say it are not neatly discrete.

To illustrate: If one person addresses another as "you old rascal," the analyst who seeks to interpret the intent validly will want to know if the addressee is an old man or an infant. If it is a baby, one infers that the speaker's intention is affectionate and simultaneously describes the content as endearment. There is a mutually interdependent set of assumptions here. One has not established the intent independently and derived the content interpretation from that, nor has one established the affectionate meaning of the phrase "you old rascal" independently and derived the intent from that. The two propositions are part of an interdependent set of inferential hypotheses.

The closeness of this relation, which goes beyond that found in most forms of systematic content analysis, is described briefly here as a preliminary to a more specific discussion in Chapter 10.

The formation of a hypothesis—that is, the assertion of a relation between a content indicator (or set of indicators) and some communicator variable—is often very difficult in propaganda analysis. This difficulty reflects the relatively poor state of scientific knowledge about political communication and, in particular, the lack of generalizations or of a good theory as to relations between content indicators and communicator variables. The nonexistence of well-developed generalizations of this type makes it difficult for the propaganda analyst to determine what terms and categories he should use in describing content for different purposes.

The problem of how content indicators and communicator variables are related is of course by no means confined to propaganda analysis or to studies of other instrumental communications. It is also encountered in many other applications of content analysis. Thus, for example, in a sober assessment of the results of their effort to employ symbols as indices of the political values, attitudes, and ideological dispositions of the communicator, the chief investigators on the RADIR content-analysis project emphasized that the scientific study of political communication was hampered by the absence of relevant theory and hypotheses:

There is as yet no good theory of symbolic communication by which to predict how given values, attitudes, or ideologies will be expressed in manifest symbols. The extant theories tend to deal with values, attitudes, and ideologies as the ultimate units, not with the symbolic atoms of which they are composed. There is almost no theory of language which predicts the specific words one will emit in the course of expressing the contents of his thoughts. Theories in philosophy or in the sociology of knowledge sometimes enable us to predict ideas that will be expressed by persons with certain other ideas or social characteristics. But little thought has been given to predicting the specific words in which these ideas will be cloaked. The content analyst, therefore, does not know what to expect.[11]

Essentially the same deficiency, noted by investigators working in other areas of communication analysis as well, was alluded to in various contexts during a work conference on content analysis, held at the University of Illinois in February, 1955, by the Committee on Psychology and Linguistics of the Social Science Research Council. For example, on one occasion George Mahl deplored the lack of a "theory of the dynamics of content categories selected as indicators." A similar point is implied by two investigators, Frank Auld, Jr., and Edward J. Murray, in a recent review of the growing list of content-analysis studies of psychotherapy:

> The problem of how the verbal behavior of the client, which is taken note of in content analysis, is related to his nonverbal behavior, is a difficulty not only for the D.R.Q. [Dollard and Mowrer Discomfort-Relief Quotient] but also for every other system of content analysis.[12]

This deficiency has important consequences for content analysis. It means that there are relatively few theories or general hypotheses about symbolic behavior available for testing by means of rigorous quantitative content analysis. As a result, some investigators collect large quantities of content data without the guidance of clear-cut hypotheses, in the hope of discovering, at the end of the study, new relationships and new hypotheses. Disappointing results with such fishing expeditions are particularly likely when large quantities of material are processed and the chief investigator has to employ clerical personnel to do the coding. As a result, there is insufficient opportunity to refine categories, and it is usually not possible to re-code the bulky material as many times as necessary in order to produce content data appropriate for testing interesting hypotheses.

Since relatively few general hypotheses exist, propaganda-analysis investigations necessarily give unusual emphasis to the formation of hypotheses. In reading and rereading propaganda communications, the investigator is engaged in a search for content indicators which may serve as a basis for the types of inferences he is interested in making. He attempts to spot content evidence for any one of a variety of relevant inferential hypotheses. During the course of his reading he formulates impressions of many content features present in the material. All of this activity is description of content. *At the same time* that it is taking place, the investigator tentatively considers whether some of these content features can be considered as content indicators in inferential hypotheses. This requires him to make a preliminary assessment of inferential hypotheses—to consider, however impressionistically, the reasoning for and against particular inferential hunches.

The propaganda analyst's procedure is thus one in which description of content and assessment of inferential hypotheses are intimately intertwined and overlap. The process of deciding whether a content indicator can be designated (and, if so, which one) for a particular intelligence problem has to be undertaken in close conjunction with a consideration of inferential hypotheses. And both of these processes, in turn, proceed in close conjunction with a weighing of other considerations which support the various hypotheses.

The question arises as to whether the content-analysis procedure outlined here does not entail the danger of circularity,[13] or analytical bias. That is, by not distinguishing more sharply—as in quantitative content analysis—between the descriptive and inferential phases of research, does not the investigator risk the possibility that a hypothesis formulated early in the course of his description of content will determine what he subsequently sees and regards as significant in the content?

This danger is indeed potentially present in the procedure described above. Many low-grade propaganda and political analyses undoubtedly fall prey to it. However, the disciplined analyst guards against it in several ways. He does not read through the propaganda materials just once but rereads as many times as necessary to satisfy himself that the inference he favors is consonant with all of the relevant portions and characteristics of the original propaganda material; he considers not just one inferential hypothesis in reading and rereading the original propaganda materials but also many alternatives to it; and he systematically weighs the available evidence for and against each of the alternative inferences.

Thus, the results of his analysis explicitly or implicitly include not merely (*a*) the favored inference and the content evidence for it but also (*b*) alternative explanations of that content evidence, (*c*) other content evidence which may support alternative inferences, and (*d*) reasons for considering one inferential hypothesis more plausible than others.

To the extent that the analyst is successful in thus controlling the dangers of circularity, his procedure duplicates the procedure of making successive approximations frequently encountered in scientific investigations.

It is important to recognize that the analyst of contemporary propaganda communications cannot easily utilize the preferred scientific procedure of first deriving a hypothesis and a set of relevant categories from one set of materials and then testing that hypothesis by a systematic content analysis of a new set (or a larger body) of materials. Such a procedure requires assurance that the body of material used for the initial, hypothesis-forming phase of the investigation be a good sample or replica of the material to be utilized for testing the hypothesis. But this assumption cannot be easily made in the case of propaganda communications which are in historical flux. Propaganda analysis is cumulative in character. New material in the second (or larger) body of material may force the investigator to alter his hypothesis or to employ additional or different content categories. Moreover, a skillful propagandist changes his strategy to prevent his future plans from being easily read from the pattern of his past conduct. For these reasons, in the type of applied content analysis being considered here, there is no assurance that the initial body of communication is homogeneous with the body of communication used for testing purposes or that it contains all the content features necessary to enable the investigator to formulate an interesting and useful hypothesis.

In practice, as a matter of fact, the propaganda analyst is not reluctant to use the scientific procedure of testing an initial hypothesis more systematically against a larger body of material. But he is reluctant to invest time and manpower doing so when he expects that, in exposing himself to a larger body of propaganda material on the same subject, he may have to revise his hypothesis and note new types of content evidence. When the subsequent systematic appraisal for which the propaganda analyst is willing to settle does not take the form of a quantitative content analysis, it is usually either because such an analysis would be inappropriate in principle (as when the analyst does not utilize frequency indicators) or because he considers it unnecessary (as when the added precision would not appreciably increase the certainty of his judgments).

NOTES

1. The author is indebted to Irving L. Janis for pointing out the usefulness of an explicit application of this distinction to many of the procedural problems of propaganda analysis discussed here.

2. For the sake of brevity the unqualified term "propaganda analysis" will be used throughout the rest of Part II to mean the type of propaganda analysis engaged in by the FCC for purposes of political and psychological intelligence.

3. Bernard Berelson, *Content Analysis in Communication Research* (The Free Press, Glencoe, Ill., 1952), p. 17. As Berelson notes, quantitative content analysts stress this requirement as a safeguard against "partial or biased analyses in which only those elements in the content are selected which fit the analyst's thesis."

4. On this point see also below, pp. 99–100.

5. On the distinction between content features sensitive to and independent of the speaker's communications strategy and its implications for the problem of the method of making inferences see Part I, pp. 38–40.

6. In the funeral oration in Shakespeare's *Julius Caesar,* for example, Mark Antony achieves his purpose by starting with praise for Caesar's opponents, in accord with the predispositions of his audience, gradually moving on to the new position to which he wishes to bring the audience.

7. Jacob Goldstein, "Content Analysis: A Propaganda and Opinions Study," Ph.D. thesis, New School for Social Research (New York, February, 1942), pp. 38–41, contains a useful discussion of this problem.

8. For an explicit statement of this important (but often ignored) assumption of quantitative content analysis see Berelson, *op. cit.,* p. 20.

9. In this respect, the implications of structure for the propaganda analyst's procedure appear to be analogous to the situation in linguistics. Thus, as Floyd G. Lounsbury has recently noted: "In the procedure of contemporary structural linguistic analysis, frequency of occurrence (of a given unit in a given context, or of a given contrast) is not a relevant criterion. Only the *possibility* of occurrence—as represented by some one instance or by many instances of it—is relevant. The answers which are sought from data are of a simple yes-or-no type rather than of a how-much type. In statistical analysis on the other hand, frequencies are the immediate goal of analysis, *e.g.,* the *probability* of occurrence. Statistical procedure usually ignores, however, a matter which is basic to linguistics—the distinguishing of levels of structure" (Charles E. Osgood and Thomas A. Sebeok [eds.], *Psycholinguistics: A Survey of Theory and Research Problems* [Waverly Press, Inc., Baltimore, 1954], p. 94).

10. This point is explicitly discussed in Goldstein, *op. cit.,* pp. 26–27, 38–40, and 150.

11. H. D. Lasswell, Daniel Lerner, and Ithiel de Sola Pool, *The Comparative Study of Symbols* ("Hoover Institute Studies," Series C: *Symbols,* No. 1; Stanford University Press, Stanford, Calif., 1952), p. 49. See also their discussion of models of symbolic behavior and the problems of "index ambiguity" and "index instability," pp. 64 ff. and 75–78.

12. Frank Auld, Jr., and Edward J. Murray, "Content-Analysis Studies of Psychotherapy," *Psychological Bulletin* (September, 1955), p. 380.

13. The problem of circularity of course is a familiar one in many types of research, though it is often referred to in other terms. The author is indebted to Charles E. Osgood for raising the question in this form and to other participants in the work conference on content analysis at the University of Illinois for their discussion of it.

NINE

Frequency and Nonfrequency Content Analysis

The Difference between Frequency and Nonfrequency Content Indicators

The terms "quantitative" and "qualitative" are applied, as was noted in the Introduction to Part II, to a variety of different matters in research operations. Here it may be useful to distinguish between the application of these terms to (*a*) the type of attribute which is the object of content description and (*b*) the type of indicator utilized for purposes of making inferences.

A differentiation between statistical content analysis [1] and propaganda analysis on the basis of the type of attribute with which they are concerned cannot be justified. Statistical content analysis does not concern itself solely with language and meaning attributes which permit of strict quantitative measurement, that is, features of content (such as size of print, length of sentences, etc.) which can be measured along a true quantitative scale comprised of equal intervals and a zero point. Rather, most statistical content analysis, as well as propaganda analysis, has also dealt with qualitative attributes, that is, dichotomous attributes which can be predicated only as belonging or not belonging to an object. For example, when the quantitative analyst studies the amount of attention received by a designated symbol or theme in a body of communication, he operates with a dichotomous attribute, namely, the presence or absence of that designated symbol or theme in each of the counting units into which he has divided that body of communication. In other words, he is interested in the frequency with which the symbol or theme appears, that is, the number of counting units in which it was present at least once.[2]

Statistical content analysis, therefore, does not exclude from study the qualitative attributes of language. Its concern lies with their frequency distributions for purposes of making inferences.[3] Similarly, what is distinctive about propaganda analysis is not that it studies qualitative attributes of language but that it often utilizes the mere occurrence or nonoccurrence of a qualitative attribute (as against its frequency distribution) for purposes of making an inference. The difference between statistical content analysis and propaganda analysis, therefore, concerns the type of indicator used in making inferences rather than type of language attribute recorded as content data.

Since the terms "quantitative" and "qualitative" have several usages in the analysis of communication, it seems desirable to employ new terms to distinguish between these two types of content indicators:

A descriptive statement of content which, for purposes of making inferences, refers to the number of times *one or more characteristics are present in a body of communications is defined as a "frequency content indicator."*

A descriptive statement of content which, for purposes of making inferences, refers merely to the presence or absence *of a certain content characteristic is defined as a "nonfrequency content indicator."*

The distinction between frequency and nonfrequency indicators is not unfamiliar. It corresponds roughly to the difference between the "more-or-less" and the "either-or" types of observation in science.

In a more detailed account of frequency analysis it might be useful to show how various types of frequency indicators are related to quantitative or nonquantitative aspects of the behavior being inferred. Thus, as Ithiel Pool has suggested in a personal communication, a distinction should be made between (a) analyses in which the *frequency* of content characteristic X is related to the *magnitude* (or frequency) of behavior Y; (b) analyses in which a frequency of occurrence of content characteristic X at least as great as (n), or as low as (n), attests to the *existence* of behavior Y; and (c) analyses in which one or more occurrences of content characteristic X attest to the existence of behavior Y.

Both (*a*) and (*b*) are analyses using frequency content indicators, while (*c*), of course, uses a nonfrequency indicator. Inferences of type (*b*) seem to have been quite rare in the FCC's work; it may be that the FCC analysts were usually unable to specify (*n*). But this, of course, does not invalidate the concept.

Ithiel Pool has also suggested that some of the FCC studies interpreted in this report as making use of nonfrequency indicators may actually have been implicit cases of (*b*).

It should be noted that in any content-analysis problem the investigator designates as his indicator only those aspects of the communication which are relevant to his problem. As in all explanation, propaganda-analysis inferences are strictly limited to characteristics of the event singled out by the investigator. Moreover, he is under no obligation to explain or make use of all the occurrences within the communication of the content feature which he selects as an indicator.

Thus, for example, if a content characteristic occurs sixty times in a given body of material, the investigator has four possible ways of using that content feature for purposes of making inferences:

1. The investigator may make an inference from the fact that the content characteristic in question occurred sixty times in a certain body of communications. (In this event, he is setting up a *frequency* content indicator.)

2. The investigator may make an inference from the fact that the content characteristic in question occurred at all, that is, from its mere presence in that body of material. (In this case it is a *nonfrequency* content indicator.)

3. The investigator may decide that only one of the sixty occurrences of the given content characteristic should be singled out for purposes of making inferences, on the ground that the particular context (situational, behavioral, and/or linguistic) in which it appeared gives it distinctive value as a content indicator for the inference of interest. (This is also a *nonfrequency* content indicator.)[4]

4. The investigator may also base his inference on several occurrences of the content characteristic in one particular type of context. (This is a *frequency* content indicator.)

Thus, it is not possible to say that a single occurrence of a content feature in the original communication determines that it will be a nonfrequency content indicator or that a multiple occurrence makes it a frequency content indicator. The investigator decides what it is about the content which it is useful to explain; the content phenomenon to be explained is not rigidly prescribed by the content itself.

The Nonfrequency Approach and Selection of Content Categories

Not only does quantitative, or statistical, content analysis generally ignore nonfrequency content indicators; in practice it also often tends to rule out for purposes of making inferences content characteristics having an infrequent occurrence. In doing so, it overlooks the fact that low frequencies, too, may be amenable to statistical analysis. In other research fields well-trained investigators seem able to apply quantitative techniques without ignoring the possible importance of content characteristics which occur infrequently. However, it is probably correct to observe that few efforts have been made thus far to utilize low-frequency analysis in the quantitative study of political communication.

Instead, most of the problems of political communication selected for quantitative analysis seem to have been defined in terms which require content characteristics occurring with at least a certain minimal frequency, so as to permit the application of techniques of statistical analysis which require large numbers. In such studies investigators often regard the occurrence of low frequencies as disappointing because they feel it rules out or reduces the possibility of statistical analysis.[5]

In some quantitative investigations, therefore, this technical requirement of relatively large numbers for statistical analysis appears to exercise an important influence on the *choice of content categories and the size of the sample*[6] of raw materials to be coded. The selection of content categories may be consciously guided by the investigator's impressionistic observation as to which symbols and themes occur with considerable frequency within the body of communications being studied. Symbols and themes with a low frequency of occurrence may be either ignored or grouped together under a broad content category with other symbols and themes thought to have essentially the same general referent, though this often excludes the possibility of a more discriminating analysis.

The conscious selection of content categories with an eye to satisfying technical requirements of statistical analysis may be justified when the research objective is to make general inferences. But such a criterion for selection of categories has severe drawbacks when, as in propaganda analysis, the object is to make specific inferences about events at particular times and places. Valuable opportunities for making specific inferences are lost if investigators ignore or minimize the value of nonfrequency indicators.

Investigators who are aware of this try to formulate ever more discriminating content categories. They deliberately try to narrow the content categories and make them more specific. The fact that this results in low frequencies, in a single occurrence, or no occurrence at all of the content feature in question is not of concern to them since they expect to employ nonfrequency indicators for making inferences. Thus, in propaganda analysis, it is typical for the investigator to be concerned with establishing slight changes in propaganda lines or minute and subtle differences in wording employed by different speakers or by the same speaker to different audiences.

The Nonfrequency Approach and the Size of the Coding Unit

It has been questioned whether the logical distinction between frequency and nonfrequency content indicators is of great importance in practice. To some the question of choosing between frequency and nonfrequency indicators has seemed identical with the problem, familiar in quantitative content analysis, of determining *the size of the coding unit* to be employed. The two problems may be related, but, in the opinion of the present writer, they are not identical.

It is true that in quantitative content analysis the occurrence or nonoccurrence of a theme or symbol may be recorded per meaningful assertion, or per sentence, paragraph, article, etc. The question of which of these to select as the coding unit is often a difficult one to answer in specific studies as well as for quantitative content analysis generally. Thus, quantitative investigators are often acutely aware of the fact that the frequency data obtained on certain content features of interest (for example, certain symbols or themes) will depend upon the size of the coding unit selected. Too often in the past, selection of the coding unit has been unduly influenced by considerations of achieving reliability and of simplifying coding procedures. Among sophisticated practitioners, however, it is increasingly recognized that the decision should depend upon which coding unit is considered likely to be most highly predictive of the communicator variables (or types of effects) in which the investigator is interested. Nevertheless, it is often difficult to apply this sound criterion in the absence of a good theory or likely hypothesis, a limitation to which reference has already been made.

The problem of selecting a coding unit in quantitative analysis is evidently thought to overlap or coincide with nonfrequency analysis for the following reasons. If the quantitative investigator chooses a relatively large coding unit, such as the paragraph or article, it is quite possible that the aspect of the communication content of interest to him will occur more than once within individual units of that size but will get recorded as a single instance of the content category to which it is applicable. For example, the investigator may specify the paragraph as the coding unit and therefore count *the number of coding units (paragraphs) in which a certain symbol or theme appears* rather than *the number of times that symbol or theme appears within each coding unit* (i.e., each paragraph). Thus, even if the word "democracy" appears six times within a paragraph, it would be coded and counted as a single instance of the content category "democracy."

In other words, in the example above the investigator makes a *qualitative* type of observation the basis for obtaining content-descriptive data. Thus, the *mere presence or absence* of the word "democracy" within a coding unit, not the number of times the word appeared within each individual coding unit, is recorded as an instance of the content category being employed.

Now it is true that the manner in which the quantitative analyst treats multiple occurrences within a single coding unit *for purposes of content description* appears to be similar to the way the nonfrequency analyst deals with multiple occurrences *for purposes of making an inference*. In both cases, note is taken (but for different purposes!) of the mere presence or absence of the word rather than the number of times it appears. Awareness of this similarity in treatment of multiple occurrences evidently leads some investigators to conclude that the difference between the frequency and nonfrequency approaches is more apparent than real.

But closer inspection shows that the similarity in question is a superficial one and in any case is indecisive. As already suggested, emphasis upon the similarity obscures or overlooks the fact that two radically different research operations are involved: content description and inference. Of greater significance than the apparent similarity in handling multiple occurrences is the fact that the quantitative analyst does not make his inference on the basis of the presence or absence of a word or theme in a single coding unit but, rather, on the basis of the frequency tabulation of the number of coding units in which the word or theme in question appears. In contrast—and this is the basis for the proposed distinction between the two approaches—the nonfrequency analyst does base his inference on the presence or absence of the word or theme in a single meaningful context, which may be called his coding unit.

It is clear that in both the frequency and nonfrequency approaches the investigator must establish the size of the coding unit in which the presence or absence of a designated theme or symbol will be said to occur. That such a decision is logically necessary, and is tacitly if not explicitly made, is perhaps obscured in much nonfrequency analysis. Since the nonfrequency analyst in effect utilizes single coding units in making inferences, he is often under no immediate compulsion to describe explicitly the bounds of the single meaningful context within which he notes the presence or absence of the relevant content feature. In contrast, the quantitative analyst, since he ultimately operates with frequencies as his content indicators, must make explicit the size of the coding unit which will be employed in counting.

It should be clear, finally, that neither of these two approaches—the frequency and the nonfrequency—prejudges the size of the coding unit that will turn out to be best for propaganda analysis or communication analysis. Rather, the situation in both approaches is that a unit of one size may be best for one specific inferential problem and a unit of another size best for another problem.

Quantitative Tests of Nonfrequency Inferences

The relationship between nonfrequency content analysis and quantitative research methods in general may be easily confused unless a distinction is drawn between the character of the *content indicator* (which is nonfrequency) and the character of the *test* (which may be quantitative) for inferences based on nonfrequency indicators.

As a hypothetical example, a propaganda-analysis inference might hold that the single appearance of a certain theme in a speech by a political leader (or in a certain context within the speech) was indicative of a secret change in political policy. This hypothesis could be tested systematically (quantitatively), in principle, by examining all known past instances in which that type of theme occurred in a speech by that leader (or by similarly placed leaders) to determine in how many cases there was subsequent evidence of the type of policy change in question.

In practice, however, this type of quantitative test of an inferential hypothesis is often difficult. There may be no such past instances, or only a few; evidence of policy changes following the occurrence of the theme in the past may be fragmentary, inconclusive, or equivocal.

In any case, whether or not such verification is feasible, it is important not to *confuse* (*a*) the systematic test (which may be quantitative) of an inference based on a nonfrequency indicator and (*b*) quantitative content analysis itself, which is based on frequency indicators. Propaganda-analysis inferences, whether they are based on frequency or nonfrequency indicators, may indeed ideally require quantitative verification. But although the test may be quantitative, propaganda analysis based on nonfrequency indicators is itself nonquantitative.

It may be the blurring of this distinction that leads proponents of quantitative methods to argue sometimes that what is here called nonfrequency content analysis is not really very different from frequency content analysis. Thus, the argument goes, a nonfrequency content indicator can be used with greater confidence in making inferences if it is known to have been a valid indicator on other occasions as well; *therefore,* it is argued, the value of nonfrequency indicators also depends upon the frequency of their occurrence.

What this argument obscures, however, is that frequency of occurrence in this sense—in many individual inferences—does not make the nonfrequency indicator into a frequency indicator. What determines whether it is a frequency or nonfrequency indicator is its role *within one inference.* The fact that a certain nonfrequency indicator has been successfully employed on previous relevant occasions does, perhaps, provide additional support for the new inference. But this does not alter the fact that in each instance such an inference is based upon a nonfrequency indicator. Thus, if a minor theme appeared not merely in one but in several separate propaganda communications, the analyst might be able to use it each time as a nonfrequency indicator to make the same inference. The fact that he could make the same inference several times from different communications would strengthen his confidence in the inference. But the minor theme used as an indicator would remain a nonfrequency indicator. That is, the inference—each time it was made—was based on the *presence* of the minor theme, and not on the frequency of its occurrence, within each individual communication.

Examples of Nonfrequency Propaganda Analysis

Several examples drawn from FCC materials will illustrate the nature of nonfrequency content analysis and some of the limitations of an exclusive frequency approach.

1. Following the German disaster at Stalingrad, domestic morale sank in Germany, and rumblings of discontent with the Nazi regime were heard. In this crisis German leaders addressed the nation. Goebbels, in one of his speeches, used the word "counter-terror." From the context in which this word was used, and from a recognition of what the situation was, the FCC analyst inferred that Goebbels had in mind pogroms against the Jews. The inference rested upon a nonfrequency content indicator. The mere presence of the word "counter-terror" in a particular context sufficed to make it a content indicator in an inferential hypothesis. The word may or may not have appeared several more times in Goebbels' speech or in other propaganda materials at the time; the FCC analyst was interested only in the presence of the word in a particular linguistic and situational context.[7]

2. In another instance the FCC analyst inferred that the Nazi Propaganda Ministry was attempting to discourage the German public, albeit indirectly, from expecting a resurgence of the strength and effectiveness of the U-boats. This inference was also based in part upon a nonfrequency content indicator. Hans Fritzsche, a leading radio commentator, had asserted, in discussing a recent success achieved by German U-boats: "We are not so naïve as to indulge in speculation about the future on the basis of the fact of this victory."[8] In focusing upon this statement, the FCC analyst was not concerned with the frequency of the theme in Fritzsche's talk or in other German propaganda accounts of the same U-boat "victory," or with the question of whether it now appeared more or less frequently than in earlier propaganda on the U-boats. For his purpose it sufficed that the content theme was present even once in the context of Fritzsche's remarks about the latest German U-boat victory.

It is interesting to speculate on what would have happened had a frequency (quantitative) approach been employed in this case. In the first place, it is problematic whether a content category would have been set up that would precisely catch the meaning of this one phrase in Fritzsche's talk. Second, since the phrase (or its equivalent) appeared at best only a very few times in German propaganda at the time, the propaganda analyst, in looking over the quantitative results, might well have dismissed it as a minor theme or lumped it together with other items in a miscellaneous category. In other words, if this single phrase from Fritzsche's talk had been tallied under a frequency indicator, it might well have lost its inferential significance.[9]

3. The third example is quite similar. Mussolini had set up a new Republican-Fascist government following his so-called "liberation" by German parachutists. German propaganda gave quite a play to these events and celebrated Mussolini's re-establishment of a pro-Axis Italian government. In looking at this propaganda, the FCC analyst noted that, after a few days, a minor theme of some sobriety was introduced into the otherwise enthusiastic publicity on Mussolini and his new government. Only a few Nazi papers carried the new message, and, where it did appear, it was rather well hidden. The significance of the new theme to the FCC analyst lay in the fact that it appeared at all. In other words, he made use of it as a nonfrequency content indicator. Had this new theme been coded under a general frequency-type indicator in a quantitative study, it would probably have passed unnoticed. But, when singled out as a nonfrequency indicator, the theme, although repeated only a few times in the total Nazi propaganda on Mussolini, provided the basis for an important inference, which has since been verified.[10]

4. In another case, the *absence* of a certain type of statement served as one of a set of content indicators for the inference that German leaders were not planning to undertake a major military offensive on the Russian front during the summer of 1943. The fact that Nazi propaganda did not predict future operations or successes was utilized by the analyst as a nonfrequency indicator.[11]

NOTES

1. "Statistical content analysis" may be considered synonymous in this study with systematic quantitative content analysis, that is, content analysis in which the counting of frequencies is done by means of a systematic, rigorous procedure and which results in precise numerical frequencies or statistics. There is also a more narrow meaning of "statistical content analysis"—that in which the counting procedure is sufficiently detailed in objective instructions that the coding can be done by clerical personnel. (This is usually possible only when the coding judgments are of a fairly simple character, as in word counts.) Perhaps a

better term for the latter meaning, although it is awkward, is "statistical-clerical content analysis."

2. For a detailed discussion see Paul F. Lazarsfeld and Allen H. Barton, "Qualitative Measurement in the Social Sciences: Classification, Typologies, and Indices," in Daniel Lerner and H. D. Lasswell (eds.), *The Policy Sciences: Recent Developments in Scope and Method* (Stanford University Press, Stanford, Calif., 1951), pp. 155–92. See also Dorwin P. Cartwright, "Analysis of Qualitative Material," in Leon Festinger and Daniel Katz (eds.), *Research Methods in the Behavioral Sciences* (The Dryden Press, New York, 1953), pp. 421–70; esp. pp. 440–54.

3. An explicit reminder of this is given by the investigators on the RADIR content-analysis project: "It is useful in reaching conclusions to remain aware that such totals are a summation of the frequency distribution of qualitative variates even though they may look like quantitative variables" (H. D. Lasswell, Daniel Lerner, and Ithiel de Sola Pool, *The Comparative Study of Symbols* ["Hoover Institute Studies," Series C: *Symbols,* No. 1; Stanford University Press, Stanford, Calif., 1952], p. 38).

4. In the further development of the nonfrequency approach, it might be desirable to distinguish terminologically between this type of nonfrequency content indicator and that in the preceding hypothetical case.

5. See, for example, Lasswell, Lerner, and Pool, *op. cit.,* pp. 60–61.

6. A relatively large sample may be required, and the cost of the study may therefore be relatively high. On this point see *ibid.,* p. 60.

7. While direct verification has not been possible, some indirect support for the inference has been found in an entry in Goebbels' diary made shortly after his speech; see Louis P. Lochner (ed.), *The Goebbels Diaries, 1942–1943* (Doubleday & Co., Inc., Garden City, N.Y., 1948), pp. 261–62, 177, 290, for references to Goebbels' plans for ridding Berlin of Jews —plans that were partly carried out.

8. *CEA* (*Central European Analysis,* the weekly report of the German Section of the Analysis Division of the FCC) #38, October 1, 1943, pp. B-5 and B-6.

9. For a fuller account of the inference see Part III, Chapter 13, Case Study No. 13.9, p. 246.

10. For a fuller account of the inference see Part III, Chapter 13, Case Study No. 13.4, p. 235.

11. For a fuller account of the inference see Part III, Chapter 11, Case Study No. 11.5, p. 155.

TEN

Contextual Factors in Propaganda Analysis

Our next subject of discussion is the way in which the various components of a communication act must be taken into account by the propaganda analyst in inferring the speaker's intended meaning and his purpose.

Two Approaches to the Study of Meaning in Content Analysis

The principal components in an act of communication are contained in the formula: *Who* says *what, how,* to *whom,* under what *circumstances,* for what *purpose,* and with what *effect.*

The use of content analysis in what is known as propaganda analysis involves, principally, an effort to infer the *purpose*[1] (goal, objective, or intention) of the communication. Other antecedent conditions of propaganda, not specified in the above formula—such as attitudes of the communicator, unconscious motivations, etc.—are also often inferred, but propaganda analysis is less often employed to infer the *effects* of communications.

In attempting to infer the purpose of a propaganda communication, the analyst does well not to focus exclusively upon the content of the message, i.e., what is said. He must also take into account who says it, how, to whom, and under what circumstances. That is, the purpose of a communication can be reliably inferred only by viewing its content in the context provided by other components of the communication act in question.

In considering the content of a propaganda communication, the analyst seeks to identify features of it which provide clues as to the speaker's purpose in making that particular communication. The content clues may be lexical or nonlexical. That is, they may consist of the meanings contained in the communication (semantical characteristics) or other characteristics of the communication. Two types of content analysis may be distinguished, therefore, depending on whether the meaning of the words is singled out by the investigator or whether only nonmeaning, or nonlexical, characteristics are recorded as possible content indicators of a speaker's purpose and other communicator variables.

There are, in turn, two essentially different types of semantical content analysis. Not only do these two types of semantical analysis employ different criteria of meaning; they also entail important procedural differences.

The content of a communication may be described in terms of the *usual* meanings which the words in question have for all users of that language or for a designated person or group; or it may be described in terms of the speaker's actual *intended* meaning in that instance of communication. The first type of semantical analysis, known as "manifest" content analysis, is associated particularly with the work of H. D. Lasswell and some of his associates. In fact, their definition of statistical or quantitative content analysis usually includes the requirement that *only* the manifest content, that is, the usual or ordinary meanings, of communication be described.[2] It will be recognized that it is important in this type of content analysis for the investigator to specify usual meaning *for whom,* since not all the users of a language employ it uniformly.

A further discussion of the exact meaning of the concept "manifest content," the circumstances which led to its adoption, and its scientific status and value is unnecessary to the purposes of this paper.[3] However, it may be noted that the criterion of manifest content is not generally accepted, especially in fields of communication research other than propaganda analysis, as being essential to the technique of quantitative content analysis.[4] Even in the area of political communication research, for which Lasswell's version of content analysis has been primarily developed, many—if not most—quantitative content analyses do not in practice employ the criterion of manifest content.

The second type of semantical content analysis attempts to record the actual *intended* meaning of the communicator (or the meaning *comprehended* by a designated audience).[5] It is obvious that in many cases the intended or comprehended meaning will be the same as the usual meaning of the words in question. But many words and combinations of words have alternative meanings, depending upon the context in which they appear. And a given speaker may use words in different ways at different times in order to convey different meanings. The usual or most frequent way in which he uses words is not always a sure guide to his intended meaning in a specific instance. If the investigator relies solely upon his knowledge of the usual meaning of words in order to ascertain a speaker's intended meanings, incorrect and invalid determinations may very well result.

The two types of semantical analysis which have just been described differ significantly in the procedure by means of which judgments of meaning are made. It is important to recognize that estimates of a speaker's intended meaning are specific inferences. Each judgment of an intended meaning is a separate inference arrived at by taking into account all relevant aspects of the context. In contrast, a judgment of the manifest meaning of words is not an inference in the sense that word is used in this report; rather, it is an estimate arrived at by applying to the words in question a set of external, explicit criteria of their usual or most frequent meaning [6] for all users of that language or for designated groups or persons.

In coding content for its usual or manifest meaning, therefore, the investigator needs to be familiar with the general rules of the language, with the customary meanings of words for all users of that language, and, in some applications, with the usual or most frequent language habits of the source. This knowledge is also essential in estimating a speaker's intended meaning. But, in order to make a valid inference of the speaker's intended meaning in each specific instance of communication, the investigator must also take into account the *situational* and *behavioral* contexts of that communication. He does so in order to determine which of the possible meanings of the words in question the speaker intends to convey in this instance and the precise shading of his intended meaning. The analysis of intended meaning differs in this essential procedural respect from the analysis of manifest meaning, in which only *communication* or *linguistic* context is taken into account by the investigator or coders.[7]

In propaganda analysis the investigator is concerned chiefly with the speaker's intended meaning and little, if at all, with his manifest or usual meaning. Quantitative content analysis, too, as was indicated above, often records intended meaning rather than manifest meaning.

The procedure for inferring intended meaning cannot easily be made explicit. That is, relatively flexible and interpretive procedures must usually be utilized in the interest of obtaining valid characterizations of intended meaning. If this is a disadvantage of propaganda analysis from a scientific standpoint, however, it is one present to some extent also in quantitative content analyses which record intended meaning rather than manifest content. The difference seems to be one of degree. For one thing, well-trained quantitative content analysts are likely to push further than most propaganda analysts the effort to introduce at least some explicit rules for coding intended meaning, thus reducing to some extent the purely interpretive character of such judgments. And, certainly, they are more alert than most qualitatively oriented analysts to the fact that even if the procedure for obtaining content data on intended meanings is highly interpretive, its results are still subject to reliability tests.

In any event, the chief criticism of highly qualitative propaganda analysis should perhaps be directed at another aspect of its procedure. In propaganda analysis, as the preliminary discussion of this problem in Chapter 8 indicated, the process of inferring intended meanings is closely related to, and overlaps, the process of inferring the speaker's purpose or propaganda goal. The lack of a sharp operational separation between these two tasks is, at first glance, subject to methodological criticism on the grounds that the reasoning on behalf of the two types of inference is not clearly separated, that the processes may be circular, and that a procedure with such deficiencies does not lend itself to adequate testing and verifying of inferential hypotheses.

To what extent can this aspect of propaganda-analysis procedure be made more explicit and possible methodological deficiencies be corrected? The situation is perhaps not as hopeless as it may appear. Closer examination of the procedure in question suggests that the fact that the two inferential processes proceed in close conjunction does not in itself exclude the possibility that the investigator may consider relatively systematically the plausibility of his inferential hypotheses. Moreover, some progress can be made toward greater formalization of this type of procedure. The present report hopes to accomplish this by identifying the major *noncontent contextual factors* to which both intended meaning and speaker's purpose are related and hopes to demonstrate the importance of giving explicit attention to such contextual factors in propaganda analysis.

Three types of contextual factors are identified and discussed below. Following this discussion, the close connection between the process of estimating the speaker's intended meaning and his purpose is examined in greater detail.

Situational, Behavioral, and Communication Contexts

In estimating intended meanings, the propaganda analyst takes into account three types of context: [8]

1. *Communication context:* the syntactic, linguistic, and structural features of the communication.[9]
2. *Situational (or historical) context:* who says it, to whom, and under what circumstances.
3. *Behavioral context:* the instrumental aspect of the communication (the speaker's purpose) and the relationship of the communication to *other* behavior of the speaker and of those with whom he is associated.

Only the situational context of propaganda communications is singled out for detailed discussion here; certain aspects of the communication context were discussed on pages 89–90, and the behavioral context was examined in Part I.

Propaganda communications always have a setting which influences the meanings the speaker chooses to convey and which, he knows, others will take into account in arriving at an understanding of what he has said. Three components of any act of communication —*who* says it, to *whom,* and under *what circumstances*—comprise the most important elements of the historical or situational context.

In order to appraise these aspects, the investigator must have rather specific, detailed knowledge of the propaganda organization whose output he is analyzing.

Who Says It

Numerous speakers, writers, and sources contribute to most organized systems of political propaganda. While these individuals and sources may be co-ordinated and share a common political orientation, differences in the content and style of their communications can usually be noted. Whether such differences stem from a purposeful allocation of propaganda roles, an unco-ordinated and deliberate assertion of different points of view, or inadvertent and unconscious projections of individual characteristics, they are often useful in making inferences. This problem has already been considered from the standpoint of "control structure," in Chapter 7; certain aspects of it are considered in more detail at this point.

The speakers and writers making up a propaganda organization may differ in one or more of the following respects: (*a*) degree of accuracy, (*b*) degree of authoritativeness, (*c*) degree of responsibility as propagandists, (*d*) degree of frankness and objectivity, (*e*) personal political and ideological views, (*f*) degree of adherence to propaganda directives, (*g*) specialized vocabulary and language habits, (*h*) access to special sources of inside information or propaganda direction, (*i*) personally held policy preferences at variance from official policy, (*j*) personally held estimates and expectations at variance from those entering into official policy calculations.

If such differences can be detected or reasonably postulated by the propaganda analyst, a discriminating treatment of the who-says-it component of propaganda becomes possible, and valuable opportunities for inferences arise. The frequency and nonfrequency approaches to propaganda analysis can be usefully contrasted in this respect. Analysts using the quantitative approach, when they apply it crudely, tend to overlook and to make little use of the fact of the individuality of different speakers. They tend to code propaganda statements made by different speakers rather arbitrarily as equivalent occurrences of a general theme or content category. They are often satisfied to record only the explicit, more common, and more superficial meaning of propaganda statements. In contrast, qualitatively oriented investigators make special efforts to gain insight into individual differences among communicators and to appraise the subtler meaning and purpose of propaganda statements in the light of the individual characteristics of the communicators.

To Whom It Is Said

The intended meaning of a given propaganda statement, as well as its inferential significance, can often be grasped only by taking into account the precise audience for which it was intended. It is well known that the propagandist, as indeed anyone interested in communicating effectively, uses language appropriate to the language habits, attitudes, and behavioral dispositions of the audience addressed.

Various characteristics of the intended audience may influence the speaker's choice of language. An elite may differentiate the language of its communications according to the intended audience's intellectual level, its position in the social and political structure, its political background and orientation, its system of values, the political dialects to which it is accustomed, its level of knowledge of and interest in governmental affairs and political developments, the extent to which it has been favorably or unfavorably affected by the regime's policies, and its assumed trustworthiness and loyalty to the regime.

In addition, various aspects of the relationship of a given speaker (or writer) to a particular audience may exercise a subtle effect on the speaker's way of expressing himself and the meanings derived from his discourse by the audience in question. Thus, the speaker-audience relationship may be more or less intimate in terms of shared historical experiences, common origins, common ideological and political beliefs, a similar position in the social structure, the fact that both have access to certain information which is not publicly and generally known, etc. Individuals may be chosen to serve as specialized propaganda spokesmen on the basis of already existing relationships of this type with certain audiences. For propaganda purposes certain speakers may be encouraged to develop special relationships with a particular audience.

Unless the investigator is aware of the characteristics of the audience which affect the speaker's choice of language and of other aspects of the speaker-audience relationship, he will fail to grasp the full meaning and significance of many communications. The language habits evinced in the communications of any single leader may vary considerably, especially in the case of high-level political leaders who address different types of audiences on different occasions. Comparisons of two or more communications made by the *same* individual (a frequent mode of analysis in propaganda and political research) involve fewer problems of interpreting meaning and purpose when the communications in question were made on similar occasions to a similar audience—for example, the yearly Hitler speeches on certain ceremonial and Party days. The complexity of the analyst's task is substantially greater when he attempts to compare the content of separate communications by the same speaker to different audiences. For example, a speech by Hitler before gatherings of Nazi Party leaders had a speaker-to-audience context different from that of a Hitler address to gatherings of military officers on memorial occasions. In these two situations the body of shared experiences, political interests, tacit understandings, political idioms and symbols, etc., between speaker and audience differed in significant respects. A reference to 1923 (the date of the unsuccessful but "glorious" Nazi *Putsch*), for example, would have different meanings for a Party audience and for a military audience, both as intended by the speaker and as understood by his audience.

In propaganda analysis the to-whom aspect of communication is often so important for assessing a speaker's precise meaning and purpose that the careful investigator making a quantitative analysis would not usually include in one sample communications known to be addressed to different audiences.

The specialized audience being addressed by a propagandist, however, is not always self-evident or easily established. It may take some time and investigation to learn that one speaker (General Dittmar, for example, in the Nazi propaganda system) speaks primarily to a relatively sophisticated audience, which he presumes has some knowledge and appreciation of military strategy and military problems, and that another propagandist writing in a certain journal (for instance, Goebbels in *Das Reich*) hopes to reach a sophisticated international audience, including enemy leadership groups.

Once such differences of speaker-audience context are discovered, there is often little justification for treating statements appearing in one specialized communication as equivalent to those in another specialized communication or to those appearing in the general communications directed to a relatively undifferentiated mass audience, even if the wording is similar. Opportunities for making inferences occur, that is, both when propaganda communications are differentiated according to the speaker-audience relationship and when political communications are not differentiated in this manner. Thus, as Hans Speier has noted,[10] the use of the same language in propaganda to different audiences may reflect:

1. The propagandist's knowledge that certain expectations and attitudes are shared by various audiences, despite differences among them in other respects.

2. The propagandist's lack of awareness of differences in the specific expectations and attitudes held by his audiences (which he might have taken into account, if he had known of them).

3. The propagandist's disregard of differences among the audiences addressed when speaking about beliefs which he holds firmly or which are firmly required of him.

UNDER WHAT CIRCUMSTANCES IT IS SAID

A speaker's intended meaning and purpose can often be grasped only if the circumstances of the communication are appreciated. This is particularly so in the case of political communications which—like the wartime propaganda analyzed by the FCC—are highly situation- or event-oriented. The *time* and *place* of a communication and, especially, the *events preceding and accompanying it* may be highly relevant in shaping the meanings which the speaker intends to convey.[11] These same factors also play a role in determining the propagandist's goals.

For example, relatively sober predictions of ultimate German victory made by Hitler in speeches before the same audience on two separate occasions might well have different intended meanings and different significance for purposes of making inferences. If, for example, an important Allied setback took place in the interim between the two speeches, the fact that the two sober predictions of victory were virtually identical in content would not justify regarding them as equivalent in meaning. The second prediction might have this connotation: *despite* the recent Allied setback, we can still be no more than moderately confident of ultimate victory.

The precise timing of a propaganda statement in relation to events often endows it with meaning that would otherwise be different or lacking. For example, "We will go over to the offensive" may have different meanings (and a different import in making inferences) depending upon whether the speaker's forces are still retreating or have succeeded in stabilizing the front.

Finally, it should be noted, key phrases and symbols in propaganda may be redefined as time passes because of the course of events. The propaganda analyst must be alert to the possibility that the meanings of many propaganda symbols and themes have a developmental history, that the way in which a word or phrase is used today may be related to its use earlier, in different situations, and that the intended meaning of the word or phrase may change as the historical context in which it is used changes. Such changes of meanings may take place without the active collaboration of the propagandist; however, propagandists have also been known to redefine terms consciously and with purpose.

The Relation between Inferring a Speaker's Intended Meaning and His Propaganda Goal

In Chapter 8 attention was called to various circumstances which account for the fact that the processes of description of content and formation of inferences are often intimately interrelated in propaganda analysis. The problem of circularity, or analytical bias, arising from the failure to distinguish more clearly between content-descriptive and inferential procedures was considered in general terms.

In the present chapter it has been pointed out that in semantical content analysis, which records intended rather than manifest meaning, the process of obtaining content data (usually known as "content description") becomes inferential in character, since it involves making inferences about the individual meanings intended by the speaker. Accordingly, the problem of the interrelationship between description of content and formation of inferences appears in a special light, for it is in fact no longer a relationship between description and inference (as when manifest meanings are recorded) but one between *two* inferential processes, that of inferring a speaker's intended meanings and that of inferring his purpose or goal. Therefore, the problem of overlapping procedures in propaganda analysis needs to be reconsidered.

From a formal standpoint, of course, an inference as to a speaker's intended meaning is logically distinct from an inference as to his purpose, or what he hopes to accomplish by conveying such an intended meaning. In practice, however, the two inferential processes are interrelated. In this respect propaganda analysis is quite different from statistical content analysis, in which the process of recording manifest or, for that matter, intended meanings is usually distinct from the effort to draw inferences from the recorded data as to the speaker's purpose or other communicator variables.

In propaganda analysis the two inferential processes overlap not only in the qualitative phase of the investigation, in which the analyst seeks to discover new relationships and to formulate new hypotheses; they seem intertwined also in the phase of the investigation in which the plausibility of the inferential hypotheses is weighed. It is for this reason that this procedure in propaganda analysis seems methodologically suspect and that questions can be properly raised as to whether the reasoning is circular and the evaluation of hypotheses adequate. Prior to a consideration of this problem, some of the reasons for the close conjunction between the process of inferring the speaker's intended meaning and the process of inferring his purpose may be examined in greater detail than in Chapter 8.

In the first place, the intended meaning which the investigator attributes to the speaker's words must generally be consonant with the propaganda goal or purpose which he attributes to the speaker in any given instance. This follows from the general assumption that the speaker's activity is purposive; his choice of an intended meaning to be conveyed by certain words is assumed to have been governed by the purpose or objective which he hopes the communication will achieve.

In the second place, consideration of the speaker's intended meanings and of his purposes, or goals, cannot be separated because, as was noted earlier, a propagandist's strategy and tactics may fluctuate at any time in response to events. Therefore, if the investigator is to make certain that his inferences of the speaker's intended meanings will be consonant with his judgments of the speaker's purposes, he cannot very well devote himself first to the task of collecting data on the intended meanings being expressed in the flow of propaganda communications. Rather, in order to insure that these inferences of intended meaning are valid, the investigator must simultaneously relate them to the speaker's purposes, or goals, which may be changing abruptly in the course of his effort to concentrate on recording intended meanings. Similarly, the analyst must assume that situational and behavioral contexts which affect the speaker's choice of intended meanings are highly unstable and may change from day to day or, in some cases, from hour to hour. Hence, especially in trend analyses— which are frequently employed in propaganda analysis—the investigator needs to make for each specific instance of communication a fresh and relatively intensive assessment of contextual factors likely to be related to intended meaning and to the purpose in that instance. (These contextual factors include the propagandist's over-all strategy. Thus, as indicated on pages 63–65, the interpretation of a change in the propaganda treatment of any given topic must take into account the possibility that it was dictated primarily by considerations of over-all propaganda strategy rather than by events directly affecting the topic in question.)

The assessment of contextual factors in the two inferential processes tends to coincide in part because much of the situational context (who says it; to whom; under what circumstances) relevant to establishing the precise intended meaning of the speaker's words may be relevant also to establishing his purpose. The relationship between the two inferential processes is necessarily intimate, too, because the speaker's purpose or goal is part of the behavioral context which is taken into account in estimating his intended meanings. That is, when more than one intended meaning can be attributed to the speaker's words, the investigator chooses between them by taking into account what he knows or can postulate about the speaker's purpose and other aspects of the behavioral context in which that particular propaganda statement has been made.

When analyzing a specific instance of communication, the investigator considers alternative hypotheses as to the speaker's purpose at the same time that he ponders the precise meaning which the speaker intended to convey by the choice of the words in question. Such a procedure is not necessarily unsystematic, though certainly it may be complicated and is usually not fully articulated. What the investigator does, ideally, is to consider alternatives for *two* different variables, as it were, simultaneously. He considers alternative combinations of intended meaning plus purpose in the light of whatever else he knows or can reasonably postulate about the behavioral and situational context of the communication being examined. Such mental rehearsals or experiments are capable of being performed either rigorously or intuitively. In any case the analyst can assess the plausibility of an inferred purpose in the light of his general knowledge about the propaganda behavior of the source. And, moreover, the inferential results achieved thereby are subject, at least in principle, to systematic verification.

It may be useful, by way of summarizing this discussion, to indicate in general terms the various components of a propaganda-analysis inference and the formal relationship among them. Such a summary will also serve to relate the discussion of the qualitative character of propaganda analysis in this part of the report to the discussion of methods of making inferences in Part I.

In propaganda analysis, the investigator's insight consists in seeing a connection between the content, its presumed intended meaning, the speaker's purpose, and possibly other antecedent conditions which help to determine the speaker's purpose and the characteristics of his communication. The connection is supported by a set of considerations which may be referred to as "reasoning."

Insight is selective. Many content characteristics, alternative ver-

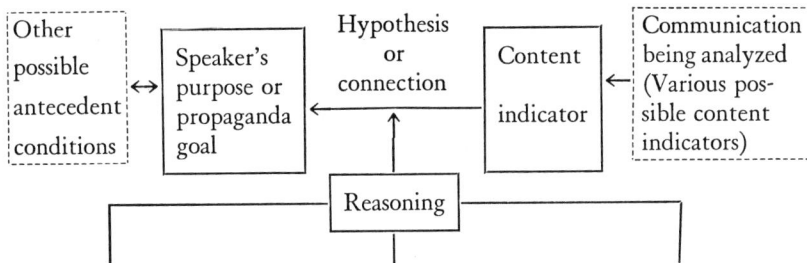

Other possible antecedent conditions	Speaker's purpose or propaganda goal	Hypothesis or connection	Content indicator	Communication being analyzed (Various possible content indicators)

Reasoning

1. *Semantical meaning intended by speaker:* Determined by knowledge of the general rules of the language and of special language habits of the speaker, and by an appraisal of:

   a) *Communication context:* Relation of content indicator to syntactic, linguistic, and structural aspects of the communication of which it is a part.

   b) *Situational context:* Who is speaking to whom under what circumstances.

   c) *Behavioral context:* Independent signs of the speaker's purpose and the relationship of what he says to other behavior on his part or on the part of his associates.

2. *Generalizations:* About propaganda and political characteristics of system under scrutiny. (See Part I, pp. 45–57.)

3. *Logic-of-situation assessment.* (See Part I, pp. 58–66.)

sions of the speaker's meaning, purpose, and other antecedent conditions, and a wide variety of considerations supporting one or another inferential hypothesis compete for the analyst's attention. Insight consists in recognizing the few alternative connections considered most plausible in the situation. The final inference, or set of interconnected inferences, should be the result of a more or less prolonged and systematic consideration of these alternatives.

The general components comprising the connection or whole of an inferential hypothesis in propaganda analysis may be recapitulated in the schema on page 119.

In this schema, it will be noted, the estimate of the speaker's intended meaning was placed under "Reasoning." But, as emphasized previously, the speaker's intended meaning is itself a matter to be inferred. Strictly speaking, therefore, it would be more logical (though schematically more cumbersome) to have made the semantical meaning intended by the speaker a part of the connection, or inferential sequence. Thus, the schema—in an abbreviated form—would be as follows:

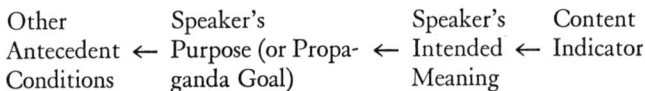

Other Antecedent Conditions	←	Speaker's Purpose (or Propaganda Goal)	←	Speaker's Intended Meaning	←	Content Indicator

NOTES

1. This applies, of course, to the *indirect* method of making inferences, in which an inference about the speaker's propaganda goal (or purpose) is always the first in what may become a chain of interrelated inferences about other antecedent conditions as well.

2. See, for example, the discussion of these definitions in Bernard Berelson, *Content Analysis in Communication Research* (The Free Press, Glencoe, Ill., 1952), pp. 14–18. The early development of content-analysis terminology was influenced by Charles Morris' statement of the general theory of signs, with its now familiar distinction between "pragmatics," "semantics," and "syntactics" ("Foundations of the Theory of Signs," *International Encyclopedia of Unified Science*, Vol. I, No. 2, 1939). The theory of signs was restated by Morris from a behavioral standpoint in his later work, *Signs, Language and Behavior* (Prentice-Hall, Inc., New York, 1946).

3. The concept of "manifest" (as against "latent") meaning was taken over from Freudian theory and introduced into content analysis by H. D. Lasswell (see his "A Provisional Classification of Symbol Data," *Psychiatry*, May, 1938). An important effort to codify Lasswell's theory of content analysis and to restate it from the standpoint of the general theory of signs was made by Abraham Kaplan, "Content Analysis and the Theory of Signs," *Philosophy of Science* (October, 1943), pp. 230–49.

For a brief review and a preliminary effort at systematic analysis of the various "meanings" of "meaning" see Floyd G. Lounsbury's contribution to *Psycholinguistics: A Survey of Theory and Research Problems* (edited by Charles E. Osgood and Thomas A. Sebeok; Waverly Press, Inc., Baltimore, 1954), pp. 171–77. The problem of the "meaning of meaning" is reviewed from the standpoint of experimental psychology by Charles E. Osgood, "The Nature and Measurement of Meaning," *Psychological Bulletin* (May, 1952), pp. 197–237.

On different types of semantical content analysis and the problem of validity, the major sources are Irving L. Janis, "Meaning and the Study of Symbolic Behavior," *Psychiatry* (November, 1943), pp. 425–39, and his "The Problem of Validating Content Analysis," in Harold D. Lasswell, Nathan Leites, and Associates, *Language of Politics* (George W. Stewart, Inc., New York, 1949), pp. 55–82. The writer hopes to consider these questions in detail in a future publication.

4. See, for example, the explicit rejection of the criterion of manifest content by Dorwin P. Cartwright, "Analysis of Qualitative Material," in Leon Festinger and Daniel Katz (eds.), *Research Methods in the Behavioral Sciences* (The Dryden Press, New York, 1953), p. 424.

5. Since propaganda analysis is concerned with intended meaning, this report will refrain from discussing further its counterpart, comprehended meaning.

6. The most explicit statement of the requirements of this approach is the discussion of the "frequency criterion" in Janis, "Meaning and the Study of Symbolic Behavior," pp. 433–34. This problem is referred to again in his "The Problem of Validating Content Analysis," pp. 55–82, esp. p. 58.

7. It may be noted that in manifest content analysis, which employs relatively rigid rather than flexible coding procedures, the investigator often places limits even on the extent of the linguistic context which coders are permitted to consider in classifying words under content categories. The reason for this is usually the investigator's desire to increase inter-coder reliability.

8. It may be helpful to point out that these distinctions offer a somewhat arbitrary but convenient way of dividing up the total context and labeling its parts in order to facilitate an *analytical description,* such as is attempted here. But in practice the content analyst would not have to compartmentalize and label in order to take account of the relevant context in any specific problem.

9. This includes various matters, such as the dependence of the semantical meaning of certain words (or, in the more precise technical terminology, sign-vehicles) upon the presence of other words, the dependence of the explicit content on the hierarchical arrangement of sentences, the relationship of parts of a communication to each other, the physical properties of words, etc.

10. In a personal communication to the author.

11. Frequently, the circumstances of a communication will be closely connected with who said it and to whom it was said, but this does not negate the usefulness of a formal distinction between these three contextual factors.

Part *III*

Methodology and Applications

Introduction

Part III of this report will indicate how the indirect method, and particularly its logic-of-the-situation approach, may be applied in attempting to solve a propaganda-analysis problem. The earlier discussion of this approach in Part I indicated the desirability of developing catalogues of all the possible propaganda goals that may be pursued in given types of situations (see p. 63). The task of doing so is undertaken here as part of the effort to provide a general framework for the indirect method of propaganda analysis. In terms of mathematical theory such catalogues are simply lists of all the elements (possibilities) in a sample space. A further systematization along mathematical lines is perhaps possible in principle but is not attempted here.

An important prerequisite to the systematizing of any particular application of the logic-of-the-situation approach is that the situations under which propaganda is issued be of a relatively *standardized* character. It would seem difficult to satisfy this requirement in propaganda analysis given the fact, noted earlier, that it is the novel and unusual aspects of the situation to which the actor responds that must be taken into account in applying the logic-of-the-situation approach. Despite the diversity and variety of the FCC inferences examined in this study, however, it became evident that they exemplified a small number of basic situations. It proved possible to classify most FCC inferences into three general groupings on the basis of the situation under which the propaganda had been issued and, then, to work out a general approach for making indirect inferences within each of these three categories.

The fact that certain basic patterns of conflict and interaction can be observed in world politics satisfies the requirement that the situations studied in propaganda analysis be of a relatively standardized character. Situations in international politics fall into three groups on the basis of what the agent or instrumentality is that causes, or seeks to initiate, changes in the power relationship between opponents. A threefold grouping is adequate, at least for the relatively simple case in international politics in which only two states (actors) contem-

125

plate or undertake moves in order to change some aspect of the situation in a direction more favorable or less unfavorable to themselves.

1. Actions to change the status quo may be taken by the propaganda analyst's side.
2. Actions to change the status quo may be taken by the opponent.
3. Other situational changes (a residual category) may occur as a result of
   a) Events partly under the control of one side, partly under control of the other side, and, perhaps, partly controlled by neither.
   b) Actions initiated by third parties.
   c) Events (leading to situational changes) which are natural occurrences.

Propaganda analysis, as employed by the FCC, is a means of obtaining various kinds of specific information about each of these three types of situational changes. Disregarding, for the moment, specific aspects of any individual inferential problem, it can be seen that each of the three types of situational changes offers the propaganda analyst a set of *general* intelligence problems. He may address himself to any one or even all of them. He may be concerned with the *character, magnitude, location,* and *timing* of any move to change the situation. If the move is one contemplated by the opposing elite, the propaganda analyst may be interested in predicting that action before it takes place, that is, in attempting to infer the opponent's *intentions.* If the move is one contemplated or already taken by the opposing elite, the propaganda analyst may be interested in inferring the set of *expectations* and *calculations* which accompany it and the *objectives* assigned to it.

If the move is one contemplated but not yet taken by the propaganda analyst's side, he may then be interested in inferring whether the opponent *anticipates* it and correctly *estimates* its character, magnitude, location, and timing. If the move is one contemplated or already made by his side, the propaganda analyst may also be interested in inferring the opponent's estimate of its objectives, the opponent's expectations regarding the outcome of the move directed against him, and his plans for countermoves.

In the case of other situational changes, not set into motion by the initiatives of the opponent or those of his own side, the propaganda analyst's task is somewhat different. Changes of this type in the opponent's milieu are not always known to outsiders; they may not be directly observable, or they may be difficult to assess. The first task of the propaganda analyst, therefore, may be to infer whether favorable or unfavorable changes of this type have taken place, or are expected to take place, in the opponent's milieu. In either case, the propaganda analyst may also be interested in inferring the opponent's estimate of the magnitude, duration, and consequences of such changes, and his plans for exploiting favorable developments or for checking unfavorable developments.

In summary and recapitulation, the three general types of situational changes of interest and each of the corresponding set of general problems of inference which the propaganda analyst faces are as follows:

GENERAL TYPE OF SITUATIONAL CHANGE (From the Standpoint of the Propaganda Analyst)	GENERAL PROBLEM IN MAKING INFERENCES (For the Propaganda Analyst)
1. A situational change introduced by the opponent's action (i.e., an intended or accomplished initiative).	To predict the character, magnitude, location, and timing of the opponent's initiative, and to infer the calculations and expectations which accompany it, and the objectives assigned to it.
2. A situational change introduced by the action of the propaganda analyst's side (i.e., the initiatives of his own elite, intended or accomplished).	To infer whether the opponent anticipates and correctly estimates the character, magnitude, location, and timing of the initiative, and to infer the opponent's estimate of the objectives of the move, his expectations regarding the outcome, and his plans for countermoves.
3. Other situational changes which favor or hamper the opponent's pursuit of his goals and aspirations.	To infer whether favorable or unfavorable shifts have taken place in the environment of the opponent or are expected by him, and to infer the opponent's estimate of the magnitude, duration, and consequences of such changes.

Each of these three problem areas in making inferences is taken up in a separate chapter. In each case a catalogue is presented of the possible propaganda goals [1] that might be adopted, in the type of situation in question, by the elite whose communications are being analyzed. Next, a general analytical approach for applying the indirect method is described. Then a number of case studies from the FCC's wartime experience are reviewed in some detail in order to demonstrate concretely how the indirect method can be used.

In the chapters on the second and third of the problem areas listed above, some attention is also given to the use of the *direct* method. (This is not done for the first problem area because the FCC made little use of it for this purpose.)

From the standpoint of theory or of the construction of a set of propositions which would encompass *the relationship of propaganda to action in different types of situations,* the analytical framework presented here and its elaboration in the next three chapters makes but a modest contribution. A critical omission from this standpoint is the failure to state systematically all of the *conditions* under which one or another propaganda goal is likely to be pursued. This task has been met to some degree in the following chapters by subdividing each list of possible goals according to type of *audience addressed* by the propagandist and his *estimate of the impact (indulgent or deprivational) of the change in the situation* upon the audience in question. In developing the theory further, each of the three general situations would have to be supplemented by statements of additional conditions which favor the adoption of one rather than other possible propaganda goals. Only occasionally in cataloguing possible goals have we suggested some additional conditions or considerations which favor selection of a particular propaganda goal.

Acceptable formulations of these conditions are likely to be complicated in structure and difficult to state; eventually, perhaps, efforts will be made to employ some form of mathematical model for this purpose. Any more rigorous work in this direction may benefit, however, from the type of abstract formulation of possible propaganda goals undertaken here. When generalized in this fashion, the list of possible goals is at least readily applicable to many different instances and to the behavior of different elites and propagandists.

From a theoretical standpoint the present effort is incomplete in another respect as well. The analytical frameworks of the following chapters, it will be noted, focus on propaganda *goals* rather than on propaganda *techniques,* which are ways of implementing goals. In cataloguing possible propaganda goals, we have only occasionally referred, by way of illustration, to propaganda techniques for implementing a goal.

Admittedly, a more rounded theory of propaganda would list possible propaganda techniques as systematically as propaganda goals have been here. (A fuller theory would also include the conditions under which one or another of the possible propaganda techniques would recommend itself.) The focus of the present study on propaganda goals, however, is defensible on several counts. First, systematic exploration of the nexus between situations and the choice of propaganda goals is more important for propaganda analysis than systematic consideration of the possible ways in which propaganda goals may be implemented by propaganda techniques.

Second, there is nothing very mysterious or exciting about propaganda techniques as such. Goebbels' merit as a propagandist, for example, can be analyzed more profitably by examining his use of propaganda as an instrument of national policy in various types of situations than by studying the (not unfamiliar!) propaganda techniques which he employed to implement specific propaganda goals.

Various efforts have been made to state or to codify the techniques employed by Goebbels and other clever propagandists. They do not throw much light on why these propagandists were particularly successful; nor do they contribute much to the development of a theory of propaganda. More useful for this purpose is an analysis of the ways in which propaganda can be employed in various types of *situations* in order to facilitate the desired impact of national policies and actions, and of other events, upon various types of audiences, or in order to alleviate undesired impacts of this sort. The Kris-Speier study of German wartime propaganda, to which reference has already been made, was a pioneer effort along these lines. The present study, and particularly this part of it, attempts to carry further this situational approach to a theory of propaganda and a theory of propaganda analysis.

The broad situational framework outlined here and its elaboration in the following chapters stems in part from an analysis of Goebbels' uses of propaganda as an instrument of wartime policies. Some indication is given, therefore, of the scope and sophistication of Goebbels' operational theory of propaganda and, in particular, of the intimate co-ordination he effected between high policy itself—including the calculations and intelligence upon which it was based—and the selection of propaganda strategy. The primary objective of the study, however, has been to *abstract* and *generalize* from Nazi wartime propaganda in order to outline a framework or general theory of propaganda analysis. Only occasionally (as on pp. 223–27) has it been necessary for this purpose to give an explicit account of portions of Goebbels' operational theory of propaganda.

NOTE

1. The catalogues are probably not exhaustive. They undoubtedly reflect the preoccupation of the present study with the Nazi elite and with wartime propaganda; additions to the list might well be suggested by a fuller consideration of peacetime propaganda and by a study of the performance of other elites.

ELEVEN

Prediction of an Elite's Major Actions

How the propaganda analyst makes inferences in situations where change occurs or may occur as a result of the opposing elite's action is the subject of this chapter. A general analytical framework is developed for predicting, by means of the indirect method, certain major actions,[1] or intentions, of a ruling elite.

Prerequisites and Limitations of the Indirect Method

The indirect method can be used to predict only those intended actions of an opponent which involve some measure of deliberation and policy planning on his part. It is a prerequisite of the method that a propaganda strategy exist, that is, that the opponent use *preparatory* propaganda as a means of enhancing or exploiting in some way his forthcoming action.[2] Excluded from the possibility of being inferred by this method, therefore, are spontaneous elite actions, i.e., those made in reaction to some event, usually a move of the opponent, which are likely to be undertaken without the usual co-ordination of policy and action with propaganda.[3]

Nonetheless, this is not so severe a limitation on the usefulness of the indirect method as it might appear to be, since modern elites so often find it to their advantage to prepare in advance some of those groups who will be affected by their major actions. Whatever form this preparation takes, its general purpose is simply to maximize the expected gains and to minimize the unfavorable consequences of the forthcoming action. Preparatory communications may be directed toward domestic audiences, groups in an opponent's camp, or groups in neutral states. The propaganda analyst takes into account the possibility that preparatory communications may be directed to one or many audiences, that the objective or intent of the preparation may be different for each of the specific audiences addressed, and that the objective may be implemented with considerable subtlety and indirection.

The possibility of predicting an elite's action from its preparatory effort depends, obviously, upon the elite's use of a communication channel that is open to the propaganda analyst's scrutiny. It is usually safe to assume that mass-media channels will be used for preparatory propaganda directed toward relatively large audiences and toward smaller audiences that cannot be reached easily and quickly enough in another way. Selected, specialized public media may be used in attempting to prepare smaller groups. However, there is no assurance that public channels will be used in every instance. Preparation may take place, for example, through confidential orders, private messages, word of mouth, and other channels of communication not readily accessible to the analyst.

Another limitation on the use of this method for predicting actions is the possibility that the elite may decide to forego any preparation and may instead employ propaganda to facilitate its action only at the time the action is taken or shortly thereafter. In such cases the best that the indirect method can do is to aid in assessing the nature and objectives of the major action once it is taken and to enable the analyst to say something about the opponent's estimate of the prospects of its action. The value of such inferences to the policy-maker should not be underrated; in many cases they overshadow in importance the usefulness of having predicted the action before it occurred.

Types of Inferences of Interest to the Policy-Maker

It is useful to emphasize that several aspects of an opponent's forthcoming action or initiative may be of interest to the policy-maker. There is, first, the question of whether a certain action is actually being planned by the opponent, i.e., the question of his intentions. But equally interesting in many cases, and sometimes of greater value, are questions concerning the *timing* of the action, its precise *nature and magnitude,* its exact *location,* the *objectives* assigned to the action, the elite's *expectations* concerning its success, and the extent and nature of any *opposition* to that particular initiative within the elite group.

Which of these questions is of primary interest will vary from case to case. In some instances there is little doubt that a certain type of action (e.g., a military initiative) is being planned by the opponent; the interesting question, then, may be that of the precise timing and location of the action, or perhaps its magnitude and objectives. In other cases, the opponent's expectations concerning the success or failure of his contemplated action, or perhaps his concern over some of the consequences of the action for certain groups, may be of paramount interest.

Mode of Reasoning

In attempting to apply the indirect method to individual instances of possible preparatory propaganda, the propaganda analyst makes use of existing generalizations about the types of situations and circumstances in which the elite under scrutiny tends to employ preparatory propaganda in support of its forthcoming actions. Such generalizations should cover the following interrelated questions:

1. For what *types of actions* does the elite generally regard preparatory propaganda as desirable?

2. What *types of audiences* does the elite consider it useful to prepare (for each type of action)?

3. What *types of goals* does the elite consider it useful and feasible to pursue in preparatory propaganda (for different types of audiences in the case of different types of actions)?

4. What *communication channels,* or types of communication, does the elite usually employ, or is it likely to employ, when attempting to achieve a certain type of goal in preparatory propaganda (for different types of audiences in the case of different types of actions)?

In attempting to solve any individual inferential problem, the propaganda analyst does not rely solely upon available generalizations which answer questions like these. He employs generalizations, rather, in conjunction with a logic-of-the-situation assessment. The propaganda analyst keeps in mind that the elite, in considering whether to employ preparatory propaganda for a certain action, is guided not merely by its own past practice or by a rigid operational doctrine. Rather, the elite is presumed to make an assessment of the factors upon which the success of its contemplated action is likely to depend, and from this assessment it decides whether any preparatory propaganda support is required. Finally, the analyst further assumes that the choice of any particular preparatory propaganda strategy has also been influenced by the propagandist's estimate of how feasible and effective various different propaganda strategies and techniques would be likely to be.

For example, in one case total surprise may be deemed essential by the elite if the success of its intended major action is to be assured or maximized. Consequently, propaganda preparation in this case may consist exclusively of attempts to mask the forthcoming action. In another instance of the same type of action, however, the elite may consider it expedient to precede the action by a propaganda of bluffs and threats. Or in another type of major action—for example, the intended use of unconventional weapons—the elite may elect to use an extended preparation which aims at unnerving the opponent in advance and increasing his sense of helplessness and despair once the unconventional weapon has been used.

Since several deductive patterns enter into the strand of reasoning typical of the indirect method, it is difficult to characterize the analyst's reasoning processes in general terms. Any effort to do so risks giving a picture which is oversimplified or overstandardized. There is, nonetheless, some value in attempting a general sketch of the pattern of reasoning or, rather, in suggesting it by formulating some of the questions an analyst must cope with in attempting to clarify the intentions of an opposing elite.

In skeletal form, the analyst's reasoning is as follows: "The opposing propagandist would not adopt these propaganda goals for implementation through these media channels at this time and in this situation unless an action of the type I am inferring were indeed planned or intended, and certain related estimates and expectations were being privately held by him." Thus, the analyst's inferences about the character and scope of the action or about elite expectations concerning it are the last steps in a sequence of inferences. As suggested in Part I (p. 61), the analyst's reasoning may be likened to an effort to reconstruct and fill in the missing pieces in a mosaic.

First, the analyst must decide whether the contents under scrutiny are indeed part of a preparation campaign for a major action. Does the propaganda material in question seem to give evidence of propaganda goals which may be part of a preparation of various audiences for forthcoming action? Would such propaganda goals be pursued at this time unless an action were being planned? Are there alternative explanations of the contents in question and/or of the propaganda goals inferred?

Is the hypothesized preparatory propaganda strategy consistent with the total propaganda output? Is it consistent with the elite's previous patterns of action preparation? With available generalizations about its theories? With its usual methods of using psychological warfare to enhance the effectiveness of its major actions? Are there special reasons for supposing that the present case may not be consistent with available generalizations and previous patterns? Do any available generalizations regarding the propaganda skillfulness or unskillfulness of the elite in question support or weaken the inferential hypothesis?

Answers to questions like these help the propaganda analyst to refine his hypothetical explanation of the content he is studying to the point where he feels justified in making an inference.

Possible Goals of Preparatory Propaganda

A crucial step in the inferential chain, it has been noted, is that of determining whether any propaganda goals are being implemented in current communications which are likely to be part of a preparation campaign preceding a major action. The analyst could determine this more easily if he had a general framework of analysis which would enable him to consider systematically whether any of the possible preparatory propaganda goals were reflected in the communications under scrutiny.

An effort has been made to develop, below, a catalogue of such possible propaganda goals. The goals are phrased in general and abstract terms, so as to be applicable to as many types of actions, audiences, and channels as possible.

There is no intention in the present study to imply, by listing *possible* goals, that any of them will necessarily be adopted by a particular elite. Nor can the frequency of their adoption by the Nazi elite be taken to indicate how frequently other elites will pursue them. Other elites may not concern themselves at all with some of these preparatory goals or may do so less frequently. Different political elites will not necessarily select the same preparatory goals in what seem to be identical situations. The propaganda analyst must guard against the assumption that the selection of preparation goals is a purely technical problem, approached alike by all elites; he must remember that an elite will adopt the preparatory goals that its propaganda theory, operational code, and assessment of the situation render desirable in its eyes. On the other hand, it would be surprising if this list of general goals were totally inapplicable to analyses of the preparatory propaganda efforts that other elites may engage in from time to time.

The list of goals presented here is subdivided according to two elements which probably exert a major influence on the selection of goals: the *audience addressed* (domestic, neutral, or enemy) and the *expected impact* (indulgent or deprivational) of the initiative upon the audience in question. Additional subdivisions (for example, according to type of action or media channel) might be meaningful and might make the list even more useful. But it seems unprofitable to elaborate the scheme more fully at this time.

It is important to keep in mind that some of these preparatory goals, which are stated quite explicitly and plainly here, would be implemented in a subtle fashion by the propagandist in order to enhance the effectiveness of his communication. The propagandist's preparation might, for example, take the form of an effort to build up in the minds of his audience certain frames of reference and to strengthen certain predispositions which, in his judgment, would be likely to facilitate the desired psychological response to the major action when it occurred. It is for this reason that some of the *techniques* for implementing a goal, as well as the goal itself, are included in the following list.

POSSIBLE GOALS OF PROPAGANDA PREPARATORY TO MAJOR ACTIONS

   I. Directed at domestic or friendly neutral audiences:
      A. In the case of major actions expected to have a *deprivational* effect on *domestic* audiences:

> *Examples:* A declaration of war which shocks domestic audiences; the use of an unconventional weapon against the enemy which violates the moral values of the domestic audiences; the arrest and trial of members of the domestic elite for treason; the announcement of severe measures against a segment of the domestic population.

1. To reduce the possibility of shock (as by hinting at the nature of the forthcoming action in gradually more explicit terms, combined with appropriate assurances).
2. To manipulate blame and/or responsibility for the deprivation.
3. To identify and encourage the reaction which the elite would like its own people to adopt when the prepared action takes place.
4. To strengthen the public's predisposition to accept demands to be made upon it by the elite in connection with the intended action.
5. To lay the basis for moral justification of the forthcoming action.
6. To prepare for a better understanding of the necessity for the forthcoming action by prior disclosure of the estimates and expectations upon which it is based—either the real ones or ones chosen for their propagandistic value in achieving the desired public acceptance.

B. In the case of major actions expected to have an *indulgent* effect on *domestic* audiences:

Examples: The announcement of a military or diplomatic offensive; the use of a new powerful weapon which does not violate the moral values of domestic audiences; a victorious battle; enemy diplomatic concessions; increase in food rations.

1. To control the degree and manner of expression of the public's expected rejoicing in order to prevent excesses which lower efficiency (e.g., wild outbursts of rejoicing, disruptions of work schedules and of labor discipline, etc.).
2. To control public expectations aroused by the good news so as to prevent unrealistic hopes that might be disillusioned later on.
3. To moderate the public's expectations as to the indulgent character of the forthcoming action, in order to produce relatively greater satisfaction with the results of the action when it occurs.
4. To increase the authority and prestige of the ruling elite by making appropriate claims of strength and foresight on its behalf which will be validated by the coming action.
5. To alleviate currently prevailing low morale by forecasting the expected indulgence.
6. To manipulate in politically desirable directions the gratitude and satisfaction that will be engendered by the forthcoming indulgence.

7. To exploit the public's gratitude in order to create greater support for the regime's policies.

8. To prepare the public for the possibility that the elite's forthcoming action will be followed by a strong and successful counteraction by the opposing elite.

C. In the case of major actions whose outcome cannot be foreseen, or is difficult to foresee:

Examples: A military offensive against the enemy or a program for improved welfare at home in whose successful outcome the elite has relatively little confidence.

1. To insure that the domestic public's conception of the aims of the action remains within modest bounds. (This may entail countering the enemy propagandist's efforts to commit the elite to more far-reaching aims than it can attain.)

2. To justify the decision to take the action in terms other than achievement of its manifest objectives (as by indicating that the action in question is in any case necessary and is worth while, even if it does not achieve all of its objectives).

II. Directed at groups in the opponent's camp:

A. In the case of major actions expected to have an important *deprivational* effect upon groups in the opponent's camp:

Examples: See those under I, B, above.

1. (When surprise is important to the magnitude of the deprivational effect achieved) to mask the forthcoming action or veil its time, place, character, and scope.

2. (When advance demoralization of groups in the opponent's camp will facilitate the success of the forthcoming action and reduce its costs, and when surprise is not essential) to publicize the forthcoming action confidently and in detail in terms which emphasize the powerlessness of the opponent and the futility of resistance.

3. To reduce the audience's confidence in the efficacy of possible countermeasures by its own leaders against the forthcoming action.

4. To strengthen predispositions which will increase the demoralizing impact of the action when it takes place.

5. (In anticipation of the likelihood that the forthcoming deprivation may set into motion efforts within the opponent's camp to fix blame and responsibility for the setback) to prepare the ground for the forthcoming action in such a way as

   a) to maximize disruptive effects of the action on relations among members of the opposing elite, between elite and masses, and among members of the opposing coalition.

b) to minimize the possibility that the action might unify the opponent's camp and strengthen his determination.

6. To give prior moral justification for the forthcoming action, when necessary, to prevent strengthening of hatred against the propagandist's side on the part of the opponent and neutrals.

B. In the case of major actions expected to have an important *indulgent* effect upon groups in the opponent's camp:

Examples: See those under I, A, above.

1. To encourage groups in the opponent's camp to form unrealistic and/or incorrect assessments of the advantages accruing to them from the action (unrealistic either in seriously under- or overestimating the potentialities of the new situation created by the action in question; incorrect in diverting the opponent's attention from feasible to unfeasible avenues of exploiting the new situation militarily, politically, or psychologically).

2. To encourage an initially overoptimistic reaction to the event which is bound to result in subsequent disillusionment.

Case Studies

The case studies of wartime propaganda analysis presented here and in the next two chapters have been selected to illustrate the broad range of intelligence problems to which the general approach outlined previously can be applied. Each case study attempts to indicate how propaganda contents serve as evidence for inferences, the nature of the reasoning in support of an inference, and the way in which the plausibility of alternative inferences may be weighed. For these purposes the materials of the original FCC propaganda analysis fre quently had to be reorganized and subjected to critical assessment. To make the case studies as nontechnical, readable, and brief as possible, however, the writer has not adhered rigidly to a standard format. Historical background is frequently provided in order to convey the intelligence setting in which the propaganda analyst worked and to recapture some of the timeliness and interest of the problems on which he worked. Wherever possible, some assessment is made of the accuracy of the FCC inferences by matching them against the available historical record of Goebbels' propaganda operations and the Nazi conduct of the war.

The general point has already been made (p. 8) that much may be learned from errors in inference as well as from the successes achieved by the FCC analysts. The possibility of making a balanced selection from the FCC work in this respect was limited by the fact that relatively few FCC inferences that could be scored turned out to be wrong. Therefore, the writer decided upon the alternative of presenting many FCC inferences which, though they could not be scored as correct or incorrect, were in any case essentially ambiguous or overly general or contained defective reasoning. To the same end, reference is made in the case studies to many occasions on which the FCC analysts, though not actually making an erroneous inference, did in fact miss an opportunity to make a correct and useful inference. (See, for example, the detailed discussion in Case Study No. 11.1, which follows, of the failure of the FCC analysts to do as well as the British analysts on the problem of German V-weapons.)

In reviewing FCC propaganda analyses from this broader critical standpoint the writer attempts to convey concretely to the reader the general point made several times elsewhere in this report (p. 8 and esp. Part IV). Whether or not inferences attempted by the FCC were correct cannot be the sole criterion of the worth and potential of the propaganda-analysis method. One must also take into account the relative importance of the matters on which FCC analysts did and did not attempt to make inferences, whether their inferences were phrased in terms so general or ambiguous as to dilute their value as intelligence results, whether the inferences clearly rested upon propaganda-analysis evidence and were supported by adequate reasoning, etc.

CASE STUDY No. 11.1: * GERMAN V-WEAPON (A COMPARISON OF BRITISH AND AMERICAN PROPAGANDA ANALYSIS)

Background. For over a year prior to the launching of the V-1 in mid-June, 1944, German leaders and propagandists had threatened reprisals with a new offensive weapon. The British High Command was sufficiently concerned to undertake extensive exploratory reconnaissance and bombing missions. Their concern was strengthened by intelligence reports which confirmed the existence of secret-weapon

---

* For purposes of convenient reference the case studies in this book are referred to by chapter as well as by number. For example, "Case Study 11.1" means "Case Study 1 in Chapter 11."

factories.[4] Aerial reconnaissance showed the construction of an unusual type of concrete installation in northern France pointed toward England.

The British Air Ministry was certain that the installations in Pas de Calais were launching-sites for a new type of weapon. "But the missiles were so long in coming," writes Gen. Walter Bedell Smith, Chief-of-Staff to Eisenhower during the war, "that some of our officers—highly placed, too—advanced the theory that the platforms were a gigantic hoax, constructed by the Nazis with great cunning to divert our bombers from vital targets."[5] The opposite point of view prevailed, however, and a certain weight of the Allied bombing offensive was directed to suspected factories and launching-sites of the secret weapons.[6]

"The development and employment of these [secret] weapons," wrote Eisenhower, "were undoubtedly greatly delayed by our Spring [1944] bombing campaign against the places where we suspected they were under manufacture . . . [and] the suspected launching sites."[7] A sober reminder of the consequences of an incorrect appraisal of the German secret weapons is contained in Eisenhower's further appraisal:

It seemed likely that, if the German had succeeded in perfecting and using these weapons six months earlier than he did, our invasion in Europe would have proved exceedingly difficult, perhaps impossible. I feel sure that if he had succeeded in using these weapons over a six-month period, and particularly if he had made the Portsmouth-Southampton area one of his principal targets, Overlord [the cross-Channel invasion in 1944] might have been written off.[8]

How good was Allied intelligence on the German secret weapons? "During this long period," reports Eisenhower,

the calculations of the Intelligence agencies were necessarily based upon very meager information and as a consequence they shifted from time to time in their estimates of German progress. Nevertheless, before we launched the invasion, Intelligence experts were able to give us remarkably accurate estimates of the existence, characteristics, and capabilities of the new German weapons.[9]

What contribution did propaganda analysis make toward the correct assessment of German V-weapons? This question is difficult to answer. Many different types of intelligence activities contributed data for over-all assessments, but none of the accounts examined clearly distinguish the weight of each.[10] On the other hand, it is possible today to note at least the accuracy of the propaganda-analysis reports, whatever their utility at the time. The British report, to be examined here, is without doubt one of the most skillful of the propaganda analyses undertaken during the last war. The FCC analyses of this problem, on the other hand, were markedly less successful. A comparison of the two, therefore, serves to spotlight elements in procedure and analysis which make for more or less successful inferences.

The British Report. A special propaganda analysis of German V-weapon propaganda was issued in early November, 1943, by the British Political Warfare Executive.[11] It listed a number of inferences about a German secret weapon drawn solely from analysis of German propaganda.

Inferences. The British analyst's systematic approach and his ability to identify the precise components of the inferential problem are impressive in themselves. Equally striking is the clear-cut manner in which degrees of plausibility are assigned to different inferences.

In close paraphrase, the report stated that:

1. It is *beyond reasonable doubt* that Germany possesses an offensive weapon which her leaders believe:
   a) Is of a type unknown to the Allies.
   b) Cannot be countered within a short period.
   c) Will be used for the first time on a scale sufficient to produce very striking results.
   d) Will create in British cities havoc at least as great as that in German cities, and probably much greater.
   e) Will have a more shocking effect upon civilians than air-bombing on present scales.
2. It is further *highly probable* that:
   f) By the end of May preparations for the use of this weapon were past the experimental stage.
   g) Something occurred on or a little before August 19th which substantially postponed D-day.
3. It is further *probable* that:
   h) Something occurred between the 3rd and about the 10th of September which further postponed D-day.
   i) The schedule for the offensive weapon has lagged in relation to that for a type or types of defensive weapon, and Germany's leaders now expect a diminution in the weight of Allied air attacks to precede German retaliation.

4. It may be *tentatively estimated* that Germany's leaders expect this offensive weapon to come into use *not before the middle of January, 1944, and not later than the middle of April.* There is unlikely to be an error of more than a month each way in the first of these estimated dates, but there might well be an error of two months either way in the latter.

The estimate for the earliest date of use is based partly upon estimates of the schedule existing in June, in early August, and in early September. If these estimates from propaganda can be confirmed by independent evidence, it would be possible to regard the final estimate (mid-January) with slightly less caution.

The estimated schedule at these earlier periods was:

In June: Earliest use, mid-September.
In early August: Earliest use, beginning October.
In early September: Earliest use, beginning December.

Reasoning and Verification of British Report. Many of these inferences, it turns out, were remarkably accurate and well reasoned. (The British analyst's reasoning is reproduced here only in part.)

Inferences 1, *a–e,* appear to have accurately described the German leaders' estimate of their new weapon. Hitler was particularly gratified by the fact that the V-1 flying bombs did not depend upon radio beams for their aiming, a fact which made it technically impossible for Allied defense to deflect them from their course.[12]

That the Germans had some sort of new weapon, and were not merely bluffing, was firmly believed by the propaganda analyst. This inference rested upon the fundamental assumption, confirmed on many past occasions, that *German propaganda never deliberately misled the German people in questions involving an increase of German power.* (Excluded from this were relatively petty instances, such as figures of losses.) In view of this, the British analyst felt it necessary to accept at face value the repeated statement in German *home* propaganda that Germany was preparing, and expected to employ, a new weapon of reprisal.

A number of characteristics of the propaganda in question permitted insight into the nature of the new weapon. Thus, the British analyst noted that references to forthcoming "retaliation" by German propagandists seemed to be predicated on the idea that something new existed, that retaliation would not be carried out by normal air attack, and that German scientists, engineers, and constructors were playing a particularly important part.

Inference f cannot be verified, but g and h appear to be quite accurate. These two inferences rested upon an interpretation of the fact that propaganda references to reprisal weapons ceased abruptly for a period of time after August 19 and again after September 10. (A fuller account of this interpretation is given on page 147.) To be sure, direct evidence that German propagandists were ordered to cease all references to the secret reprisal weapon for a while after August 19 and September 10 is lacking. But that such orders were given in response to events occurring approximately on or before these two dates, events which caused substantial postponements in the scheduled use of the V-weapon, seems to be a safe assumption in view of Hitler's remarks to Goebbels on the latter date to the effect that:

> Unfortunately the English raids on Peenemuende and on our OT work in the West [presumably the launching-sites for the new weapons in the Boulogne-Calais area] have thrown our preparations back four and even eight weeks, so that we can't possibly count on reprisals before the end of January (*Goebbels Diary,* September 10, 1943, pp. 435–36).

The analyst's reasoning on behalf of inferences g and h is discussed below (pp. 147–49).

Inference i was based upon the observation that after August 19 German propagandists spoke of coming defensive measures against Allied air bombardment in such a manner as to suggest that these would precede the use of the secret weapon against England. (Prior to August 19 the development of new defensive countermeasures had *not* been mentioned in the same breath as preparations for retaliation.) These subtle shifts in propaganda, reasoned the analyst, could hardly be accounted for except on the premise that the relative schedules for defensive and offensive weapons had changed after August 19 in favor of the former. The hypothesis that the offensive weapon had been delayed was more plausible to the analyst than the hypothesis that the schedule for the defensive weapon had been speeded up. For, unless this were the case, there would have been no need for German propagandists to make, as they did, an excuse for not having the offensive weapon ready. Once again, direct verification of this inference is lacking, but new German antiaircraft defense measures which proved to be effective against Allied night bombing raids were applied in the early spring of 1944, several months before the use of the V-1.[13]

Finally, the British analyst's tentative estimate, *made in early November, 1943,* that *at this time* German leaders expected to have the new offensive weapon ready for use sometime between mid-January and mid-April, 1944, proved to be amazingly accurate. For, on *September 22, 1943,* Hitler gave Goebbels his estimate that the V-weapon could be used by the end of January or the beginning of February; and in late November, 1943, Speer, Minister of Armaments and War Production, told Goebbels that reprisals could begin only in March.[14]

The British analyst's remark that his second estimated date—i.e., mid-April, 1944—might be off by *two* months in either direction was the basis for Wallace Carroll's observation that the British propaganda analysts predicted D-day for the new weapon right on the nose—i.e., June 15.[15] However, at the time of the British report (November 8, 1943), as is clear in the two entries in *Goebbels Diary,* German leaders expected to have the V-weapons ready at an earlier date which was well within the narrower range of time predicted by the British analyst. In other words, the British estimate in November, 1943, was even better than Carroll's assessment implies. At the time of the report, events which would further delay the German timetable for V-weapons had not yet occurred. As British Air Marshals Sir Arthur Harris and Lord Tedder both note, in December, 1943, the launching-sites for the V-weapons were so effectively destroyed by Allied bombing that the Germans were forced to improvise new sites, inferior to the first.[16] In the estimate of Harris and Tedder, this delayed the V-weapons' timetable another six months.

The deduction concerning the German leaders' private estimate of the timing of the V-weapon was based upon ingenious use of a general observation about Nazi propaganda practice. The British analyst reasoned that Goebbels would be careful not to give the German public a promise of retaliation too far ahead of the date on which the promise could be fulfilled. For Goebbels had shown himself to be astute enough to realize that, if a promise of this sort were not made good within a reasonable time, the public would become disillusioned, skepticism and hostility toward German leaders and propaganda would set in, and Goebbels would have aggravated the very morale problem which his retaliation promises were designed to allay. Taking a number of factors into account, the British analyst reckoned that Goebbels would give himself about three months as the maximum period for which it would be safe to propagandize forthcoming retaliation in advance.

While this estimate cannot be checked directly today on the basis of available verification material, indirect evidence supporting it was available at the time and was cited in the British report. Goebbels' propaganda commitment on new reprisal weapons was launched in June, 1943; and by mid-August, some two and a half months later, local Nazi speakers were finding it necessary to deal with skeptics. By mid-September, public skepticism was a considerable problem; and in October, Nazi party speakers were devoting a large part of their time to reassuring doubters that retaliation would come, after all. (In a previous phase of the war, too, as the British report observed, it took about three and a half months after an authoritative promise of retaliation—made by Hitler on April 26, 1942—for the German public to begin to ask awkward questions about the unfulfilled promise.)

FCC Analyses. FCC analyses of the same German V-weapon propaganda have been examined in order to discern, if possible, why the results were of lower caliber than those made by the British analyst. Three major explanations for this divergence emerge.

1. *The FCC analysts, in contrast to the British analyst, were reluctant to tackle the main inferential problems growing out of German propaganda on retaliation and secret weapons.* Assuming that other intelligence specialists with techniques more appropriate than propaganda analysis were at work on the problem, the FCC analysts stuck pretty closely to description of the content of German V-weapons propaganda.[17] They ventured few inferences—and these cautiously and sporadically—on such crucial questions as whether secret weapons for reprisal actually existed, what the nature of such weapons was, how soon the Nazis expected to use them, against which targets, and with what expected effects.

Moreover, the FCC analysts worked on their own and were not asked to co-ordinate their analysis of German V-weapons propaganda with that of other intelligence specialists. This may be contrasted with the experience of the British analyst, whose report of November 8, 1943, was clearly in reply to a request, and who was taken into the confidence of his superiors and asked to match his inferences against information about the presumed significance of targets attacked by the R.A.F. at Peenemünde and by Allied aircraft in the Pas de Calais area. The FCC analyses, on the other hand, were made on a week-to-week basis; a systematic retrospective analysis of all preceding propaganda on this subject was not undertaken. It is obvious today that such a retrospective analysis, had it been made, would have sharpened the FCC analysts' insights and analytical procedures.

2. *The FCC analysts did not develop analytical techniques and hypotheses of sufficient refinement for this problem.* It is, or should be, a truism in propaganda analysis that the investigator is likely to develop more discriminating and fruitful analytical techniques only in the process of stating and attempting to assess alternative inferences when confronted with a concrete problem. As the following paragraphs will indicate, the reluctance of the FCC analysts to attempt inferences on the subject of German secret weapons kept them from making optimum use and needed refinements of the analytical equipment they brought to the task.

The fundamental proposition employed by the British analyst (p. 143, above)—that German propaganda never deliberately misled the German people in questions involving an increase of German power—was not unknown to the FCC analysts.[18] Reluctant to make inferences about the V-weapons, however, the FCC analysts apparently overlooked the relevance of this proposition as a basis for evaluating Goebbels' propaganda commitment on retaliation by means of secret weapons.

Another deficiency of the FCC's procedure was its failure to make use of systematic, quantitative procedures in evaluating certain aspects of Nazi V-weapon propaganda. The British analyst, it may be noted, employed highly systematic procedures for a trend analysis of the occurrence and volume of such Nazi reprisal threats. The FCC analyst used only impressionistic methods.

It is because of this, no doubt, that the British analyst, but not the FCC, discovered several *time intervals in which reprisal propaganda dropped almost to the zero point.* Unknown to the public and to the propaganda analysts, the R.A.F. attack of August 17, 1943, upon Peenemünde had the German experimental secret-weapons station as its target. Similarly, Allied air raids of September 7–8 between Boulogne and Calais had as their secret target the installations suspected of being launching-platforms for new German weapons. The purpose of these two raids became known to the British analyst only later. He did notice, however, that references to retaliation suddenly dropped out of German propaganda for ten days, beginning

August 19. Similarly, for a week after September 11 not a single item on retaliation appeared in German domestic propaganda.

Some time later, in preparing his report of November 8, the British analyst was apprised of the significance of the targets in these two raids. His problem, therefore, was to consider alternative explanations for the gaps he had noted in German reprisal propaganda and for possible shifts in the character of this propaganda following resumption of reprisal threats. For this purpose, he took into account and attempted to explain the following: (1) the *suddenness* with which the gap began; (2) any *change in the quality* of propaganda on retaliation and on the forthcoming new weapon *after the gap* in attention passed; (3) the *coincidence* of the beginning of the gap *with events* which might have been *connected with retaliation* and/ or a new weapon; and (4) the *coincidence* of the gap *with other events* or with changes in the war situation which might be expected to cut off the flow of reprisal propaganda.

It was discovered that the gap beginning August 20, 1943, had been sudden, that it was followed by a watering-down of the propaganda commitment on reprisal (i.e., propaganda allusions now put the date of use of the V-weapons further into the future than they previously had), and that the gap in propaganda on the new reprisal weapon did not coincide with other events. (Other events, those not directly connected with German preparations of the reprisal weapon, might be, for example, Allied air raids on Germany, and German morale.) References to reprisal usually occurred either in propaganda diatribes against Allied air raids or in conjunction with propaganda efforts to salve the poor morale of the German public. Therefore, an absence of reprisal talk might be correlated with an absence of Allied air raids on Germany or an improvement in German morale. *Only when these possibilities were ruled out was it reasonable to deduce that not other events but some consideration directly connected with the retaliation weapon itself was responsible for the gap in reprisal propaganda.*

The necessary explanation, then, was that something must have happened just before August 20 which was connected with the preparation and schedule of the new reprisal weapon. (This, of course, confirmed the effectiveness of the Peenemünde raid.)

Another gap, beginning September 11, 1943, also fulfilled these criteria, but not so clearly. Therefore the analyst inferred that it was only slightly less probable that something had occurred in early

September which further postponed the Nazi schedule for the use of the reprisal weapon. Thus, once again, confirmation was obtained of the effectiveness of the Allied air raids, this time of those on Boulogne and Calais.

The four considerations listed above were not articulated by the FCC analysts, an omission which followed from their failure to do a systematic time analysis of trends in reprisal propaganda.

The FCC analysts, however, were not insensitive to the possible significance of *shifts in propaganda commitments as to the date of reprisal*. They were aware, as will be seen, that shifts toward *increased ambiguity* in setting the time of reprisal meant that D-day for use of the new weapon, as estimated by the Nazi leaders, had been further deferred. This type of reasoning was essentially the same as that employed by the British analyst but was applied less systematically and less boldly. Thus, in late November, 1943, an FCC analyst noted that Goebbels' current reprisal threat remained "undated"; "in fact, the wording makes the prospect of realization seem less definite than in many previous announcements which have come from German leaders and, in particular, from Goebbels himself." [19]

3. *The FCC and British analysts both recognized the connection between reprisal propaganda and the German elite's preoccupation with internal morale. But only the British analyst explored this relationship to its logical conclusion and, thereby, formulated an assumption crucial for the high-grade inferences which he made.*

The FCC noted as early as did the British that public disillusionment in Germany with Nazi propaganda promises of reprisal was beginning to set in.[20] Increasing public skepticism on this issue was noted in subsequent FCC reports, but its significance in terms of Goebbels' astuteness as a propagandist was never squarely faced by the FCC. It was certainly not beyond the analytical proficiency of FCC analysts to note that Goebbels' propaganda promises (of reprisal by means of new weapons) must have been made in the expectation that they would be realized in time to save him from severe embarrassment. For Goebbels, of all Nazi leaders, was known by the FCC to be most cautious about making propaganda commitments to the German people which could not be fulfilled and which might, therefore, prejudice public attitudes toward their leaders.[21]

Given this appraisal of Goebbels, the FCC analysts too might have concluded that the propaganda commitment on reprisal would not have been made by Goebbels too soon before the date on which he expected reprisals to take place. And, accordingly, when the continued deferment of D-day for reprisals created increasingly difficult morale problems for the Nazi leadership, the inference should have followed that something had happened to delay the timetable for the reprisal weapon. The closest an FCC analyst came to making such inferences was in mid-November, 1943, when heavy Allied raids on Germany made retaliation even more urgent from a morale point of view. Taking note of the fact that Nazi propaganda promises of retaliation to the German public were continuing, the FCC analyst commented:

> The propaganda intent clearly appears to be to help tide German morale over its severest crisis. . . . In the interest of home morale a realized threat would seem a matter of utmost urgency. . . . Delay may be attributable to unfinished technical preparations, or retaliation may be timed for a certain strategic moment, which has not arrived yet. But this much is certain; *Nazi propagandists could hardly risk taking so many chances with an impatient domestic audience, were it not for cogent reasons* (*CEA* #45, November 19, 1943, p. A-10; italics supplied).

Had this general hypothesis been further refined, and, especially, had it been applied to the whole history of the V-weapons propaganda, the FCC would doubtlessly have approximated the findings of the British analyst more closely.

CASE STUDY No. 11.2: GERMAN PREPARATIONS FOR HOSTILITIES WITH BRAZIL, 1942

In June, 1942, it seemed possible that the German government might change its official diplomatic policy toward Brazil. Relations between the two countries had for some time been critical, amounting in mid-1942 to a virtual state of undeclared hostilities. Brazil had taken action against German nationals, and a number of hostile incidents between German U-boats and Brazilian forces had occurred. However, Berlin broadcasts to Brazil had maintained the tone of an "injured friend," as the FCC put it. During the last week of June the tone of these broadcasts became more belligerent. Now Berlin radio broadcasts directly accused Brazil of arresting German nationals without cause and of subjecting them to medieval mal-treatment. To these accusations emphatic threats were added that, if such behavior did not cease immediately, the German government would answer promptly.

Was this threat a mere bluff, or was the German government prepared to take some forceful action? The FCC analyst reasoned that such threats and accusations, if no more than bluff, were extremely unsound propaganda.

Behind-the-scenes pressure and muscle-flexing may privately impress certain key officials in Latin-American countries. But publicly calling a nation to account and threatening it is something to which no Latin-American nation could or would permit itself to bow, short of the blackest necessity.[22]

Therefore, because he assumed that Latin-American psychology was not lost upon the Germans, the FCC analyst suggested that these open threats were not a matter of unskillful propaganda but indicated, rather, that Berlin was ready to drop its earlier role of injured friend.

The precise relation between the change in these German broadcasts to Brazil and German plans for action against Brazil has not been ascertained. However, there is some indirect evidence that the change in propaganda tone and content may have been co-ordinated with military plans. Thus, in a so-called "Führer Conference" (a high-level conference of German leaders) on May 14, 1942, a memorandum entitled "The Opening of Hostilities against Brazil" and naval plans for a "powerful blow" were discussed, and Hitler authorized a strong U-boat attack in Brazilian waters for the beginning of August.[23] The "powerful blow" planned in May was struck on August 15, 1942, when five Brazilian ships, including a troopship, were torpedoed off the Brazilian coast. Another Brazilian ship was sunk on August 19. Thereupon, on August 22, Brazil declared war on Germany and Italy.

CASE STUDY NO. 11.3: POSSIBILITY OF AN AGGRESSIVE GERMAN MOVE IN SPAIN AND SPANISH MOROCCO, MARCH, 1943

From the very beginning of the North African invasion, the Allied command had to consider the possibility of a German countermove on the Iberian Peninsula. This might take the form of German occupation of Spain and Portugal; it might include an attack upon Gibraltar or upon the Allied rear in Morocco.

In mid-March, 1943, the German news agency for the foreign press, Transocean, put out a dispatch purporting to be an eyewitness account by its chief editor of activities on the border between Spanish and French Morocco. The dispatch read, in part:

The Caudillo had placed his best divisions in the Morocco protectorate. The troops are camping under complete wartime conditions. . . . A surprising number of troops . . . at least amounting to the same number as the formations of General Eisenhower in French Morocco. . . . Spanish officers and men in Morocco impress one as excellent and seasoned troops . . . [with] the most modern war implements. . . . General Juan Yague, who earned his fame during the Spanish Civil War by his initiative and his spirit of attack . . . (*CEA* #10, March 19, 1943, p. C-10).

The FCC analyst noted that although the Transocean dispatch stated that Spanish military preparations were for defense purposes, the impression that the Spaniards were capable of aggressive action was easily aroused by the emphasis on Spanish strength. The dispatch also reported that Spanish antiaircraft guns were firing warning salvos against American reconnaissance planes.

This dispatch provoked close attention because of the tense expectation it managed to convey of some sort of imminent military action. What was the intention behind the dispatch?

FCC

Several inferences may be drawn as to the intention behind this story. The most plausible is that *the Germans now want Americans to worry about the threat to their rear* in French Africa. Another possibility is that an American move is expected and that the Germans want to forestall it by stressing Spanish strength. Still another hypothesis, that they are imputing aggressive intentions to Americans as a justification for a German or Spanish countermove, appears less plausible . . . (*ibid.*, p. C-11).[24]

Goebbels

It is understandable that Spain has an appetite for Algiers, but for the present there seems to be no practical way of gaining possession of Algiers except by entering the war. But that is exactly what the Spaniards do not want to do (*Goebbels Diary*, March 17, 1943, p. 304).

The FCC inference suggested as most likely cannot be directly confirmed. However, Goebbels' statement would appear to rule out the possibility of a Spanish initiative. Furthermore, available evidence strongly suggests that a German initiative was not contemplated either. In December, 1942, Admiral Raeder had spoken to Hitler about the strategic advantages of occupying the Iberian Peninsula, but, recognizing that such a move would require large German forces, he recommended instead that such an action be taken only if it were necessary to forestall an attempt by the Allies to seize Spain and Portugal. Hitler concurred.[25] The operation plan, GISELA (occupation of the Iberian Peninsula), was discussed at a Führer Conference on April 11, 1943. The discussion was focused upon the possibility that the Allies had a similar operation in mind and waited only for the Germans to take the first step in order to have an excuse to go ahead.[26] Later, after the cessation of Axis resistance in Tunis, Hitler turned down Admiral Doenitz' proposal for an occupation of Spain to forestall further Allied initiatives in the Mediterranean. Hitler's reason was that such an operation was feasible only with Spanish consent or first-class divisions, neither of which was available.[27]

In sum, then, available evidence suggests that, at the time of the Transocean dispatch in question, German strategic plans involving the Iberian Peninsula were purely defensive; the only move contemplated was a countermove in the event the Allies attempted to extend the war into the peninsula.

Analyst's Reasoning. The third possibility—a Spanish or German initiative—was considered less plausible by the analyst for two reasons.

1. The Transocean dispatch in question had been given only to an *American* audience (in English to America); if the dispatch were serving the propaganda purpose of a *justification* for a German or Spanish initiative, presumably it would have been directed to a world audience. And presumably a profusion of similar propaganda material, rather than just this one item, would have been issued.

2. It was unlikely, reasoned the analyst, that the Germans would give away their forthcoming initiative by employing a propaganda device which they had used in the past to cloak an aggression and which would now have the disadvantage of being generally recognized as an indicator of an initiative. In other words, the analyst thought that the Germans would not at this juncture of the war resort to the shopworn propaganda device of projecting their own intentions onto the enemy (as they may have done, for example, preceding the invasion of Norway).

Therefore, the other two interpretations appeared more plausible to the analyst—the first, in particular, because of the small amount of propaganda on this subject issued by the Germans and the fact that it had been aimed exclusively at America.

CASE STUDY NO. 11.4: GERMAN OFFENSIVE AGAINST RUSSIA, 1942

In this case, the analyst did *not* speculate about the possibility of a forthcoming German offensive in Russia but confined himself to a straight description of the content of Nazi propaganda on the subject. The following discussion, therefore, merely illustrates one of the opportunities which the FCC analysts missed.

The Nazi plan for 1942 called for a concentration of offensive power into a drive for the oil fields of the Caucasus. The only other sector on which offensive operations were to be undertaken was on the Baltic flank. Thus, while the Germans had attacked along the entire front in 1941, in 1942 Hitler had to limit himself to a southern offensive.[28]

Goebbels has described his efforts to camouflage the impending offensive. Under his aegis German military periodicals carried a number of planted items which pointed out that possession of the enemy capital is always the determining factor in war, but, Goebbels ruefully admitted, "The opposition thus far hasn't bitten." International observers continued to speculate about forthcoming German activity on the southern section of the Russian front. Therefore, "the task of German propaganda will . . . consist of focusing international attention on either the central or northern front." To this end, Goebbels sent Dr. Kriegk, a journalist well known in Germany, to the central front in Russia for a week. Afterwards Kriegk was to be dispatched to Lisbon

to commit several indiscretions on orders from me. He is to get tipsy and . . . spread the assertion that the German attack is planned not for the south, but for the center. I hope it will be possible in that way to launch this canard as a rumor in the world organs of publicity.[29]

At the same time, Goebbels tried another bit of deception to divert attention from the southern sector. An "unauthorized" article, which discussed "the economic and operational possibilities of an attack on Moscow," was planted in the *Frankfurter Zeitung*. (This newspaper was chosen, as Lochner observes, no doubt because it was still considered abroad to be somewhat liberal, an impression cultivated by the Propaganda Ministry to preserve the organ's usefulness as a possible medium for veiled propaganda.) When the article in question appeared, it was "officially suppressed and denounced in the [daily] press conference" held by Goebbels, but not, of course, until copies for foreign consumption had already left Germany.[30]

Goebbels made still another attempt to camouflage the forthcoming offensive. He reports that he induced the German High Command to plant a misleading article either in the Turkish or Portuguese press.[31]

Throughout June the FCC analyst did no more than note the refusal of German propaganda to foreshadow future German operations or to predict future successes. This reticence was interpreted by him as being part of Goebbels' plan for rehabilitating the credibility of Nazi propaganda, which had suffered because of false forecasts in the previous year. In early June the analyst noted that in the previous week Nazi propaganda had made only one reference to a German spring offensive, about which it had talked so much previously. Moreover, the fighting at Kharkov, Kerch, and Sevastopol was being handled with marked propagandistic restraint.[32]

In the next few weeks, too, the FCC analyst refused to commit himself on whether, when, or where a German offensive might be coming. After the German drive in the direction of the Caucasus began, he merely recorded that, after "a three month's background of extreme reticence about the previously-heralded 'great offensive,' "[33] Berlin had announced on July 1 that the long-expected offensive in Russia had begun.

Thus, the FCC had not contributed explicitly to a clarification of German offensive intentions. Perhaps this type of problem was not deemed appropriate for clarification through propaganda analysis, or perhaps the analyst was too uncertain in this case to go out on a limb. Or perhaps the FCC's propaganda analysis in 1942 had not developed to the point which would permit responsible predictions on such questions. In any event, one year later, in 1943, the FCC analysts not only tackled a similar problem but scored an impressive success (see Case Study No. 11.5, below).

Case Study No. 11.5: Speculation over a German
Offensive against Russia in 1943

In 1941 and 1942 the German Army had launched powerful summer offensives against Russia. After the disaster at Stalingrad, in January, 1943, it was uncertain whether the German forces would be capable of another large-scale offensive in 1943. The highly publicized "total mobilization" measures, launched concurrently with the announcement of the Stalingrad defeat, had as their avowed aim the restoration of "the fighting efficiency" of German manpower and arms. In this context, promises of another German offensive against the Russians were made for a while in February, 1943, but disappeared completely at the beginning of March. Moreover, the increase in German military capability due to total mobilization could be employed otherwise than in another offensive against the Russians. German forces were not only engaged in North Africa but faced the possibility of further Allied invasions during the year. Therefore, the question for Allied intelligence was this: Would Hitler give the order to attack on the Russian front (if the offensive potential of German arms could be restored), or would he prefer to remain on the defensive during the coming year to conserve his strength in order to deal more effectively with forthcoming Allied invasions?

What was the Allied intelligence estimate on this question at the time? This has been only indirectly ascertained. Harry Butcher relates that in late May of 1943 General Walter Bedell Smith returned to Eisenhower's headquarters, after attending joint British-American conferences in Washington, with the following "Washington" appraisal of the Russian situation: The Germans were prepared to attack shortly on the Russian front on a "monstrous" scale; the offensive was designed to knock Russia out of the war or paralyze the Red Army. Smith's opinion, as reported by Butcher, supposedly reflected the highest intelligence estimate in Washington. Smith added that Washington was confident the Russians would defeat the German offensive and exact huge casualties.[34]

Available German sources indicate that the above estimate grossly exaggerated the scope of German offensive plans. Available documentary evidence indicates that Hitler planned only in terms of a limited, spoiling attack, which would disrupt Russian preparations for an offensive of their own.

Operations Order No. 5 (March 13, 1943), issued to the German armies in Russia by Hitler, stated:

> It is to be expected that the Russians will continue their attacks at the end of the winter and the muddy season and after they have rehabilitated and reinforced their forces to some extent. . . . *Therefore it is important for us to take the initiative at certain sectors of the front if possible before they do, so as to be able to dictate their actions at least at one sector,* as is the case at the present time at the front of the Southern Army Group.[35]

This order also specified that Army Group A was to contract its positions as soon as weather permitted in order to free forces for the Southern Army Group, the northern wing of which was to make the planned attack at the end of the muddy season, prior to the Russian offensive. The order directed the Central Army Group merely to shift positions and the Northern Army Group to concentrate on defense for the first half of the summer. Finally, the order revealed a plan for the Northern Army Group to attack Leningrad around the beginning of July, in the second half of the summer (an attack, be it noted, which never materialized).

As revealed in Liddell Hart's conversations with German generals, Hitler refused advice to go over to a purely defensive strategy in the East.[36] Instead, his strategy was to gain "a resounding tactical victory to re-fortify German morale and *upset the offensive he knew the Russians were planning.*"[37] Available portions of Goebbels' diary support the interpretation that Hitler planned merely a limited offensive to spoil the Russian plans for 1943:

Our military offensive in the East is expected for the end of May. One imagines something terrific by it. I let reports to that effect pass uncontested. . . . It is quite good that the enemy credits us with more in one or the other respect (Microfilm Goebbels diary,[38] April 27, 1943).

In the East the Fuehrer will soon start a *limited offensive* in the direction of Kursk. He may, however, delay it to see whether the Bolsheviks want to beat us to it. That might offer us an even more favorable chance than if we took the initiative (*Goebbels Diary,* May 7, 1943, p. 352; italics supplied).

The eastern offensive is now expected in some quarters and regarded as not coming in others. In London people believe that an eastern offensive is near but that it will fail and that a German catastrophe will follow. Both sides involved in the eastern offensive are sticking to the principle of "After you, my dear Alphonse". . . . The Fuehrer intends to let the Bolsheviks start things (*ibid.,* May 23, 1943, pp. 391–92).

Goebbels' suggestion that Hitler delayed the German attack is neither supported nor disproved in other sources examined. Whether he delayed or not, Hitler apparently tired of waiting for the Russians to start matters, for he launched the limited offensive on the Kursk salient on July 5.

FCC Analysis. The FCC analyst's handling of this intelligence problem was marked by great caution. Although he repeatedly reported evidence in German propaganda during the spring which implicitly suggested that the German command planned no major offensive against the Russians, it was not until the beginning of June that the analyst finally stated an explicit inference to that effect. The earlier evidence presented by the analyst will be briefly summarized here; the analyst's reasoning in support of his inference will be examined in detail.

One of the first propaganda pieces to attract the analyst's attention was a talk by General Dittmar, the most important German military commentator. Dittmar's espousal of the "elegance" of defensive strategy interested the analyst, who remarked: "Dittmar . . . (implicitly) links the insistence on offensive military strategy with the impatience of *civilians* who are ignorant about strategy."[39] Such a pointed rebuke by Dittmar, noted the analyst, came "at a moment when Goebbels' propaganda for total war and Sauckel's manpower laws bring the Napoleonic principles of *offensive strategy* and *mass warfare* to an unprecedented historical climax." By this the analyst intended to imply the existence of some sort of behind-the-scenes conflict between military and civilian leaders regarding the proper military strategy for 1943. While this implicit inference cannot be verified one way or the other, Liddell Hart's interrogations of German generals indicate that it was about this time (before Operations Order No. 5, quoted in part on p. 156, above, was issued on March 13) that Hitler was turning down the advice of his generals to go over to a strictly defensive strategy.[40] Dittmar's rebuke of "civilians," then, quite possibly reflected the point of view of German generals, which was being presented at this time to the "civilians" and was encountering their opposition.

In subsequent reports the FCC analyst repeatedly noted that German propaganda avoided any commitment concerning a German offensive. But, finally, in early June the analyst ventured the inference that no major German offensive in the East was planned for the summer of 1943:

It is difficult to decide whether or not this propaganda is a screen to hide offensive operations on a major scale . . . it is unlikely, however, that Nazi spokesmen should wax so eloquent on the merits of the defensive unless one assumes they are forced by events to do so . . . unless the situation leaves him [Goebbels] no other choice . . . (*CEA* #21, June 4, 1943, p. A-2).

Analyst's Reasoning and Assumptions. The following is an attempt, admittedly difficult, to reconstruct the factors which influenced the analyst's inference.

The FCC analyst had noted the abrupt cessation of predictions of a forthcoming German offensive in the East in early March, 1943. But, he felt, the sudden propaganda silence was equivocal as an indicator of German intentions:

> Berlin's sudden silence on this subject may be due to the desire to avoid predictions which cannot be realized. It may also be due to the fact that talk about a coming offensive would interfere with objectives which are militarily less and politically more ambitious than victory, namely peace or a virtual truce with Russia (*CEA* #8, March 5, 1943, p. A-1).

Later, the FCC analyst stated another obvious alternative explanation: namely, that German propaganda silence on the subject of another offensive was motivated by security considerations or by a desire to camouflage an intended German initiative (see, especially, *CEA* #18, May 4, 1943, p. C-4).

In order to choose between these alternative explanations, the analyst had to bring additional considerations into his reasoning. It was only several months later, at the beginning of June, that he was able to say with some degree of confidence that a German offensive was not likely. What factors led him, finally, to make the inference? The answer appears to be that the FCC analyst now interpreted Nazi propaganda behavior on the subject *in the context of German domestic morale considerations.* Accordingly, additional considerations were taken into account:

1. In the past, Nazi propaganda had characteristically extolled the virtues of the *initiative* and had claimed that Germany held and would continue to hold it.

2. Because of the state of depressed morale in Germany, the traditional assertion of German initiative was almost obligatory upon German propagandists as a morale measure.

3. *General, vague* predictions of a forthcoming German offensive in the East would hardly tip off the Russians, since in any event the only elements of a modern land offensive of this type that could be camouflaged were its exact time and place.

4. Instead of predicting an offensive, however, German propaganda had recently begun to extol the merits of the defensive.

5. If the propagandists' refusal to predict an offensive was really motivated by security considerations, then it was most unlikely that German propaganda would simultaneously be preparing its domestic public to accept the unpopular idea that Germany would henceforth play a defensive role in the war. For such a propaganda line, implying German weakness and a turning point in the war, aggravated an already serious domestic morale problem (following the Stalingrad disaster).

Therefore, the analyst concluded, the refusal of Nazi propagandists even implicitly to predict a German offensive could be explained most plausibly on the assumption that it was based upon knowledge of the fact that no major offensive was in the offing. In the words of the FCC analyst:

Given the inclination of Nazi propagandists to present German initiative as a consequence of Germany's might and historic role, it is unlikely . . . that Nazi spokesmen should wax so eloquent on the merits of the defensive unless one assumes they are forced by events to do so. Also, the pessimism which pervades German home opinion makes it appear unlikely that the Nazis should sacrifice one of their major propaganda slogans merely in order to execute a ruse. Since the preparation of important military campaigns cannot be effectively concealed it would be odd to conceal it verbally in such a way as to give new food to pessimists at home. Goebbels is not the man to indulge in lengthy oratory abounding with metaphorical thinking . . . and sweeping historical views in which Germany's present dilemma is meant to shrink to a tolerable size, unless the situation leaves him no other choice. Like every other propagandist, Nazi or non-Nazi, he would surely prefer to predict that an irresistible offensive is coming (*CEA* #21, June 4, 1943, p. A-2).

Consideration 5, above, played an important role in the analyst's reasoning. Thus he noted that

Nazi spokesmen continue to adjust their interpretations of the war and its prospects to the defensive role into which Germany has been forced. . . . The impression [is created] that Nazi propaganda wants to prepare the Germans for a long war with the paradoxical implication that Germany will not take the initiative in waging another major offensive and will yet win.

In this connection, the analyst was impressed, too, by General Dittmar's recent radio talk, which struck him as being "an attempt to dissuade Germans from associating defensive warfare with military weakness." "The question—who *can* attack," Dittmar had said, "is less relevant at present than who *must* attack." The FCC analyst commented: "Thus, initiative is presented, at this stage of the war, as a sign of weakness, because the Germans appear to have lost it."

Critique. Despite the high quality of its reasoning, the propaganda analysis in question suffered from poor presentation, which no doubt detracted from its clarity and impact. (The inadequacy of the presentation has not been conveyed in this summary, the purpose of which is, rather, to disentangle and identify the separate elements in the reasoning underlying the inference.) Unsystematic presentation and the fact that the inference itself was buried in a long paragraph must have made it difficult for readers to grasp the inference and to appreciate the reasoning underlying it.

CASE STUDY NO. 11.6: GERMAN THREATS TO DENOUNCE
THE GENEVA PRISONER-OF-WAR CONVENTION

Manacling of British Prisoners-of-War and the German Order to Shoot Enemy Commandos. On October 7, 1942, the German High Command's official communiqué announced that because German prisoners captured at Dieppe and Sark had been bound, all British prisoners taken at Dieppe would be put in chains from noon October 8 on. The British government promptly announced that, if this threat were carried out, a like number of German prisoners would be manacled and chained. This brought the rejoinder that the German High Command would fetter three British prisoners for every German prisoner chained. On October 13 Churchill informed the House of Commons that British countermeasures would be withdrawn at once if the Germans would desist. The affair was settled only the following December through the good offices of the Swiss government.

The German communiqué of October 7 contained an even more significant announcement that

in future all terror and sabotage troops of the British and their accomplices who do not act like soldiers but like bandits will be treated as such by the German troops and will be ruthlessly eliminated in battle wherever they appear.[41]

Following the announcement of these two actions, German propaganda let loose a heavy barrage of atrocity propaganda against the Anglo-Americans, but primarily against the British, who were accused of a wide variety of evil deeds. The FCC analyst advanced three possible interpretations of the function of this atrocity propaganda:

1. It might pave the ground for a renewed air offensive on England, which Hitler and Goering, Nazi air minister, had referred to in recent speeches. (This interpretation was based on the assumption that in this case, as previously, the Nazi leaders deemed it necessary to precede aggressive moves on their part by a renewed effort to prove the enemy's immorality and their own virtue.)

2. It might be intended to bolster domestic morale—an interpretation supported by the fact that a month earlier Goebbels had told Germans that they must hate their enemies. (This interpretation was based on the assumption that the Nazis considered that intense hatred of the enemy increased cohesion at home.)

3. The atrocity propaganda might be designed to counteract the effect in Germany and abroad of recent statements by Roosevelt and the British government that Axis war criminals would be tried and punished. (This interpretation was apparently suggested to the analyst by the fact that various German commentators referred in the same breath to "British atrocities" and the "impertinent arrogance" displayed in the idea of "phantom trials." [42])

In the following week the FCC analyst noted certain changes in the continuing atrocity propaganda campaign which led him to advance a new explanation of its function. The campaign was intensified, observed the analyst, through (*a*) the increased luridness and crudity of the atrocity charges, (*b*) increased emphasis given the charges by means of such familiar journalistic devices as headline banners, facsimile reproductions of "atrocious" military orders given by the enemy command to its troops, dramatic radio reporting, etc., and (*c*) increased emphasis on the *legal* implications of the alleged atrocities, stressing that *England had in effect torn up the Geneva Convention.*

These observations led the analyst to the following inference: "One is almost led to believe that Germany, on her part, is about to commit a major violation of international law herself." [43]

This interpretation was strengthened in the following week. For German propaganda stepped up its insistence that the British had violated the Geneva Convention and added the new theme: *If Germany denounced the Geneva Convention, she would be fully justified by prior British and American violations of it.* The analyst commented: "The stage is set." [44]

Verification. No data are available, unfortunately, on the propaganda directives and calculations behind the atrocity campaign in question;[45] therefore, direct verification of the analyst's inferences is not possible. Although the analyst's three inferences were not mutually exclusive, his interest focused on the more important questions regarding the Geneva Convention.

The analyst's interpretation on this score was defective because it blurred essential distinctions as to the variety of actions which the German government might take vis-à-vis the Geneva Convention. At first (in *Weekly Review* #47), the analyst inferred that Germany might be getting ready to violate the Geneva Convention. Later (in *Weekly Review* #48), he referred to a possible German denunciation of the Convention. The difference between a *forthcoming violation* and a possible *denunciation* is, of course, significant; a violation need not be revealed or necessarily accompanied by an open denunciation. Actually, there is no indication in the rather considerable historical data available that Hitler was considering an open denunciation of the Geneva Convention at this time. Evidence at the Nuremberg Trial, mainly with reference to the role of Jodl (chief of the operations staff of the High Command of the German Army) and Keitel (chief of the High Command of the German Army) at this time, indicates that the point of discussion among Nazi leaders was, rather, with respect to the question of whether the order to kill the "terror and sabotage troops" (i.e., commandos) did or did not violate the Geneva Convention and the rules of war. The possibility that Hitler *privately* flirted with the idea of denouncing the Convention without informing his associates must also be ruled out. For it is quite unlikely that Hitler would have seriously considered an open denunciation of the Geneva Convention without discussing it with his top military and political advisers. Indeed, later in the war— in February, 1945—when in fact such a step was seriously considered, prolonged discussions took place among the top leadership, as a result of which Hitler dropped the idea.[46]

Finally, the possibility that the atrocity propaganda was *the accompaniment to* rather than *the precursor of* a violation of the Convention was overlooked by the analyst, although this was perhaps the simplest explanation for the atrocity propaganda campaign. It is difficult to account for the FCC analyst's failure to consider this explanation. For the official German communiqué of October 7 had explicitly announced: "The High Command of the Wehrmacht is therefore compelled to decree the following,"[47] namely, the shackling of British prisoners taken at Dieppe and the policy of killing "terror and sabotage" commandos in combat when they behaved as "bandits" instead of "soldiers." While there had been some propaganda and diplomatic preparation for the first of these two moves, according to Jodl's testimony, the order to kill commandos was apparently added to the communiqué (otherwise written by Jodl) *quite abruptly* by Hitler himself. It was only after the communiqué was issued that Hitler took steps to issue appropriate directives to the German armed forces confirming what he had openly announced in the communiqué of October 7. Because of delays and some obstruction in staff work, Hitler finally issued two orders himself on October 18, the first addressed to the troops, the second an explanatory decree addressed to commanders-in-chief. These are Documents 498-PS and 503-PS presented at Nuremberg, the famous "Commando Order," which played an important role in the conviction of several defendants on the war-crimes count.[48] The ostensible purpose of the Commando Order was to dissuade the Allies from continuing activities which had proven irksome in the past.[49]

The German Reaction to the Japanese Execution of American Fliers. On April 21, 1943, Washington disclosed that some of the American airmen brought down during the raid on Tokyo of April 18, 1942, had been executed by the Japanese government. This news came at a time when mounting Allied air raids on Germany were posing a serious problem for German defensive forces. As the Goebbels diary discloses: "The Fuehrer gave orders to play up the execution of the American fliers in the press. It would be the big spread for the Good Friday editions."[50]

Analysis by the FCC of subsequent German propaganda on the issue disclosed that Goebbels used the Tokyo executions to bolster Axis solidarity, to combat the impression among some Germans and neutrals that the Americans were less atrocious than the British, to intensify the over-all theme of Allied immorality, and to focus Allied attention once more on the Far East.

But interspersed in this propaganda were also veiled statements that might be interpreted as threats of similar action by Germany against Allied fliers. The FCC analyst noted: "No doubt, the Germans want to convey the impression that they, at the proper moment, may feel induced to apply similar measures."[51]

How seriously were these veiled threats to be taken? The analyst noted, first, that German propaganda avoided explicit threats of similar action by Germany. "That Berlin does not go further is significant. Germany does not seem to be ready to retaliate in kind." No additional considerations were cited on behalf of the inference. (The analyst might have reasoned further: Since German propaganda was not directly preparing the German people for such a bold step, it was less likely that a move of this sort, so at variance with the predispositions of the public, could be contemplated.) The accuracy of the inference, in any event, is supported by the following entry in the Goebbels diary:

The Fuehrer has no intention of following the Japanese procedure of court-martialing aviators shot down over German soil and having them executed. He fears the English have too many possibilities for reprisals and that we may stumble into a situation about which we know . . . not where it is likely to end. I must see to it that, while we let our press mention the strong language employed by the Japanese and also more recently by the Italians, we do not suggest to the German public that we should indulge in similar practices (*Goebbels Diary*, May 10, 1943, p. 367).

Later German propaganda on this theme led the FCC analyst to re-examine the problem. This time a more refined inference was made:

Nazi Party practice has always shunned the use of legal channels for illegal objectives. Persons and issues not accessible through legal means were handed over to the organized spontaneity of the *Kochende Volks-seele* ("boiling soul of the people"). It is not impossible that similar means may be applied with regard to Allied fliers. It is likewise not impossible that they have already been applied in one case or other. Indeed, it is not even necessary that such acts be instigated by official personages. It suffices that nothing is done to prevent them from happening (*CEA* #20, May 28, 1943, p. C-1).

Such an inference was suggested, no doubt, by some of the Nazi propaganda statements noted by the analyst. (For example, in reporting a suggestion by Italian papers that "enemy fliers who come down by parachute be lynched," Radio Berlin commented: "It is understandable when these victims take immediate revenge on every one of those murderers." [52]

Verification. Whether in fact German leaders *at this early date* (April, 1943) were encouraging spontaneous actions of this sort cannot be established on the basis of documentary evidence, but it seems improbable in view of later evidence. But the analyst's insight as to *the method preferred by the Nazis* for accomplishing illegal activity of this type was an important forecast. For, as the Nuremberg Trial revealed, some time in the period of May to July, 1944, Hitler made a secret proposal to his top collaborators that captured enemy fliers who engaged in specified "acts of terror" be executed without court-martial. In the ensuing policy discussions two methods were proposed for dealing with Allied aviators in such cases: (*a*) permitting lynch law to operate and (*b*) handing over the captured airmen to the S.D. (Sicherheitsdienst) for "special treatment" (i.e., execution without court-martial).

Testimony and documents produced at Nuremberg regarding the role in the discussions played by Goering, Keitel, and Jodl shows that in June, 1944, they deemed formal *legal* procedures against captured airmen either impractical or inexpedient, the clear implication being that, if the action were to be taken, resort must be had to informal, nonlegal methods. Whether orders to this effect were ever issued could not be clearly established at the Trial, but the evidence indicated that Hitler's top-level military and diplomatic collaborators knew of lynchings of Allied airmen by the German civilian population, did nothing to prevent them, and, in fact, considered giving them official approval.[53] About this time, too, Bormann, Vice-Führer after 1941, issued an order (May 30, 1944) prohibiting police or criminal action against persons who had taken part in lynchings of Allied fliers.[54]

In effect, then, Bormann's order, together with Goebbels' propaganda inciting the public to actions of this sort, constituted the type of organized spontaneity which the FCC analyst had predicted, perhaps somewhat prematurely, a year before such a development took place.

Subsequent developments in February, 1945, are not discussed here because they fall outside the period of the FCC operations under examination. At that time, top Nazi leaders debated whether to denounce the Geneva Convention and to liquidate a number of Allied prisoners equal to that of German civilians killed in the Dresden raids (which ran into tens of thousands).[55]

German Action against Allied Prisoners-of-War as Reprisal for the Kharkov Trial. In mid-December, 1943, the Russians held an official war-crimes trial at Kharkov, which resulted in the execution of several German prisoners-of-war for having committed atrocities against the Russian population. Nazi leaders apparently considered this too delicate a topic to publicize at home, for no mention of the Kharkov trial appeared in domestic broadcasts. Instead, at this time, German propaganda suddenly began to utter threats of retaliation against *Anglo-American* fliers "accused of having committed grave violations of international law."[56] In German *domestic* propaganda such threats were made exclusively in the context of denunciations of Allied bombing "terror"; only in propaganda for *foreign* audiences was the connection with the Kharkov trials made.

The analyst's inference was that the Nazis were using the Kharkov trial "for driving a wedge between the Western Allies and Soviet Russia . . . in the hope of inducing the British and Americans to bring pressure to bear on the Russians . . . not [to] hold any more trials à la Kharkov in the future."

In fact, however, Hitler at this time had *actual* reprisals in mind; he was not thinking merely of a propaganda campaign, as the FCC analyst suggested. In top-level conferences held on December 19 and 20, Hitler ordered that the Kharkov trial be counteracted by similar trials of Anglo-American prisoners-of-war:

> In connection with the machine-gunning of shipwrecked survivors by British naval forces in the Aegean Sea, the Fuehrer spoke of his intention of retaliating for the mock-trial at Kharkov by holding similar trials in Germany for British and American officers who have violated international law. He gave orders to draw up appropriate charges.[57]

Nazi preparations for such countertrials were brought out at the Nuremberg Trial.[58] But, apparently, no such trials were ever held.

The FCC analyst may be credited with having partially illuminated the Nazi intention in this instance since the retaliation planned by the Nazis may be assumed to have been considered a means of forcing their opponents to desist from any further trials of this type. It may be noted, too (even though direct evidence is not available) that German propaganda was evidently closely co-ordinated with Hitler's decision to take this extreme step.

NOTES

1. The term "major action" is preferred to "initiatives" because it is not limited to declarations of war or to major military offensives but also includes political, diplomatic, and economic actions. The problem of predicting the latter events is essentially similar to that of predicting military initiatives; therefore the same general approach or analytical framework can be applied. Also, "major actions" does not exclude, as "initiatives" does, actions which are taken in response to conditions created by the opponent.

2. When preparatory propaganda is not employed, it is theoretically possible for propaganda analysts to predict the major action by the *direct* method, which does not depend upon considerations of propaganda strategy. This possibility is not further explored, since the FCC analysts, on whose work this study is based, appear to have confined themselves to the indirect method in attempting to predict and analyze forthcoming Nazi actions.

3. See, for example (p. 164), Hitler's sudden announcement of this decision to take action against Allied commandos.

4. For detailed accounts of the problems of intelligence and countermeasures against the V-weapons see Winston Churchill, *Closing the Ring* (Vol. V of *The Second World War;* Houghton Mifflin Co., Boston, 1951), pp. 226–40; W. F. Craven and J. L. Cate (eds.), *Europe: Argument to V-E Day, January 1944 to May 1945* (Vol. 3 of *The Army Air Forces in World War II;* University of Chicago Press, Chicago, 1951), pp. 84–106; R. V. Jones, "Scientific Intelligence," *Journal of Royal United Services Institution* (August, 1947), p. 353.

5. W. Bedell Smith, *Eisenhower's Six Great Decisions* . . . (Longmans, Green & Co., New York, 1956), p. 39. See also Capt. Harry C. Butcher, USNR, *My Three Years with Eisenhower* (Simon and Schuster, New York, 1946), pp. 468, 492, and 513; Craven and Cate, *op. cit.,* pp. 91–92.

6. According to Major Gen. J. F. C. Fuller (*The Second World War* [Duell, Sloan & Pearce, New York, 1949], p. 319), during the thirteen months of Allied bombing countermeasures against V-weapon targets, approximately 100,000 tons of bombs were dropped. This comprised 9 per cent of the total bomb tonnage dropped by the Allied Air Forces during that period. For the effects of the Allied bombardment of the launching-sites see the account based on primary sources in Chester Wilmot, *The Struggle for Europe* (William Collins Sons & Co., London, 1952), pp. 152–54.

7. Dwight D. Eisenhower, *Crusade in Europe* (Doubleday & Co., Inc., Garden City, N.Y., 1948), p. 259.

8. *Ibid.,* p. 260.

9. *Ibid.,* p. 230.

10. For example, J. P. Baxter III, *Scientists against Time* (Little, Brown & Co., Boston, 1948), pp. 6–7 and 34–36, states merely that "Allied intelligence found out most of what we needed to know about the V-1 flying bombs and V-2 long-range rockets before the close of 1943." But Baxter does not reconstruct in detail the development of the intelligence picture.

11. Political Warfare Executive, CIO, Germany and Austria, "German Propaganda and a Secret Weapon" (November 8, 1943).

12. Louis P. Lochner (ed.), *The Goebbels Diaries, 1942–1943* (hereafter referred to as *"Goebbels Diary";* Doubleday & Co., Inc., Garden City, N.Y., 1948), p. 467 (entry for September 23, 1943).

13. Wallace Carroll, *Persuade Or Perish* (Houghton Mifflin Co., Boston, 1948), p. 154.

14. *Goebbels Diary,* pp. 467 and 532 (entries for September 23 and November 27, 1943).

15. Carroll, *op. cit.,* p. 154.

16. Sir Arthur Harris, *Bomber Offensive* (William Collins Sons & Co., London, 1947), p. 198; Lord Arthur W. Tedder, *Air Power in War* (Hodder & Stoughton, London, 1948), pp. 95–96.

17. This type of self-imposed restraint is nicely conveyed in the discussion of V-weapons propaganda in Ernst Kris and Hans Speier, *German Radio Propaganda* (Oxford University Press, London, 1944), pp. 457–58. The implicit assumption in their discussion is that it is simply not possible to deduce from mere propaganda threats whether such weapons actually exist, although common sense indicates that German scientists, like all other scientists in wartime, are constantly at work on new weapons.

18. A similar proposition had been formulated and used by the FCC analysts in inferring the existence of a Nazi *defensive* weapon from Goebbels' explicit promise of one: "Since Goebbels is extremely cautious in making predictions . . . it seems safe to assume that Germany is going to introduce new weapons into the air war over Germany" (*CEA* #11, March 26, 1943, p. A-1).

The German Section of the Analysis Division of the FBIS (of the FCC) originally made weekly contributions to the over-all report, the *Weekly Analysis,* of the Analysis Division. The title of this report was changed to *Weekly Review* with issue #36, dated August 8, 1942. After the beginning of 1943 the German Section produced a special weekly report of its own, the *Central European Analysis,* in this study abbreviated to *CEA,* which gave a fuller and more analytical review of German propaganda than did its earlier contributions to the Analysis Division's reports.

19. *CEA* #47, December 2, 1943, p. B-1.

20. *CEA* #32, August 19, 1943, p. B-8.

21. Toward the end of the war Goebbels departed from this otherwise invariable rule only to the extent of reluctantly permitting Party propagandists to use the idea of a miracle weapon in word-of-mouth propaganda. He made this concession in part because he felt that he, as official propagandist, would not be compromised by such irresponsible rumors, the official inspiration of which could not be traced: "No one will ever be able to reproach us for having circulated this rumor. No one will ever be able to nail us down for having made such a prediction, because we never did make it" (quoted in Curt Riess, *Joseph Goebbels* [Doubleday & Co., Garden City, N.Y., 1948], p. 303).

22. *Weekly Analysis* #31, July 4, 1942, pp. 13–14. See ftn. 18, above, for identification of the *Weekly Analysis.*

23. U.S. Navy Dept., *Führer Conferences on Matters Dealing with the German Navy, 1942* (Washington, D.C.), pp. 89 ff. For additional details on implementation of the decision to take action against Brazil see Admiral Raeder's testimony at Nuremberg in I.M.T. (International Military Tribunal), *Trial of the Major War Criminals* (Nuremberg, 1948), Vol. XIV, pp. 122–25.

24. Hereafter, where the same FCC report is quoted repeatedly or consecutively within one case study, identification of it will be made only at the first instance of quotation. The reader may therefore assume that materials quoted from FCC reports are from the report most recently identified in each case study unless otherwise indicated.

25. Anthony Martienssen, *Hitler and His Admirals* (E. P. Dutton & Co., Inc., New York, 1949), pp. 148–49.

26. U.S. Navy Dept., *Führer Conferences on Matters Dealing with the German Navy, 1943* (Washington, D.C.), pp. 25–26.

27. *Ibid.,* p. 67.

28. B. H. Liddell Hart, *The German Generals Talk* (William Morrow & Co., New York, 1948), pp. 194–96. Hitler's directive for operations in Russia, dated April 5, 1942, is quoted in Winston S. Churchill, *The Hinge of Fate* (Vol. IV of *The Second World War;* Houghton Mifflin Co., Boston, 1950), pp. 342–45.

29. *Goebbels Diary,* pp. 162–63, 221–22, 223 (entries for April 6, May 20, and May 21, 1942).

30. *Ibid.,* pp. 214, 221 (entries for May 15 and 20, 1942).

31. *Ibid.,* p. 226 (entry for May 23, 1942).

32. *Weekly Analysis* #27, June 6, 1942, p. 6.

33. *Weekly Analysis* #31, July 4, 1942, p. 3.

34. Butcher, *op. cit.,* p. 314.

35. U.S. Army, A.G.O., Departmental Records Branch, T.A.G.O., *Führer Directives* . . . *German Armed Forces, 1942–1945* (Washington, D.C.), p. 74; italics supplied.

36. Liddell Hart, *op. cit.,* p. 212.

37. This interpretation is from Fuller (*op. cit.,* pp. 276–77; italics supplied). Fuller's further interpretation—that Hitler hoped that such a military setback inflicted at that time would persuade the Russians to consider a separate peace proposal—however plausible, finds no support in sources examined by the present author. Moreover, Fuller presents no documentation on behalf of this hypothesis.

38. Portions of Goebbels' diary not published by Lochner are available in microfilm at the Hoover War Library, Stanford University, Stanford, Calif. Quotations from the microfilm diary in this report were translated into English by Eric Willenz of the RAND Social Science Division. Portions of the microfilm diary referred to in this report are identified for the sake of brevity as "Microfilm Goebbels diary."

39. *CEA* #8, March 5, 1943, p. A-1.

40. Liddell Hart, *op. cit.,* p. 212.

41. I.M.T., *op. cit.,* Vol. XV, p. 316.

42. *Weekly Review* #46, October 17, 1942, pp. 6–8. See footnote 18, above, for identification of the *Weekly Review.*

43. *Weekly Review* #47, October 24, 1942, pp. 1–2.

44. *Weekly Review* #48, October 31, 1942, pp. 8–9.

45. The relevant period is missing in the Goebbels diaries.

46. See I.M.T., *op. cit.*, Vol. XV, pp. 318–29, 479–91; Rudolf Semmler, *Goebbels: The Man Next to Hitler* (Westhouse, London, 1947), pp. 182–85; Riess, *op. cit.*, pp. 307–8.

47. I.M.T., *op. cit.*, Vol. XV, p. 317.

48. See I.M.T., *op. cit.*, Vol. I, p. 228; Vol. X, pp. 589–90; Vol. XV, pp. 314–29, 479–91; Vol. XXVI, pp. 100–115, 140–47.

49. The British government made no open protest to the Commando Order. Jodl, in his testimony at Nuremberg, stated that he had not wanted to issue such an order and indicated that he had expected a British protest at the time and hoped that it would throw the matter into diplomatic channels. The lesson would appear to be that an official diplomatic protest, such as was not made in this case, *might* have strengthened the hand of those members of the Nazi elite who were opposed to the Commando Order. This was apparently the case in February, 1945, when a timely official British warning may have helped restrain Hitler from denouncing the Geneva Convention. See Semmler, *op. cit.*, pp. 184–85; Riess, *op. cit.*, pp. 307–8.

50. *Goebbels Diary*, p. 341 (entry for April 23, 1943).

51. *CEA* #16, April 30, 1943, p. C-12.

52. *CEA* #20, May 28, 1943, p. C-1.

53. See, especially, *Nazi Conspiracy and Aggression* (U.S. Government Printing Office, Washington, D.C., 1946), Vol. II, pp. 508–12, 535, 545–46, 568–69; and Documents 728-PS, 729-PS, 731-PS, 735-PS, 740-PS in English translation, *ibid.*, Vol. III, pp. 526–35, 537–38.

54. See the judgment of the International Military Tribunal (I.M.T., *op. cit.*, Vol. I, p. 340). Bormann's order is Document O57-PS; the original German version is recommended over the English translation (see *ibid.*, Vol. XXV, pp. 112 f.). That such lynchings took place was fully established in a series of American Military Commission proceedings, which resulted in the conviction of German civilians for the murder of Allied fliers (see Documents 2559-PS, 2560-PS, 2561-PS in *Nazi Conspiracy and Aggression*, Vol. V, pp. 294–301).

55. For details, see I.M.T., *op. cit.*, Vol. XIII, pp. 406, 468–71; Vol. XV, pp. 297, 423, 504–7, 606–97; Semmler, *op. cit.*, pp. 182–85; Riess, *op. cit.*, p. 307.

56. *CEA* #50, December 23, 1943, p. C-7.

57. U.S. Navy Dept. *Führer Conferences* . . . *1943*, p. 149.

58. See, particularly, Document UK-57 in *Nazi Conspiracy and Aggression*, Vol. VIII, pp. 539–45; see also, I.M.T., *op. cit.*, Vol. X, p. 642.

TWELVE

Analysis of Propaganda Anticipations of an Opponent's Actions

The preceding chapter considered the use of propaganda analysis for predicting the initiatives of an opponent. The present chapter is concerned with the converse of this situation—namely, when the opponent is confronted with the possibility of an initiative by the propaganda analyst's side. This chapter takes up the possible use of propaganda analysis to throw light upon the opponent's estimates, expectations, and counterintentions when confronted by such an initiative.[1] This is the second of the three general problem areas in making inferences mapped out in the Introduction.

There are many examples of successful inferences by the FCC in this general problem area, a number of which are presented as case studies in this chapter. Most of these inferences appear to have been derived by a procedure resembling the indirect method, but there are a few cases of procedure resembling the direct method.

Prerequisites and Limitations of the Indirect Method

Modern elites often find it to their advantage to talk publicly about the actions which an opponent may take, especially when such actions are likely to affect the position and interests of the elite, its public or friends, and neutrals elsewhere in the world. This type of propaganda may be termed "anticipatory," in contrast to that put forth in connection with the elite's own forthcoming actions, which this study has termed "preparatory" propaganda.

In this general problem area the indirect method can be employed only if the opposing elite engages in such anticipatory propaganda. Otherwise, propaganda-analysis inferences concerning anticipations of an opponent's actions can be made only by using the direct method.

If an elite were interested solely in security—in not revealing anything it might know or suspect about a forthcoming action of its opponent—it would not engage in anticipatory propaganda. But even the most security-minded elites undoubtedly find this type of propaganda expedient and preferable in certain situations, hoping thereby to gain any one of a variety of objectives.

Types of Inferences of Interest to the Policy-Maker

The task of the propaganda analyst in the case of anticipatory propaganda is not merely that of inferring whether the opposing elite knows of the major actions which the propaganda analyst's side plans to take. He is also interested in the opposing elite's estimates of this action and in its intentions with regard to it. The problem of intentions has many ramifications, a number of which need to be identified and clearly distinguished as specific problems. Which of these problems is of primary interest varies from one individual case to another. There are at least nine specific inferences which the propaganda analyst may try to make when analyzing the propagandist's anticipation of his opponent's actions:

1. Degree of certainty with which opponent's action is expected.[2]
2. Estimate of character and scope of expected action.[3]
3. Estimate of location of expected action.[4]
4. Estimate of timing or degree of imminence of expected action.[5]
5. Expected outcome of expected action (confidence in ability to counteract it effectively; extent of loss expected, etc.).[6]
6. Estimate of specific defensive capabilities for meeting or countering expected action.[7]
7. Plans for counteraction to thwart expected action.[8]
8. Plans for defensive strategy with which to meet expected action.[9]
9. Effort to force delay of expected action.[10]

Mode of Reasoning (Using the Indirect Method)

Much of what was said in the preceding chapter about the use of the indirect method in analyzing preparatory propaganda applies also to the use of this method in dealing with anticipatory propaganda. The task of identifying and interpreting possible instances of anticipatory propaganda is facilitated by the use of the types of generalizations about the elite and its propagandists discussed in Part I, Chapter 5. The propaganda analyst will particularly benefit from generalizations which characterize the types of situations and circumstances in which the opposing elite tends to employ anticipatory propaganda, that is, for what types of actions, for what types of audiences, for what types of goals, and using what types of communications channels (see p. 133).

Such generalizations are employed within the framework of logic-of-the-situation assessments. The general structure of the analyst's reasoning parallels that already indicated for the employment of the indirect method in analyzing possible uses of preparatory propaganda. Thus, in effect, the propaganda analyst reasons as follows: "The enemy propagandist would not adopt these propaganda goals for implementation through these media channels at this time and in this situation unless he anticipated an action by his opponent of the kind I am inferring, or unless he entertained estimates, expectations, and/or counterintentions of the kind I am inferring."

Possible Goals of Anticipatory Propaganda

The critical step in the application of the indirect method is, once again, that of determining whether *any* propaganda goals are being implemented in current communications which are likely to be part of an anticipatory strategy. Since any of a variety of anticipatory propaganda goals may be selected by the opposing propagandist, and since the method of implementation of a goal may be quite subtle, it is often not at all easy for the analyst to spot anticipatory propaganda. A catalogue of all possible propaganda goals that might be employed by an elite in such a context would be useful in sensitizing the propaganda analyst to the varieties of anticipatory propaganda and in facilitating his systematic consideration of anticipatory strategies. Attention is called again to the fact that the statement of possible goals is deliberately phrased in abstract terms in order to make it as useful as possible for analyzing the anticipatory propaganda of different political elites, in different types of actions, etc.[11] Some of the *techniques* for implementing a goal, as well as the goal itself, are included in the following list.

Possible Goals of Propaganda Anticipating Opponent's Actions [12]

I. Directed at domestic or friendly neutral audiences:
  A. To attempt to anticipate correctly the opponent's action (i.e., predict its occurrence, nature, scope, timing, and location) in order to demonstrate to the domestic public that its leaders are not taken by surprise and that they retain the possibility of some control over the situation (if only, or primarily, by virtue of the fact that they are able to anticipate and estimate the opponent's coming blows).
  B. To cushion the psychological shock to domestic morale (that might ensue from the sudden, unanticipated announcement of an opponent's action) by predicting the opponent's initiative in advance and by presenting it as mere reaction to an initiative of one's own.
  C. To anticipate the success which the opponent's coming action is expected to have in order to lessen its negative impact on morale.
  D. To cushion negative consequences to morale of the expected success of the forthcoming opponent's action by deliberately exaggerating the aims of his action and assuring the domestic public that these (exaggerated) aims will not be realized.
  E. To strengthen the public's confidence in the defensive assets which are presumably available for meeting the forthcoming action of the opponent.
  F. To shield the public against the impact of the war-of-nerves propaganda which may precede the opponent's action.
  G. To strengthen the public's will to resist the opponent's forthcoming action.
  H. To manipulate in politically acceptable directions—that is, away from the leadership—the blame and responsibility for the setback expected to result from the opponent's forthcoming action.
II. Directed at groups in the opponent's camp:
  A. To dissuade the opponent from undertaking the expected action by appealing directly to leadership groups or by appealing to public opinion to bring pressure to bear on leaders.
  B. To influence the timing and/or location of the opponent's action in a direction more favorable to the propagandist's side.
  C. To exploit the waiting period before the opponent's action to exacerbate his (and his public's) anxiety over the outcome; to induce overcautiousness, fear, and defeatism.
  D. To spoil the positive effect on morale of the coming action for the opponent:
    1. By representing him as being forced to act by conditions out of his control.

2. By predicting his action and proclaiming readiness for it.
3. By labeling in advance the results to be achieved by him as inconsequential and indecisive.
4. By promising that his losses in the forthcoming action will be out of proportion to any advantage gained.
5. By encouraging his public to think that its forthcoming action has relatively far-reaching goals (beyond those actually entertained by its leaders) so that any successes achieved by the action will seem disappointing (i.e., the familiar technique of committing the enemy to goals more far-reaching than he actually envisages).

E. To discredit the motivation of the enemy leadership in undertaking the action in question in order:
   1. To undermine the public's confidence in the leaders' judgment and morality.
   2. To facilitate an adverse public reaction later against the leaders.

F. To lay the groundwork for stirring up discord among factions making up the opposing elite, or between opponent and his allies over any suitable aspect of the action.

G. To hide from the opponent the fact that his action is expected. (This is similar to the "masking goal" with respect to domestic actions. It is listed here not because it was a familiar goal in Nazi anticipations of opponent actions but because it may be a more important goal to other elites. Obviously, the problem of making inferences will be complicated to the extent that this goal enters into propaganda calculations.)

The Direct Method

On several occasions, the FCC analysts made use of procedures which resemble the *direct* method. Since the FCC analysts themselves made no distinction between the direct and indirect methods, it can be no more than surmise to state that in any given instance one or the other method was used.

In Case Study No. 12.1, Inference 10 (p. 187), and Case Study No. 12.2, Inference 6 (p. 201; see esp. p. 203), the reader may see how the direct method may be applied within this general problem area. The simplicity of the mode of reasoning characteristic of the direct method and some of the problems in utilizing it are indicated in these cases. In several other instances it was not clear whether the direct or indirect method was being applied (see Case Study No. 12.1,

Inference 5, p. 182, and Case Study No. 12.2, Inference 4, p. 197). In still others, there is some reason to believe that the direct method could have been successful had it been tried (see Case Study No. 12.1, Inference 4, p. 181, and Case Study No. 12.2, Inferences 6 and 9, pp. 201 and 208).

In reviewing these cases, the reader will note how tenuous direct inferences become once the basic assumption that the content indicators employed are independent of propaganda strategy is effectively challenged (see, for example, Case Study No. 12.2, Inference 4, p. 197).

Case Studies

Some of the five case studies presented here include more than one inference; in these cases the individual inferences are numbered.

Case Studies Nos. 12.1 and 12.2, roughly comparable in subject matter, provide an interesting contrast in the level of analytical skill. Inferences about the second front in Case Study No. 12.1 were made in 1942 when the FCC's propaganda-analysis unit had been in operation a relatively short time. These inferences were definitely of a lower quality than those made in Case Study No. 12.2 in 1943, when personnel had become more experienced and also more numerous and when additional background knowledge about Nazi propaganda behavior had been accumulated. Another factor accounting for the better quality (and the accuracy) of inferences in Case Study No. 12.2 was the improved coverage of German *domestic* propaganda, which permitted comparison of what was said to domestic and foreign audiences—a fruitful approach to making inferences.

Case Study No. 12.2, therefore, provides a much better example of the potential utility of propaganda analysis. Fortunately, too, it was possible to verify most of the more important inferences made on the second-front issue in 1943, whereas historical data for validating the 1942 inferences were frequently impossible to obtain. The results of the appraisal show the FCC analysts to have been remarkably successful over a period of time in 1943 in inferring the situational estimates and propaganda calculations made by Goebbels and other Nazi leaders on the problem of the second front.

CASE STUDY NO. 12.1: GERMAN EXPECTATION IN 1942
OF AN ALLIED SECOND-FRONT ATTEMPT AND OF THE ALLIED
INVASION OF NORTH AFRICA

The possibility of an Allied second front in Europe began to be mentioned as early as the spring of 1942. Throughout the year the second front was expected by the Nazis as well as the Allies to be primarily a diversionary measure designed to draw off appreciable German forces from the Russian front.[13] Only later in the war did both sides attach broader strategic import to the second front.

The limitation in scope and strategic significance in 1942 must be kept in mind in appraising the Nazi reaction to the threat of an Allied initiative during the year. Nazi propagandists sought initially to dissuade the Allies from such an attempt. It was probably recognized by the Nazis that the Allied decision in the matter would be particularly sensitive to expediential and political considerations and that Allied strategists and decision-makers might well be divided on the issue. Consequently, it was probably reasoned, the hand of those forces in the Allied camp opposed to the venture might be strengthened directly or indirectly by Nazi propaganda manipulations. Certainly, much of Nazi propaganda over a period of months in the spring and early summer of 1942 was clearly directed toward this end.

In this situation Allied intelligence was called upon to note: (*a*) at what point the Germans realized that a decision had been reached by the Allies, (*b*) whether the Germans thought the Allied decision was for or against a second front, and (*c*) when and where the Germans expected the attempt, if there was one, to be made.

The FCC analysts attempted inferences on these questions, but in most cases the correctness of the inferences could not be determined for lack of relevant historical data. The present appraisal, therefore, focuses on the alertness of the FCC analysts to the key problems and on the quality of the reasoning underlying the inferences attempted. The appraisal begins with the FCC reports of June, 1942, earlier reports not being available.

Inference 1. In early June the FCC analyst noted[14] an increase in the frequency of explicit arguments (in Berlin broadcasts to North America) attempting to dissuade Americans from participating in an offensive against the European continent. He noted also that *factu-*

ally reasoned arguments were being employed now, whereas in previous weeks Nazi comments had taken the form of *ridicule* and *dogmatic assertions*. The analyst suggested that Berlin may have stepped up its campaign partly to offset the effect on the American public of the discussions between Molotov, Soviet foreign minister, and Roosevelt. This cannot be verified directly but can probably be assumed to be correct. For, though the fact that Molotov had been in Washington was officially made known to the public only a week after he left, German propagandists openly claimed before the announcement that they had knowledge that negotiations were going on.

Molotov arrived in Washington on May 29 from London, where he had negotiated the Anglo-Soviet Alliance. In discussions with both the British and the American leaders, Molotov attempted to obtain a positive commitment on a second front for 1942. The official public statement issued on June 11 contained the following statement: "In the course of the conversations full understanding was reached with regard to the urgent task of creating a second front in Europe in 1942." [15] During the conference Roosevelt authorized Molotov to tell Stalin that the Allies were preparing a second front and that he expected it in 1942. When he returned to London, however, Molotov was given an *aide-mémoire* by Churchill which made it clear that, while preparations for a landing in Europe were being made, no promise of one could be given. [16]

Analyst's Reasoning. The analyst focused attention upon the psychological-warfare aims, vis-à-vis the American audience, pursued by Nazi propaganda. The shift in the content characteristics of this propaganda (from ridicule and dogmatic assertions to factually reasoned arguments) plus increased Nazi attention to the second-front issue in the context of Molotov's visit suggested the inference that the Nazis were now taking the talk of a second front more seriously and were pursuing a *defensive* goal—namely, to dissuade the American audience from making a second-front commitment to Molotov. Implied in this was the additional inference that earlier Nazi propaganda, with its concentration on ridicule and dogmatic assertions, had not been defensive but, rather, had had the aggressive purpose of exploiting and exacerbating those feelings of weakness in the American audience stemming from the absence of an Allied second front.

Inference 2. At the beginning of July, 1942, the FCC analyst presented another analysis of second-front propaganda over the German short-wave radio:

> By sarcasm, taunts, and other minimization devices in place of the more reasoned and factual arguments of the past few weeks, the Nazis aim to give the *impression* of complete confidence in the security of their continent from invasion . . . [thus, they] return to the method of handling the second front threat which they ordinarily employ when the threat is at a low ebb (*Weekly Analysis* #31, dated July 4, 1942, covering broadcasts of June 26–July 2, p. 6).

Analysis of German *domestic* propaganda bolstered the impression that the private Nazi estimates on this issue were more sober than before. Thus, from German domestic propaganda the FCC analyst inferred it was "very problematic" that the Nazis "actually regard the threat as reduced." The following evidence was adduced: (*a*) warnings over the domestic radio that the German public must be prepared to receive direct blows, in view of the appointment of General Eisenhower as Commander of U.S. Forces in Europe, and (*b*) Goebbels' intimation in his latest *Das Reich* article that an invasion attempt was highly probable. (In his *Das Reich* article of the previous week Goebbels had placed a second-front attempt in the "realm of fable." In the interim between the two articles the Eisenhower appointment had been announced.)

The correctness of the analyst's inference appears to be indirectly borne out by the "Order concerning the strengthening of defense measures in the West" issued by Hitler at about this time (July 9, 1942):

> Our rapid and great victories [i.e., in the current offensive in Russia] may place Great Britain before the alternative of either staging a large-scale invasion with the object of opening a Second Front, or seeing Russia eliminated as a political and military factor. It is therefore highly probable that enemy landings will shortly take place in the area of the Commanding General Armed Forces, West . . . [cites several indications that suggest a forthcoming invasion and proceeds to outline a number of countermeasures]. In the event of an enemy landing, I personally will proceed to the West and assume charge of operations from there.[17]

Inference 3. In the third week of July, 1942,[18] the FCC presented an analysis indicating that German propaganda strategy *to* *the American audience* had suddenly shifted. From a propaganda of taunts and derision (which the analyst interpreted as having the aim of compounding the frustration of the Allied public at its inability to mount a second front and thus help the hard-pressed Russian ally), the Propaganda Ministry suddenly switched to arguments which, in the analyst's interpretation, were designed to persuade the Allied public to bring pressure upon their leaders against the advisability of an invasion destined to result in a bloody fiasco.

The analyst's reasoning was as follows:

1. An important shift in Nazi propaganda on the second front had taken place on July 21; such an overnight shift was unusual and suggested that new propaganda directives had been issued. The analyst did not speculate as to what events might have been responsible for this sudden shift. The fact is that Hopkins (assistant and adviser to Roosevelt), Marshall (U.S. Army Chief of Staff), and King (U.S. Chief of Naval Operations) flew to London on July 16 for conferences with Eisenhower and the British, during the course of which TORCH (the invasion of North Africa) was decided upon as a substitute for a cross-Channel invasion. The whole mission of the Chiefs of Staff and Hopkins was a secret one—indeed, no public announcement of it was made until several weeks later. Therefore, the FCC analysts, not given inside information in such cases, could not possibly link the sudden shift in Berlin's propaganda line and the presence of top American military planners in London. But, as Sherwood observes,

> It was extremely difficult for any of the hundreds of people who went about Claridge's to miss the fact that top-level conferences were in progress. With remarkable speed, sixteen rooms on the fourth floor of Claridge's were converted into a military headquarters . . . and a U.S. sentry posted at every door.[19]

Under these circumstances, it is not entirely out of the question that the Germans got wind that an important military conference was taking place. Hopkins, Marshall, and King left the United States on July 16; five days later the German propaganda line abruptly switched. The American party returned to the United States on July 27.

2. The major Berlin radio commentators (on short wave to North America and Great Britain) markedly increased attention to the second front following July 20, as did newscasts on these beams.

3. The thematic quality of Nazi references to the second front also shifted as of the same date and also supported the analyst's inference: (*a*) More direct propaganda efforts, stressing the cost in Allied lives, were now made to discourage the second-front attempt. The analyst noted that this type of appeal had never been stressed before and was precisely the kind of appeal calculated to influence the Allied public. (*b*) Nazi propagandists argued that the Allied invasion, if attempted, would take place wholly for *political* considerations, as opposed to military prospects. Allied listeners were thus encouraged, the analyst observed, to believe that their own political pressure upon their leaders might be influential.

The analyst concluded that the new propaganda of discouraging an Allied initiative must be based upon the estimate that a second-front attack was quite within the realm of possibility.

The analyst did not take up the questions of how imminent the Nazis considered the invasion to be, where they expected the attack, or how confident they were of the outcome.

Inference 4. In the following week, the FCC analyst noted that "for the first time in many months, German [short-wave] propaganda [to North America] shows signs of serious concern, if not anxiety, about the Second Front." [20] Several separate questions for inference were blurred in this analysis, however, and consequently the analyst's statement was somewhat ambiguous. What was the precise meaning of "signs of serious concern, if not anxiety, about the Second Front"? Did this refer to (*a*) an expectation that an attempt would be made, (*b*) a belief in its imminence, or (*c*) uncertainty as to its outcome?

However, for present purposes this ambiguity can be resolved into the following three major inferences: (*a*) that the Nazis were now more certain of an Allied second-front attempt and, in fact, took it for granted, (*b*) that the Nazis viewed the attempt as being somewhat more imminent than previously, and (*c*) that the Nazis were definitely less confident than previously that the outcome would be quickly and completely in their favor.

Despite the untidiness of the analysis, the evidence for these three inferences in German propaganda to North America, though not clearly distinguished, was striking. German propaganda not only contained explicit predictions of a second-front attempt but implied that pro-second-front elements were now in the saddle in the Allied camp. Again, propaganda references to German preparedness to meet the invasion became markedly more specific. Finally, the leading German propagandist, Goebbels himself, took pains not to underestimate the force of the forthcoming Allied blow nor to rule out the possibility of "one or two illusory successes."

The generalizations underlying the inferential significance of these three content characteristics were not stated by the analyst and perhaps were only vaguely formulated in his mind. For present purposes they may be paraphrased as follows (without regard for appropriate refinements):

1. A shift in propaganda strategy from an effort to discourage the opponent from launching an initiative to an effort to prepare the domestic audience (and friendly neutral audiences) for the opponent's action [21] reflects a new elite expectation that the opponent's initiative has been decided upon and is forthcoming.

2. Increased specificity of propaganda references to defensive preparedness vis-à-vis an expected initiative by the opponent reflects an estimate of the increased imminence of that initiative. (As stated, this generalization would be used in a *direct* inference since it apparently does not take into consideration propaganda strategy.)

3. Propaganda preparation of one's own people and friendly foreign audiences for the possibility of important or partial successes by the forthcoming enemy initiative indicates some uncertainty on the part of the propagandist as to the immediacy and completeness of his side's victory in the forthcoming battle.

Inference 5. The following weekly FCC report [22] again identified a number of interesting propaganda shifts. The analyst's interpretations were, however, once more blurred by a failure to distinguish clearly the separate inferential problems involved.

The chief inference was again ambiguous: "That the Nazis regard the *establishment* of the Second Front as a *serious probability* has become increasingly manifest in their propaganda treatment of that theme over the past month" (italics supplied). Does "establishment" mean merely that a second front will be attempted, or that it will be partially or wholly successful? To which of these possibilities does "serious probability" refer?

Two rather important types of content evidence were cited by the analyst, but their precise significance was not explicitly assessed:

1. Whereas the subject of Allied shipping shortages due to German U-boat successes had previously been the major theme in Nazi second-front propaganda, recently it had played a minor role. The

inferential significance of this shift in propaganda, not articulated by the analyst, lay in the (reasonable) presumption that the Nazis would argue that Allied shipping shortages were an obstacle to a second-front attempt *only* if they did not expect such an attempt. *Ergo,* to drop this propaganda claim might well indicate that an invasion was expected. (Note the underlying assumption that Nazi propagandists were skillful enough to realize the need for dropping the Allied-shipping-shortage theme when an invasion attempt became a definite probability.)

2. Although current Nazi propaganda argued that the defeat of the forthcoming Allied invasion was assured, the FCC analyst noted that "the hitherto fairly frequent more *general* assertion that the invasion would end in another Dunkirk is quite rare this week." The significance of this near-omission of a standard propaganda theme was, presumably, that the Nazis were less confident than previously of a clean-cut, decisive victory in the expected invasion battle.

The analyst's report gave no evidence that he had assessed the Nazi references or hints as to the time and place of the forthcoming second-front attempt, a type of analysis which might have thrown additional light on their expectations as to the imminence and location of such an attempt.

Inference 6. During the next week, August 7–13, discussion of the second front per se declined on the Radio Berlin short-wave. There was instead relatively greater emphasis on the theme of British-American discord over the second front. The analyst was content to note these content characteristics without offering an interpretation of them. This was the week before the Dieppe raid (August 19).

Inference 7. The Dieppe raid itself was depicted in Berlin propaganda as a full-fledged invasion attempt which failed. Goebbels publicly credited himself with having correctly predicted an impending second-front attempt. An important question for Allied intelligence at this time might have been to assess the Nazis' private estimate of the strategic scope of the Dieppe raid.[23] Did the Nazis really think it to be a full-fledged second-front attempt? or a diversion for the real attempt to follow later? or merely a substitute for a second-front attempt? This problem was not examined in detail in the FCC analysis, which confined itself to suggesting that Nazi propaganda had deliberately blown up what it knew to be merely a large-scale sortie into a second-front attempt: "Berlin . . . applies to Dieppe affair its favorite technique of magnifying the motives of the enemy in order then to exploit the discrepancy between intention and achievements." [24]

In the following week, however, the FCC analyst seemed somewhat less certain of this interpretation.[25] Impressed by the rather fierce and elaborate effort made by Nazi propagandists to support their contention that Dieppe had been a full-fledged second-front attempt, the analyst did no more this time than suggest that perhaps the Nazis did not really believe their own story.

Available historical evidence indicates that German military leaders in fact disagreed in their assessment of the Dieppe operation. Rundstedt, Commander-in-Chief of German forces in the West at the time, has since stated that he personally had not imagined that the landing at Dieppe marked the beginning of an actual invasion. He thought it merely an experimental attack to test German coastal defenses. Blumentritt (who arrived in the West to become Chief of Staff to Rundstedt just after the Dieppe raid) stated, however, that "the German Command was not sure whether it was merely a raid, or whether it might have been followed up with larger reinforcements if it had been more successful at the outset." [26] The German Naval Staff (Operations Division) records, however, indicate that there was an interservice disagreement on the interpretation of the Dieppe operation. After examining all the evidence in its possession, the German Naval Staff reached the conclusion that the Allied operation was definitely limited in scope. This view, according to the Naval Staff records, was contrary to that of the German Armed Forces Command:

> The Naval Staff is unaware of the reasons which caused the Armed Forces High Command to evaluate the operation as it did. . . . Probably apart from convincing public opinion on both sides that future invasions are useless, it was hoped to use the events of 19 August to justify the fact that considerable forces are committed in the West and North areas and are withdrawn from the East.[27]

Inference 8. In mid-September [28] the FCC analyst noted merely that the Axis radios were reluctant to make predictions about a second-front attempt. The following week [29] the question of whether German leaders expected a second-front attempt was taken up in greater detail, though with inconclusive results. This report is an interesting example of a logically incomplete analysis.

The analyst's reasoning was as follows: If there is no second front before the end of 1942, a full-blown Axis propaganda exploitation of the Allied failure to act may be expected. However, at present, propagandists in Berlin (and, to a lesser extent, Rome) are quite restrained in exploiting the continued absence of a second front. Therefore, it would seem necessary to conclude that *the Axis still expects a second-front attempt or is at least uncertain whether or not it will take place.*

However, the analyst was unwilling to accept this seemingly plausible conclusion. Rather, continuing the analysis, he concluded for reasons not entirely clear that Axis propagandists (in Rome and Berlin) *did not necessarily expect a second-front attempt in 1942, nor did they necessarily remain uncertain about the possibility.* He held that "the danger of a premature celebration," rather than the expectation of a second-front attempt, might account for the restraint in exploiting the absence of a second front. But, it might be queried, could they fear "the danger of a premature celebration" unless they still felt *some* degree of uncertainty as to whether a second-front attempt would take place in 1942? The apparent contradiction in the analyst's reasoning is probably to be explained in terms of a desire on his part to indicate that Nazi propagandists, being quite prudent, would not launch the propaganda celebration until it was extremely certain that subsequent events would not prove them wrong.

The analyst also noted that propaganda from Berlin was more cautious than that from Rome in this respect. An explanation for this difference was not offered until the following week's report,[30] when the analyst observed that Berlin's greater restraint might be due to Goebbels' familiar policy of propagandistic caution in prediction and also to the fact that Germany would be more directly concerned in any invasion attempt. Apart from this, the new analysis was noteworthy only for its observation of an increased boldness on the part of both Rome and Berlin in exploiting the absence of a second front. This the analyst interpreted as reflecting greater confidence on the part of the Axis that the Allies had postponed the attempt.

It may be noted that, by phrasing his inference in the new report in terms of a Nazi belief that the second front was "postponed," the analyst consciously or otherwise avoided the more specific and more difficult problem (which had perplexed him in the previous report) of whether the Nazis still expected a second-front attempt *in 1942*. While the analyst was of course justified in inferring only what he thought could safely be inferred, he would have done well to indicate explicitly to the reader that he had simplified the inferential problem under consideration by redefining it.

Inference 9. In the meantime, the nature of the intelligence problem had changed without the FCC's being aware of it. The analyst had been watching for indications of the Nazis' attitude toward a possible second-front attempt *across the English Channel or somewhere in Northern Europe.* He was not apprised of TORCH, nor was he briefed to look for indications of Nazi concern over a *possible Allied invasion of North Africa.* This helps to account for the relatively poor showing he made in analyzing German propaganda anticipation of the forthcoming Allied initiative in North Africa. For his ignorance of the forthcoming invasion led him to place a somewhat different interpretation upon Nazi propaganda references to the North African theater than he would have had he known of the prospective invasion, as will be seen in Inferences 9–12.

Since Brazil's entry into the war (August 22, 1942), the German-controlled Radio Paris had kept up a steady stream of comment about the danger of an Allied attack upon Dakar. This propaganda was intensified on the anniversary of the abortive Anglo–Free-French military action against Dakar (September 23, 1942). Shortly thereafter, when Radio Paris' concern over an attack on Dakar was further intensified and found an echo on other Axis transmitters, the FCC took note of it in a special article, "Danger to Dakar?" [31] Three major propaganda themes in Radio Paris broadcasts were identified by the analyst: (1) the Allies (and especially the United States) plan to invade Dakar and French West Africa; (2) France will defend herself against this danger to the Empire; (3) Axis military forces might be involved in the defense of the French Empire.

In interpreting this propaganda, the analyst was no doubt impressed by the fact that Radio Berlin itself took little part in the campaign: "The Berlin radio keeps to the sideline in such discussions, satisfied with broadcasting objectively a few reports from French sources, *with no implication of particular self-interest"* (italics supplied). It would appear that Berlin's aloofness was taken as an indication that the Germans did not share Radio Paris' apparent concern over a possible Allied attack upon Dakar. The analyst, searching for an explanation, turned to the possibility that Radio Paris was attempting to whip up an artificial scare for domestic French purposes. The rather precise manner in which Radio Paris used the "danger to Dakar" in order to cement and augment Franco-German collaboration lent support to this inference. Nevertheless, at this stage, the analyst cautiously listed this and two other inferential hypotheses without selecting any one of them as the most likely, though he did express some reservations about the second. He pointed out, too, that the three possibilities were not necessarily mutually exclusive. The inferential hypotheses were as follows:

1. Radio Paris propagandists are genuinely concerned over Allied intentions toward French North Africa, and Axis transmitters are simply echoing them.

2. This is the propaganda build-up for German "protection" of the region—in the classic Nazi style. In that case, however, more attention from other-than-French transmitters might be expected (and of course might be forthcoming). In addition, the very familiarity of this technique argues to some extent against its use in this context.

3. This propaganda campaign is really localized in France (other stations merely echoing it), the purpose being to further Franco-German collaboration by (*a*) diverting hostility to the outsider in a dramatic instance, thus tending to unify the insiders; (*b*) diverting attention from the poor results of the campaign to induce French workers to migrate to Germany; (*c*) influencing (French) public opinion to accept collaboration with the Germans in Africa at least, as a measure to defend the Empire; (*d*) intensifying anti Allied sentiment against an Allied attempt to establish a second front in France. . . .

Inference 10. In the following two FCC reports[32] the analyst explicitly favored the third of the above interpretations. The main reason for this preference was the continued and accelerated exploitation of the scare by Paris for purposes of collaboration politics. In addition, the manner in which Axis propaganda responded to two events—the Smuts visit to England and the arrival of American troops in Liberia—was taken by the analyst as further evidence for the third interpretation. Thus, he observed,

The clear opportunity to present the Smuts visit to London and especially the arrival of American troops in Liberia as intensifying the Allied "threat" to West Africa is neglected. Instead, these events are taken to reinterpret the threat in terms of more general United Nations designs upon Africa. Thus, the threat becomes less imminent and more general while at the same time the necessity-for-collaboration line remains strong on Paris and Vichy.[33]

The generalization underlying the latter part of the analyst's reasoning may be paraphrased as follows: The more *specifically* the geographical site of the threat is identified in propaganda accusations of enemy aggressive designs, the more likely it is that the accuser believes that a concrete enemy initiative is imminent (and vice versa). (This type of generalization or assumption implies the use of the direct method, since the question of propaganda strategy is ignored.)

Critique. The above generalization is a fairly respectable one. (For another use of it see Case Study No. 12.2, Inference 6.) A review of the content evidence cited in the FCC report, however, suggests that the analyst may have incorrectly applied the generalization. The analyst assumed that propaganda identifications of the alleged Allied threat simply shifted from specific to general geographical sites (such a content shift would have suited the generalization), but this seems doubtful. Rather, the propaganda seems to have *persisted* in mentioning specific sites (i.e., danger to Dakar) even while adding references to broader geographical areas. (This content shift does not suit the generalization.) Here, then, is a case where a systematic count might have served to correct a possibly inaccurate impression of the frequencies and, thus, might have led to a reconsideration of the inference.

The present writer's observation regarding the persistence in Paris propaganda of specific geographical references is, of course, also unreliable, since it is based upon an impression gained from the FCC article. This critique, therefore, is merely suggestive, being designed to prevent a precipitous rejection of the generalization. For if the analyst misapplied the generalization, this should not discredit the generalization itself. The generalization could be regarded as being proved erroneous only if it were (*a*) applied to appropriate content *and* (*b*) contradicted, as by establishing that the Paris propagandist's underlying estimate at the time was that an Allied initiative was imminent. Verification data on the latter point are not available. As to the former, at least a reasonable doubt exists that the content characteristics of the propaganda relevant to the generalization (i.e., how generally the Allied threat was located geographically) were correctly described by the FCC analyst. This discussion underlines the importance of accurate description of content in making inferences; it also demonstrates the cautions that must be observed by the analyst in appraising the validity of his generalizations.

Inference 11. In the next weekly report,[34] the analyst reported, under the title "Less Danger to Dakar," that Axis propaganda on the subject had subsided somewhat. The Vichy radio discussed the problem in terms of the visit of Admiral Darlan, commander of the Vichy armed forces, to inspect French defenses in Africa, and seemed content to rely upon the adequacy of French defensive strength at Dakar. Radio Paris, however, placed less emphasis on the effectiveness of the Dakar defenses and persisted in predicting an impending Allied attack there.

The FCC analyst noted that since the Stalin letter (October 4) to an American journalist on the subject of the second front and other matters, the Axis radio stations had had little to say on the second-front issue. This decreased attention certainly raised an important problem for interpretation. What did it mean? The analyst gave a threefold explanation: (*a*) there had been no dramatic events to serve as a peg for second-front propaganda; (*b*) the Nazis may have reasoned that the Allied publics had given up hopes of a second front this year and, therefore, the Axis radios were satisfied to cite Allied and neutral sources to the effect that it was now too late to expect an important move; (*c*) "the prospect of a hard and perhaps losing fight in North Africa [i.e., the British Army's offensive against German General Rommel in eastern North Africa] probably deters Axis radios from calling too much attention to the non-opening of the Second Front."

Again, the absence of relevant historical evidence makes it impossible to determine the accuracy of these inferences. Noticeably lacking in the analyst's reasoning at this time, however, was any consideration of the possibility that continued Axis reticence in propaganda on the second front (i.e., infrequent mention as well as small exploitation of Allied failure to open a second front) may have reflected the fact that the Axis was uncertain as to whether there was a forthcoming Allied initiative. Failure to consider this possible, indeed plausible, inference is all the more surprising since more than a month earlier the analyst had predicted that the continued absence of a second front in 1942 would allow the Axis propagandists a celebration (in Inference 8, above).

Inference 12. The next in the series of FCC reports covered German propaganda during the week immediately preceding the Allied landings in North Africa. During this week Axis sources speculated more heavily than ever about the possibility of an Allied invasion. Yet the FCC analysts, themselves unaware of the Allied invasion plans, evidently did not consider it possible that these propaganda anticipations of the event were based upon genuine concern that an invasion might take place. The importance of adequately briefing propaganda analysts on problems that warrant consideration was never more clearly revealed, for the FCC analysts were even more surprised by the landings than were the German leaders.

"Axis commentators," read the FCC report, "with unprecedented frequency refer to the opening of a Second Front via North Africa and an invasion of Italy."[35] The analyst related this propaganda (incorrectly) to the British 8th Army's offensive against Rommel's forces, seeing in it a manifestation of the familiar Nazi propaganda technique of deliberately exaggerating an opponent's military objectives (in this case, against Rommel's forces) in order to minimize thereby any successes he might achieve.

Had the German High Command been alerted to the possibility of an Allied attack upon French North Africa?

As early as July 9, 1941, Admiral Raeder, then supreme commander of German naval forces, had warned Hitler of a possible Anglo-American effort to dislodge the French in North West Africa. The warning, given two days after the United States sent naval forces to Iceland, represented Raeder's assessment of Allied strategic possibilities rather than a judgment based upon intelligence as to Allied plans. Hitler ignored Raeder's warning, believing rather that, if any danger existed, it was in Norway.[36]

On August 26, 1942, ten weeks before the invasion, Raeder gave Hitler a strong, urgent warning: "I continue to regard the possible attempt of the Anglo-Saxons to occupy North-West Africa . . . with the aid of the French as a very great danger to the whole German war effort. They would attack Italy from there and endanger our position in North-*East* Africa." Hitler concurred in this opinion but delayed action until some three weeks before the Allied landings in North Africa. At this time he initiated operations for taking Tunisia from the French and, as an additional safeguard, prepared for the military occupation of southern France. These plans were carried out almost immediately after the North African landings.[37]

Despite this, however, the invasion of North Africa achieved complete tactical surprise. Although an Allied armada of 850 warships and merchantmen had had to sail for many days in the open Atlantic and to pass at Gibraltar under the very nose of German intelligence, the Germans were nevertheless taken by surprise. The first battle contact of the invasion was the torpedoing on November 7, 1942, of the U.S.S. "Thomas Stone," which was preceding the convoy toward Algiers.[38] On this day the German Propaganda Ministry was in constant telephonic communication with the German Army and Navy Supreme Commands. American and British troop transports had been sighted, and the Nazis believed that the landings would take place on Sicily and Tobruk. German submarines and part of the Luftwaffe had been rushed there to trap the Allies.[39] The landings came sooner and at points other than those expected; Admiral Krancke admitted that the German Navy was caught badly off guard by this Allied move: "Neither the preparations nor the transit of the landing barges were known to the German naval staff. Consequently, U-boats were not put into operation off the African coast." [40]

Contemporary records of Goebbels' calculations in issuing the propaganda anticipations of the Allied invasion are not available. But it seems safe to assume that he was acquainted with confidential German estimates that some sort of Allied landing was imminent and that, therefore, his propaganda was based upon genuine concern over that possibility and was not, as the FCC analyst inferred, merely a device for detracting from Allied successes against Rommel.

After the invasion Goebbels was incensed that the High Command could have been duped. He knew that Canaris, head of the German Abwehr (Army Intelligence), had reported several weeks earlier that Casablanca, Oran, and Algiers would be the points of the Allied invasion.[41] Several months later (February, 1943) Goebbels was told personally by the Grand Mufti of Jerusalem that as early as September, 1942, he had passed information on Allied invasion plans to the German Foreign Office. The Mufti emphasized that he had even given the date of the invasion fairly accurately.[42] From other sources Goebbels learned that a German Foreign Office agent in North Africa, too, had supplied detailed reports on Allied invasion plans but that these warnings had gone unheeded in the Foreign Office.[43]

CASE STUDY NO. 12.2: GERMAN EXPECTATION IN 1943 OF
ALLIED SECOND FRONT AND INVASIONS OF SICILY AND ITALY

In March, 1943, the Western Allies were pushing ahead in North Africa toward their eventual victory in Tunis several months later. The Germans, still reeling from the Stalingrad disaster, were struggling desperately to bring the Russian winter offensive to a halt. As winter conditions gradually lifted, talk of a second front mounted. From an intelligence point of view, several questions were important throughout the next few months: [44] Did the German leaders expect Allied second-front attempts to be made? If so, where and when did they expect them? How did they evaluate their own defensive potentialities (i.e., relative degree of confidence or anxiety) at the several points of possible invasion? Did the German leaders intend to mount offensive actions to interfere with Allied second-front plans? What vulnerabilities could be discerned in German morale which would offer possibilities of exploitation to Allied psychological warfare?

The FCC analysts, studying German radio transcripts and domestic press excerpts, made numerous inferences about some of the intelligence problems outlined above. Fortunately, verification data for this period are readily available, especially in excerpts from the Goebbels diary. Consequently, it has been possible to evaluate the accuracy of many, though not all, of the inferences made.

The appraisal which follows shows the FCC analysts to have been remarkably successful over a period of time in inferring the situational estimates and propaganda calculations made by Goebbels and other Nazi leaders. This record must be assessed in the light of the following factors:

1. Consistently accurate inferences were made by the FCC despite the fact that, as in Case Study No. 12.1 (1942), it was not apprised of the forthcoming Allied invasions nor briefed as to which specific problems it should consider. (It is certainly possible that additional and even better inferences could have been produced had the FCC analysts been briefed.)

2. German propaganda materials available for analysis by the FCC in 1943 included a generous sampling of contemporary German newspapers (not available in 1942) and a somewhat better coverage of German domestic broadcasts. The availability of these materials permitted sharper comparisons between what was said to the *domestic* and to *foreign* audiences; comparison of what is said to different audiences is generally of considerable value in making inferences.

3. The FCC staff in 1943 was more numerous, more skilled, and more experienced than it had been in 1942. As a result, more intensive analyses of German materials were undertaken.

Since the accuracy or error of most of the important inferences was verified in this case study, the following presentation will either omit or summarize briefly nonverified inferences.

Inference 1. In the middle of March, 1943, Goebbels ordered a strong propaganda campaign on the second front, the defensive character of which was obvious:

> Inasmuch as the theme of invasion is again being given greater emphasis [abroad], I direct our news and propaganda services to beat the drum hard (*Goebbels Diary,* March 17, 1943, p. 302).

This change in propaganda policy was noted by the FCC shortly thereafter, and a number of inferences were drawn from the content of Goebbels' propaganda.

FCC	GOEBBELS
It is Second Front season again. . . . Berlin steps up its Second Front propaganda (*CEA* #11, March 26, 1943, p. C-7).[45] Dr. Goebbels has apparently decreed a state of propaganda emergency in preparation for the Second Front (*CEA* #12, April 2, 1943, p. B-11). Berlin takes it for granted that a European invasion will be attempted (*CEA* #11, March 26, 1943, p. C-7). This week's [propaganda] campaign may represent a recent conviction in Berlin that an invasion is *now imminent* (*CEA* #12, April 2, 1943, p. B-12; italics supplied).	Supreme Command West speculates on a European invasion between March 20–30 by the English which I deprecate since the English don't have enough shipping space in my opinion (Microfilm Goebbels diary, March 12, 1943). Our military men, too, have let themselves be influenced by the scope of these discussions [i.e., Allied statements] and are expecting an attempt at invasion by the English during this summer. I don't believe it will happen (*Goebbels Diary,* March 18, 1943, p. 305).

Analyst's Reasoning. 1. "The increase of references to a Second Front is more marked on the German domestic than on the German short-wave beams. There are no assertions of the impossibility that a foothold can be established. The 'Fortress of Europe' is scarcely mentioned this week to the German home listener. More significantly, he is not told (as is the short-wave audience) that the invasion will end like Dieppe."[46] The implicit reasoning was that, if a propagandist prepares his domestic audience for possible successes to be achieved by an opponent's initiative, it must be that he expects, or at least does not rule out, such an initiative. It may be noted that communications to the *domestic* audience were considered by the analyst as providing particularly sensitive indicators of the propagandist's intentions and expectations. The FCC analyst reasoned further that Goebbels, being a skillful propagandist, would want to prepare his own people for any forthcoming enemy blow in order to minimize the shock to morale that it would entail. In brief, then, the inference rested upon the identification of a preparation goal being pursued by Nazi propaganda vis-à-vis its own people.

The analyst might have carried this analysis a step further. The content characteristics noted by him could well have been taken as evidence not only that Goebbels expected an invasion attempt soon but that he was somewhat concerned as to *the degree of success which the Allies might achieve*. The evidence for this additional inference would be the absence of the customary propaganda assertions that the Allies would not be able to establish a foothold, and the propagandist's unwillingness to make the comforting prediction that the Allied attempt would end in another Dieppe. Avoidance of such a propaganda commitment about an uncertain future may be taken as an indirect preparation of the domestic audience for possible setbacks.

2. Goebbels' expectation that an invasion attempt was imminent was deduced by the analyst in another manner as well. He noted that "the present propaganda alignment resembles that which was suddenly ordered last summer [i.e., 1942], just four weeks before Dieppe. The similarity," he reasoned, "may be of some significance. The former campaign was quite possibly initiated following the receipt of intelligence to the effect that invasion preparations were already under way." The conclusion followed: "If so, this week's campaign may represent a recent conviction in Berlin that an invasion is now imminent."[47] In this case, then, the inference rested upon the identification of a propaganda pattern, the precise content of which, however, was not spelled out.

Inference 2. During the same period (late March and early April, 1943), the FCC analyst also attempted to account for certain aspects of the *propaganda strategy* behind Goebbels' talk of an Allied invasion. (In the first inference, described above, the FCC analyst deduced a Nazi expectation that an Allied invasion might be imminent.)

FCC

[Noting Berlin's "we-are-ready" boasts apropos of a second-front attempt:] This, of course, is an essential ingredient. Since the Germans obviously expect an invasion, they must put on a bold front to the outside world (*CEA* #11, March 26, 1943, p. C-8).

Dr. Goebbels' strategy is to capitalize on the anxieties which inevitably accompany the period of waiting (*CEA* #12, April 2, 1943, p. B-12).

GOEBBELS

We must under no circumstances give an impression of weakness, even though our troop reserves in the West are at present very weak and we are still taking a dangerous risk. . . .

We are therefore faced with the necessity of taking this question up with more assurance than the situation warrants. If, however, we were to give any indication of weakness, that would be nothing short of an invitation to the enemy to attempt such an invasion. I am also convinced that a firm attitude on our part will somewhat spoil the appetite of the English for an invasion. . . . The firmer the attitude we take, the stronger will those [in England] who oppose an invasion become. I issued instructions to be firmer on this question than hitherto. . . . Every day we win is a clear gain. For if the English wait four or six more weeks their invasion, assuming they planned it, would hardly have any prospect of succeeding (*Goebbels Diary*, March 17, 1943, p. 302).

Comment. The FCC analyst was correct in implying that the Nazi elite did not expect to discourage the second-front attempt altogether. He recognized the "bold-front" nature of German propaganda and correctly inferred that it was intended to stir up Allied anxieties. However, the analyst did not grasp that Goebbels' propaganda aim went further and included efforts to cover up the weakness of German defenses and to scare the British into delaying the invasion. These more refined inferences might have been possible had the analyst succeeded first in deducing that Goebbels was concerned about the outcome of the invasion attempt. (The missed opportunity to make the latter inference is discussed under Inference 1 on pp. 193–94.) Had he been aware of Goebbels' concern (confined to domestic broadcasts), the analyst might have contrasted it with the "bold-front," "we-are-ready" boasts in foreign propaganda. He could then have deduced that Goebbels was hiding his true concern from the enemy and playing for time. Here, then, is a good example of the logical interrelationship between separate inferences which may or (as in this case) may not be exploited by the propaganda analyst.

Analyst's Reasoning. Comparing current German propaganda with that preceding the Dieppe raid, the analyst noted that the propaganda intentions were different in the two cases. In 1942 "the intent was clearly to discourage the attempt." Then the German propagandist apparently had believed that Allied invasion plans would be dictated by political considerations—i.e., Russian diplomatic pressure plus demands by Allied public opinion for a second front—rather than purely military considerations. In that situation, Goebbels thought that skillful propaganda on his part might discourage the Allies from making the attempt. The situation in 1943, reasoned the analyst, was different: "This year, the Germans believe, will obviously bring one or more invasions, and attempts at discouragement would be absurd." Hence, concluded the analyst, "Dr. Goebbels' strategy is to capitalize on the anxieties which inevitably accompany the period of waiting." [48] Implicit here, too, was an estimate that Goebbels thought the Allied decision had been firmly made and was not subject to conflicting pressures within the Allied camp.

Inference 3. Shortly thereafter, the Nazi elite's expectation of an imminent cross-Channel invasion was modified by fresh intelligence reports. Goebbels was apprised of this new strategic estimate, and his propaganda policy was altered accordingly. Almost immediately, too, the FCC analyst spotted the change in propaganda and correctly inferred the underlying shift in Nazi expectations.

FCC	GOEBBELS
Hence, it may be deduced that Berlin is convinced either that there will be no early invasion attempt along the Atlantic, or that any such attempt will be repelled	In the West only diversionary maneuvers will in all likelihood take place, *assuming that the secret reports of our agents are correct.* Personally I consider this

(*CEA* #14, April 16, 1943, p. B-7).

quite plausible. I don't believe that the English and the Americans will attempt to break in on us in the West as they know only too well that they will bleed to death there (*Goebbels Diary*, April 11, 1943, pp. 324-25; italics supplied).

Analyst's Reasoning. The analyst noted a shift in propaganda to the *domestic* German audience. Previously, Goebbels had cautiously avoided predicting another Dieppe and had indirectly prepared his domestic audience for possible Allied successes (see Inference 1, p. 193). Now, the analyst noted, Goebbels permitted himself boastful predictions: "German domestic programs give great attention to the Atlantic Wall which is depicted as so formidable that it may discourage any attempt at invasion. . . . Should the attempt be made, the invaders will be thrown back into the sea. Most comments make no explicit allowance for the possibility of temporary footholds being attained—[there are] no preparations . . . to accustom German opinion to the idea that bridgeheads might be established."

The inference, then, rested upon the analyst's recognition of the fact that the earlier aim of preparing the German audience for the possibility of Allied second-front successes was no longer being pursued. The inference was supported also by an estimate of Goebbels' skillfulness as a propagandist, aptly stated by the analyst: "No responsible propagandist allows himself specific boasts if there is any likelihood that his words can soon be thrown back at him. (The fear that at some remote date they may come home to roost is not a deterrent; it is assumed that listeners' memories are short.)"

Inference 4. Concurrently with the above inference, the FCC analyst speculated also as to the *location* at which the Nazi elite expected the Allied attack to come and as to its *relative degree of confidence* in repulsing an invasion at different points.

FCC	GOEBBELS
If the Germans [Nazi elite] are apprehensive over an early invasion, therefore, it is not their Atlantic fortifications which cause them misgivings. Their uncertainty more likely has to do with the Aegean or the eastern Medi-	It would appear that the invasion of the English and the Americans will have Sardinia and Sicily, possibly also the southeast, as the target, so as to come close to the Rumanian oil fields. [Goebbels' estimate was derived from

terranean (*CEA* #14, April 16, 1943, p. B-8).

Last week's symptoms of insecurity regarding an invasion from the South continue (*CEA* #15, April 23, 1943, p. C-7).

secret intelligence provided personally by Admiral Canaris, chief of the Abwehr.] (*Goebbels Diary*, April 11, 1943, p. 324.)

If an invasion were to take place in the southeast, there would be cause to fear that large parts of the population would immediately desert us. The Balkans are still the powder barrel of Europe. It is to be hoped that the English and Americans are not aware of the chances beckoning them there. I am more than ever convinced that if they attempt an invasion, that's where it will come (*Goebbels Diary*, April 29, 1943, p. 348).

Analyst's Reasoning. The analyst noted that the strong expressions of confidence made by Nazi propagandists with respect to the impregnability of their Atlantic fortifications were not accompanied by a similar flow of confident assertions about the Mediterranean and Aegean. This difference in content was the cue for the analyst's inference. In *CEA* #14 the analyst observed that references to the Mediterranean-Aegean area were completely absent in German broadcasts. In *CEA* #15 he noted: "Specific place names are reiterated in describing Atlantic fortifications, but assurances concerning the Mediterranean are either vague or absent." (This observation was illustrated by several quotations from German short-wave commentators, e.g., "The Atlantic Wall guarantees immunity of attack from Norway to Southern France. The Southeastern and Southern extremities of Europe are provided with natural, God-given defenses. . . . The Axis is prepared with mobile defenses to take care of any effort of enemy nations to find a vulnerable spot in that portion.")

This inference appears to have been based on an implicit generalization which might be paraphrased as follows: A marked difference in the *frequency* and *specificity* of propaganda references to one's defensive capabilities in the various areas in which an enemy initiative may take place reflects a difference in degree of confidence regarding one's ability to meet an initiative in those areas, the confidence being greater for the area to which the more frequent and more specific references are made. (Such a generalization implies the use of the *direct* method, since no reference is made to propaganda strategy.[49])

Comment. The FCC analyst did not clearly distinguish between (*a*) the Nazi elite's expectation of an initiative by the opponent, (*b*) its estimate of the imminence of such an expected initiative, and (*c*) its degree of confidence in the outcome. As a matter of fact, the analyst avoided committing himself on the first two problems—i.e., whether the Nazis really feared an invasion attempt in the Mediterranean and, if so, how imminent they thought it to be. He merely stated that *if* the Nazis were apprehensive "over an early invasion," their satisfaction with defensive preparations in the Mediterranean-Aegean was less than that with the Atlantic fortifications.

That the Nazis' reluctance to speak at all about the Mediterranean in their domestic propaganda might have a slightly different explanation was recognized by the analyst: "Perhaps it is believed that there is little German [public] anxiety on that score, or perhaps, in the absence of any concrete basis for reassurance, it is deemed wiser not to arouse anxiety by vague reassurance." [50] This interpretation, of course, would not have been incompatible with the inference that the Nazi leaders themselves were dissatisfied with their defensive preparedness in the Mediterranean.

Hindsight suggests that the analyst might have plausibly inferred that the Nazis were not worried about an imminent Allied attack in the Mediterranean-Aegean. The reasoning for this would have been as follows: *If* an *imminent* attack were expected, some preparation of the home audience for the blow would have been made in domestic propaganda. The lack of such preparation indicated, therefore, that no *imminent* attack was expected.

Inference 5. At about this time, too, the FCC noted a change in the German propaganda line about the Atlantic Wall. German propaganda had previously strongly emphasized its value as a *defensive* bastion; now, noted the FCC, it was suggesting that the Atlantic fortifications could also serve as a starting point for operations of an *offensive* character. Was the FCC analyst correct in labeling this a change in propaganda line? If so, what was its significance?

FCC	GOEBBELS
[The FCC analyst infers that the recent glorification of the At-	I give our propaganda the directive not to speak any more of

lantic Wall as a defensive barrier] has lent itself to certain undesirable interpretations. The current praise of the Atlantic Wall is embarrassing because earlier in the war German propaganda had minimized the value of static defenses [e.g., the Maginot line].

The task of the week for German short-wave broadcasts is to correct these [undesirable interpretations] (*CEA* #15, April 23, 1943, p. C-6).

Instructions seem to have been given to emphasize that the fortifications were built for offensive as well as defensive operations (*CEA* #16, April 30, 1943, p. C-8).

As promises of taking the offensive such statements are vague, indeed. As propaganda, they are little more than defenses for being on the defensive (*CEA* #15, April 23, 1943, p. C-7).

Fortress Europe. We are not proposing to go on the defensive in a propaganda sense (Microfilm Goebbels diary, April 12, 1943).

[Goebbels' new directive as it appeared in the *Zeitschriftendienst* (*Z.D.*), official propaganda directives for magazines, was as follows:]

This supplement has as its aim to stimulate periodicals to undertake the writing of articles in which they can present to readers in Germany and abroad the double role which fortified zones and fortresses play in defensive-offensive warfare. . . . It is to be emphasized that fortifications do not serve solely as defensive apparatus within the framework of contemporary warfare (*Z.D.* No. 8681, April 16, 1943).

[Later a new consideration appears to have led Goebbels to modify the defensive tone of his propaganda even further:]

The *Times* [London] has suddenly discovered that our position is exceedingly weak and our propaganda equally so. As a matter of fact in recent weeks we have limited ourselves too much to a defensive propaganda. This must be changed at once. I have given suitable orders to the press and radio (*Goebbels Diary*, April 22, 1943, p. 339).

Analyst's Reasoning. The analyst discounted the possibility of any real offensive intention by correctly diagnosing the specific propaganda purpose behind innuendoes regarding the "offensive potentialities" of defensive fortifications. The inference was based upon a careful qualitative analysis of General Dittmar's talk on the subject and of other materials as well. Dittmar did not conceal the fact that the recent glorification of the Atlantic Wall by Nazi propagandists had evoked unintended negative reactions from German audiences:

> Certain foreign radio and press voices . . . have represented the great emphasis on the Atlantic Wall by the Germans as being an obvious inconsistency. . . . Once, so they say, we could not be emphatic enough in our rejection of those ideas (associated with) the conception of the Maginot Line; now it is we ourselves who have awakened this long forgotten idea.[51]

It was clear, too, that Dittmar's propaganda task was to correct these impressions. Thus, the inference rested upon a correct identification of the underlying purpose (to raise domestic morale) of a propaganda line which superficially suggested an aggressive German action.

Inference 6. With Axis forces cleared out of Tunis by early May, 1943, Nazi concern as to the locus of the next Allied move mounted. In the coming weeks it would be important for Allied intelligence to ascertain Axis expectations regarding forthcoming Allied moves and Axis plans for meeting such moves.

A brief résumé of Allied military plans at this stage will serve to throw into focus the problem facing German strategic intelligence.[52] HUSKY (the invasion of Sicily) had been decided upon at the Casablanca Conference in January, 1943, as one of two alternative plans, the other being the capture of Sardinia and Corsica. At this time, as Eisenhower observes, the ultimate objectives of the Allies in the Mediterranean had not been fixed.

Both Eisenhower and Marshall (and others) believed that the Mediterranean should remain subsidiary in Allied planning and that operations there should not interfere with the build-up for the cross-Channel invasion in 1944. Not the least factor influencing the decision on behalf of HUSKY was that it "avoided a commitment to indefinite strategic offensives in the area" and, because of Sicily's relatively small size, "its occupation after capture would not absorb unforeseen amounts of Allied strength." Eisenhower's recommendation, presented at the Casablanca Conference, had been to attack Sicily if the Allies' primary purpose was to clear the Mediterranean for use of Allied shipping, but to invade Sardinia and Corsica if the purpose was to knock Italy out of the war by invading the Italian mainland. (It is interesting to note that Hitler believed that the Allied invasion would strike at Sardinia and Corsica, whereas Mussolini thought Sicily was threatened; see p. 204, below.)

In late May, after the Tunisian victory, the Allies had to decide what additional moves to take after the coming invasion of Sicily. Churchill argued for a continued exploitation of the situation in the Mediterranean. The Marshall-Eisenhower duo, however, opposed any commitment that might have the result, if not the intention, of weakening OVERLORD (the cross-Channel invasion for 1944) or possibly replacing it with an all-out campaign for winning the war through an Italian approach. "These and other reasons," says Eisenhower, "led to an agreement which, in effect, left the exploitation of the Sicilian operation to my judgment—but expected me to take advantage of any favorable opportunity to rush into Italy—and which emphasized the great value of the Foggia airfields. Since a major port was necessary to sustain us in Italy, the city of Naples was named as the other principal locality desired by the Allies."

In sum, then, (a) Allied plans for military action did *not* include a cross-Channel invasion in 1943;[53] (b) aims in the Mediterranean were limited, flexible, and somewhat opportunistic (with some conflict among the planners as to how far the exploitation of successes in this area should go); (c) no plan for an invasion of the Balkans was agreed upon.

In *CEA* #17, May 7, 1943, the FCC analyst noted Dittmar's admission that geographical features of the eastern Mediterranean offered "specially favorable conditions" for a landing and his further implicit admission that the Allies might score certain minor successes in the eastern Mediterranean and Italy. At the same time, it was noted that Goebbels himself avoided labeling the second front an impossibility. Another important German domestic radio commentator spoke of the German determination to prevent a "permanent invasion." The analyst did little more than point out these significant statements, assuming perhaps that their meaning was clear. He added that these "best-informed Nazi spokesmen" were already drawing the next line of propagandistic defense in case of an Allied success somewhere in Europe. Apparently the analyst did not feel secure enough at this time to venture inferences about Nazi estimates of the imminence and/or location of an Allied initiative.

The following week's report[54] found the analyst still reluctant to draw further inferences. He noted merely that there was some disagreement among Nazi-controlled radio stations as to where the attempt would be made, while the Berlin radio itself preferred not to mention specific locations.

In the next week, however, the FCC produced a quantitative analysis of major import.[55] All references to possible invasion areas in Berlin broadcasts (to North and South America) were noted on a weekly trend basis for the preceding three weeks. Results of the tabulation were as follows:

1. The total number of references to places of possible invasion (including those to Europe generally) had doubled from the first week to the third. (Presumably the sample of broadcasts was held constant.)

2. A striking shift in attention from the Atlantic coast to the Mediterranean area took place. (For the three one-week periods the number of references to the Atlantic and Mediterranean areas, respectively, was 6 to 0, 9 to 10, 6 to 21.)

3. While in the first week of May references to possible invasion areas had been entirely *general* (e.g., "Europe," "Atlantic Coast," etc.), there was an increasing trend toward *specific* references in the next two weeks (e.g., "Corsica," "Crete," "Sicily," etc.). In the third and last week of the study, the ratio of specific to general references was 1 : 1.

The analyst drew no inferences from the first two findings; he brushed them aside with the explanation that the growth of attention to the Mediterranean area should be expected after the surrender of the Axis forces in Africa (see comment section, below).

The third finding, however, elicited the interpretation that the shift toward specific references reflected the "increased concreteness and imminence of the [invasion] issue" in the eyes of the Nazis. (The implicit generalization was that greater specificity of references to the geographical area of an expected enemy initiative reflects increased imminence of the issue in the propagandist's mind.[56]) The correctness of this inference seems clear in view of the operational order quoted below under "German leaders" (p. 204).

Comment. The analyst might well have used the first two findings as additional support for his inference and, as well, as support for a further inference—which he did not make—that the Nazis were now expecting an Allied initiative in the Mediterranean rather than in the Atlantic coastal area. The implicit generalization underlying such an inference would have been as follows: In the context of *heightened* propaganda speculation about the possible areas of an enemy initiative, a *narrowing of focus* to one area reflects a private estimate that the initiative will come in that area.[57]

As it turned out, the analyst did eventually make just this inference several weeks later. Available verification material indicates that Nazi leaders had formulated their estimate in early May. The analyst, though correct, therefore, was several weeks late with this inference.

FCC	GERMAN LEADERS

If Nazi propagandists now do not follow this precedent they are probably convinced that no landing will be attempted on the Atlantic Coast in the near future. [Precedent referred to is German propaganda preceding the Dieppe raid, when Goebbels explicitly predicted and discussed forthcoming Allied attempts at invasion.] (*CEA* #21, June 4, 1943, p. C-11.)

As to where the invasion is coming, analysis of German shortwave broadcasts seems to indicate that Berlin is more certain that it won't come in Western Europe than not in Southern Europe (*CEA* #22, June 11, 1943, p. D-5).

Laudations of the Atlantic Wall are considerably reduced [in German propaganda]. Attention turns instead to the fortifications and preparations in Southern and Southeastern Europe—undoubtedly reflecting German apprehensions about that region. . . . Attention remains focused on Italy, probably the first choice for the invasion locale in German guesses (*CEA* #25, July 1, 1943, p. B-11).

Operational order: telegram of May 12, 1943 (U.S. Army, A.G.O., Departmental Records Branch, T.A.G.O., *Führer Directives . . . German Armed Forces, 1942–1945,* pp. 79 f.):

Following the impending end of fighting in Tunisia, it is to be expected that the Anglo-Americans will try to continue the operations in the Mediterranean in quick succession. Preparations for this purpose must in general be considered concluded. The following are most endangered:

A. In the western Mediterranean, Sardinia, Corsica and Sicily.

B. In the eastern Mediterranean, the Peloponnesus and the Dodecanese Islands. . . .

Measures regarding Sardinia and the Peloponnesus take precedence over everything else.

Report of Führer Conference of May 14, 1943: The Führer does not agree with Duce that the most likely invasion point is Sicily. Furthermore, he believes that the discovered Anglo-Saxon order confirms the assumption that the planned attacks will be directed mainly against Sardinia and the Peloponnesus (U.S. Navy Dept.,

Führer Conferences on Matters Dealing with the German Navy, 1943, Washington, p. 63; quoted also in Anthony Martienssen, *Hitler and His Admirals,* E. P. Dutton & Co., New York, 1949, p. 171).

[Goebbels evaluated an Allied broadcast from Allied GHQ in North Africa to the French people, which suggested that they should sit at their radio sets late into the night and wait for important news, as follows:]

I think this whole matter is a gigantic bluff. The English and Americans won't stage an invasion at this time. They haven't prepared sufficiently for it, and the whole matter is still too uncertain (*Goebbels Diary,* May 18, 1943, p. 383).

[Goebbels:] I had a long discussion with Admiral Canaris about the data available for figuring out English intentions. Canaris has gained possession of a letter written by the English General Staff to General Alexander. . . . I don't know whether the letter is merely camouflage—Canaris denies this energetically—or whether it actually corresponds to the facts. In any case the general outline of English plans for this summer revealed here seems on the whole to tally. According to it, the English and Americans are planning several sham attacks during the coming months—one in the West, one in Sicily, and one on the islands of the Dodecanese.

These attacks are to immobilize our troops stationed there and thereby make English forces available for other and more serious operations. These operations are to involve Sardinia and the Peloponnesus (*Goebbels Diary*, May 25, 1943, p. 394).[58]

Inference 7. What defensive possibilities did the Nazis have? How did they evaluate, for example, the role of their U-boats for anti-invasion purposes? Detecting a significant retrenchment in Nazi propaganda claims about the U-boats, the analyst inferred that Nazi leaders no longer appeared confident of the U-boats as a major anti-invasion weapon. Nazi propaganda on the relation between the U-boats and a second front passed through several phases. At first, it was claimed that the toll the U-boats were taking would make it impossible for the Allies to attempt an invasion. This claim was withdrawn (see Case Study No. 12.1, Inference 5, p. 182) in favor of a new claim that the U-boats, by taking a heavy toll of invading fleets and by eating into Allied supply lines, would insure the eventual defeat of any invasion footholds established by the Allies.

FCC

One of the most interesting developments in this week's German discussion of the Second Front is the virtual omission of the argument that the Axis will thwart Allied invasion plans on the high seas. . . . There is extraordinary reticence this week on Axis submarine protection against the Second Front (*CEA* #19, May 21, 1943, p. C-9).

Significantly, considerable restraint is now being exercised by Nazi [domestic] propaganda not to relate U-boat warfare to a second front or to the outcome of the war at large (*CEA* #20, May 28, 1943, p. C-10).

GERMAN LEADERS

[In a conference with leaders of the Italian Navy in Rome on May 12, 1943, Doenitz, Commander-in-Chief of German U-boats, said that he:] is convinced that U-boats will never be able to stop an invasion—they would only be of nuisance value. . . . The battle on land alone is decisive; therefore the most important part of the Navy's task is to make battle on land possible, which means safeguarding the supply lines across the sea. . . .

[He urged:] We must use every available means to get as much material to the islands as possible. . . . If there are not enough small vessels, U-boats will have to

be used [to transport supplies]
. . . because U-boats are not decisive in battle (quoted in Martienssen, *op. cit.,* p. 166).

These inferences were part of a broader analysis of the major readjustment in Nazi propaganda on the U-boats that was taking
place in connection with a recent drastic slump in U-boat successes.
The FCC analyst deemed it of importance that, in addition to employing the usual minimization and compensation techniques to
cover lack of U-boat successes, the Berlin propagandists were making
"major adaptations" in their *domestic* propaganda. For example, as
the analyst noted, "unprecedented admissions of [Allied] strength
in the war at sea" [59] were being made, including explicit statements
that technical superiority had passed over to Allied anti-U-boat
weapons. It was in this context that the analyst noted the omission of
the long-standing, familiar propaganda theme that the U-boats
would thwart second-front attempts.

While the analyst's inference was phrased cautiously, it carried
with it the implication that the Nazis' estimate of the U-boats' defensive utility against a second front had appreciably declined.

Inference 8. Eisenhower describes his concern at the time lest
Axis intelligence succeed in estimating the location and timing of the
forthcoming invasion of Sicily.[60] But, as the battle reports describing
the initial phase of the invasion reached him, Eisenhower concluded
that "it was evident that the enemy had been badly deceived as to
the point of attack. His best formations were located largely on the
western end of the island," whereas the attacking forces had landed
in the south and east.

It appears that the German High Command continued to believe
in early July as in May that Sardinia and the Peloponnesus were
especially in danger, but this cannot be established conclusively on
the basis of available historical materials. Colonel-General Student,
at that time in command of German paratroops in Italy, stated
later that the attack on Sicily came as a surprise: "We believed the
Allies would invade Sardinia first." [61] But this, of course, does not
rule out the possibility that higher German military leaders had a
different estimate at the time.

The most specific FCC inference regarding the Nazi estimate as to
location of the forthcoming Allied invasion was simply "Italy": "Attention [in German propaganda] remains focused on Italy, prob-

ably the first choice for the invasion locale in German guesses." [62] Whether the analyst might have done better than this is difficult to judge, since it is not known how specific the top Nazi estimate itself was.

Inference 9. Where did the Nazis expect the Allies to strike after the conquest of Sicily? The FCC analyst for some reason did not give much attention to this problem. He noted that the German domestic radio was careful not to focus the expectations of its listeners on a single spot: " 'Obviously we must expect an enemy landing attempt at any place on the European continent. . . .' " [63] He noted, too, that further amphibious Allied operations were explicitly predicted by responsible German writers. Finally, he noted that the German wireless press service, Transocean, was busy speculating about possible invasion points all the way around the European perimeter, from the north to the southeast.[64] But the analyst did not infer, as he might have from such propaganda characteristics, that the Nazi leadership was *uncertain* as to where the next blow might fall.

The actual expectations of the Nazi leaders at this time are difficult to piece together from available materials. According to Goebbels, Hitler in late July (following the invasion of Sicily) anticipated that the Allies might land ". . . possibly in Genoa, in order to cut off the German troops stationed in southern Italy. We must anticipate this, he said." [65] This expectation may have changed in the following weeks.

Later, the analyst noted that German propaganda treated the Allied invasion of Calabria (the southern tip of Italy) "as a distinctly secondary operation." [66] He interpreted this propaganda line as an effort "to soften the impact of this attack on Europe and to dismiss its military consequences." However valid this interpretation may have been, the analyst failed to consider whether this propaganda line might not *also* mean that the Nazis regarded the Calabria landing as a camouflage for the main Allied invasion effort which was to come elsewhere. As it turned out, that was what they expected:

The Fuehrer is still convinced that the English and Americans are merely carrying out a camouflage maneuver in Calabria. He believes they will shortly try an invasion in the West. The increasing concentration of air attacks in the West and certain accumulations of shipping units in the harbors of the mother country [England] seem to point in this direction. . . . But the Fuehrer is on the lookout. He doesn't, under any circumstances, want to be surprised by Churchill and Roosevelt (*Goebbels Diary,* September 8, 1943, p. 425).

The aim of our military activity in Italy must consist in freeing a number of divisions for the Balkans. For without a doubt the spearhead of the Anglo-American invasion will be pointed in that direction in the immediate future (*ibid.,* September 10, 1943, p. 433).

The Fuehrer is somewhat worried lest the English now attempt an invasion in the West. . . . The Fuehrer expects the Anglo-American invasion attempt to come in the Netherlands. We are weakest there, and the population would be most inclined to give the necessary local support to such an undertaking. . . . The exceptionally heavy bombing attacks which the English have launched against the western lines of communication for some days are rather suspicious. Could it be that this is the prelude to an attempt at invasion? The fleet, too, has repeatedly come up close to the European western coast, has started some fireworks, but has always left again according to schedule. This time of year is the best imaginable for an invasion in the West. But only a short time remains . . . (*ibid.,* p. 434).[67]

CASE STUDY No. 12.3: GERMAN EXPECTATION OF THE DEFECTION OF ITALY AS AN ALLY

This case history is concerned not with military initiatives (as were Case Studies Nos. 12.1 and 12.2) but with what may be called "diplomatic" initiatives. Mussolini's resignation took place on July 25, 1943, and the surrender of Italy on September 8, 1943. Both events were more or less expected by the Allied leaders, whose military strategy in the Mediterranean, indeed, included precisely such aims. The surrender itself, of course, was preceded by negotiations with Allied representatives. The important problem for Allied intelligence, therefore, was to note whether these Italian developments were foreseen by the *German* leadership and, if so, what countermeasures were prepared.

While the quality of the FCC's analysis in the present case may not have been overly impressive, there is some reason to believe that better results can be achieved by propaganda analysis in cases of this kind.

Inference 1. In mid-May, 1943, the FCC analyst noted: "German propaganda gives the impression that there is nearly universal expectation among the Germans [domestic public] that the Italians will fold up soon." [68] At this early stage, in mid-May, 1943, the analyst did not take up the question of the Nazi leadership's expectations on the subject. Actually, apart from a generalized (and typical) suspiciousness on Hitler's part, [69] the Nazis were apparently genuinely surprised by Mussolini's ouster on July 25. Goebbels had commented on May 18: "We must expect the English and Americans to continue to wage a war of nerves on Italy, but I assume that Mussolini and the Fascist party will be equal to it." [70] And, again, on May 24: "I don't believe the Fascist party intends to surrender voluntarily at any point in this war. On the contrary, I am convinced the Italian people, once they defend their own soil, will fight much more bravely than they did in North Africa, not to mention the Eastern Front." [71]

This optimistic estimate of the Italian ally was not changed in the following weeks. It does not appear that German intelligence gave any forewarning. The "confidential information" which Goebbels mentions as having been received on July 24 (diary entry for July 25) reported merely that the Fascist Grand Council had been called at the instance of the Fascist Old Guard for the purpose of strengthening the war effort. [72] When the first news came through, Goebbels thought it "almost unbelievable" and noted that at Hitler's GHQ "nobody can figure out just what really happened." [73] Goebbels' account leaves little doubt but that the German leadership was completely surprised by Mussolini's overthrow. The awkward, fumbling manner in which Nazi propaganda reacted to the event, noted by the FCC analyst, also implied lack of anticipation of such an event.

FCC	German Leaders
The initial Nazi treatment of Mussolini's resignation seemed to be a confession that no line which the Nazis regarded as tenable had been formulated in advance or was formulated quickly as the news broke (*CEA* #29, July 29, 1943, p. A-1).	Everyone at the Propaganda Ministry was speechless. Finally it was decided to say that the Duce was ill. For a few days Goebbels was so upset that he failed to write his weekly editorial. What line was he to take? (Curt Riess, *Joseph Goebbels,* Doubleday & Co., Garden City, N.Y., 1948, p. 266).
	It is quite obvious that the German people are uneasy and deeply distressed because we can't tell them anything at present about

the background of the Italian
crisis. What are we to tell them,
anyway? We can't say, much less
write, what we think personally.
Anything we can write will fail
to explain the Italian crisis to our
people (*Goebbels Diary,* July 27,
1943, pp. 410–11).

The analyst presented a fairly detailed description of the Nazi
propaganda treatment of Mussolini's resignation which led him to
this inference. He noted that Berlin's first mention of the news came
five hours after Rome's announcement, which was relatively slow
reaction time for Berlin. Moreover, Berlin announcements were very
brief, sticking to the straight news bulletins issued by Rome without
any comment other than an occasional bromide as to Mussolini's
"illness." Two days later Berlin dropped the ill-health version, apolo-
gized for its reticence, and, as the analyst put it, "tried to move cautiously in a situation studded with the possibility of further shocks."
The situation in Italy was referred to as "fluid," a Nazi propaganda
stereotype borrowed from military reporting and designed to cloak
the fact that German leadership had lost control of the situation
and was uncertain as to future developments.

Inference 2. What countermeasures, if any, would the Nazi leadership take in Italy? The answer to this question depended in part on
the Nazis' estimate of the reliability of the statement by Badoglio,
Mussolini's successor as chief of state, that Italy would continue
the war. The FCC's contributions on these questions were couched
in general terms only, a fact which necessarily reduced their utility
even though they were reasonably accurate.

FCC	GERMAN LEADERS
There are indications, however, that Nazi propagandists are not unaware of the necessity to brace the Germans against more than the initial shock of Mussolini's downfall.	[Hitler's analysis of the Italian situation, as paraphrased by Goebbels, presented at a conference held on July 26 at the Führer's headquarters, to which all top Nazi leaders had been hastily summoned to consider the crisis:]
As to Badoglio, Nazi propaganda cannot afford to doubt the veracity of his declaration that Italy will continue the war . . . ;	The Fuehrer first gave us his analysis of the situation. . . . In the final analysis this crisis

on the other hand, Nazi irritation is evident in German insistence on Italy's *national* interests in continuing the war. The Nazi-Fascist marriage of true love is becoming a German-Italian marriage of convenience; . . . the Nazis could rediscover their love for persecuted *fascism* by turning against the new *Italian* power holders (*CEA* #29, July 29, 1943, pp. A-4, 5; italics partially supplied).

was of course directed against Germany. The idea was to take Italy out of the war. . . . The assertion in his [Badoglio's] proclamation that the war would continue meant exactly nothing. There was nothing else he [Badoglio] could say, for any statement to the contrary would immediately have called the German Wehrmacht into action. . . .

The Fuehrer intends to deliver a great coup [the plan to land a parachute division in Rome in order to kidnap Badoglio, King Victor Emmanuel, etc.].

The Fuehrer is firmly determined to see to it that Italy does not betray the German Reich a second time. . . .

The big question during our conference in the Fuehrer's GHQ is whether the measures planned against the Badoglio clique . . . should be prepared with great care, which would certainly require a week, or whether it is necessary to act quickly and by improvisation. [Hitler wanted to act quickly, but Rommel, now in supreme command over German forces in Italy, was more conservative. No final decision was reached. It was finally agreed, however, to exclude the Vatican from any countermeasures taken. Hitler at first had wanted to seize the Vatican also.] (*Goebbels Diary*, July 27, 1943, pp. 407–16; see also the account in U.S. Navy Dept., *op. cit.*, *1943*, pp. 102 ff., and Martienssen, *op. cit.*, pp. 180–92.)

Analyst's Reasoning. The analyst noted that German propaganda was now emphasizing the theme of German strength rather than Axis strength. Thus, three leading newspapers pointedly stressed this new theme on the same day (July 26):

Germany's confidence is based on the knowledge of its own strength (*Völkischer Beobachter*).

The German nations [*sic*] has always known that war is not an easy matter, but it knows its own strength (*Berliner Lokalanzeiger*).

The *Deutsche Allgemeine Zeitung* likewise stresses that the German people are looking forward to coming developments with supreme confidence since *they know their own strength*.

The analyst deduced that this line was based upon a new Propaganda Ministry directive. The emphasis on German rather than Axis strength, he inferred, was designed as consolation for German domestic morale and as a prop in case Italy surrendered.

Inference 3. In the next few weeks the analyst noted the continuing reticence of German propaganda on the subject of Italy. He inferred several times that the propaganda "vacuum" on Italy was causing the Propaganda Ministry considerable embarrassment because such taciturnity and, especially, the reluctance to give any assurances about future developments had the effect of seriously worrying the German public.[74] The analyst offered an explanation for the Nazi propagandists' refusal to meet the people's demand for more news:

Pending whatever developments are afoot in Rome, this is the time when the propagandist has to take his place behind the diplomat. Any premature speculations on Goebbels' part may not only disturb political negotiations, they may also seriously heighten the tension and uncertainties of the heavily tried German audience. Goebbels, in particular, can not afford to raise expectations which may not come off.

The analyst then added an inference which, while accurate in part, was phrased in general terms and was not clearly shown by him to be based upon propaganda analysis:

It is quite likely that German diplomacy, and probably the High Command as well, in the long run have written off Italy as a military ally, if not as a political one as well.

At this time, German troops were pouring into Italy without interference.[75] More aggressive German plans (Operations ASCHE,

EICHE, and SCHWARZ) were being postponed, though held in readiness for immediate implementation. Hitler himself thought that Badoglio and King Victor Emmanuel were planning "treachery," negotiating with the Germans merely in order to gain time to come to terms with the Allies. Jodl and Doenitz, on the other hand, speculated about the possibility that the Badoglio government's lack of resistance to German measures in Italy might be taken as a desire to rely upon the Germans for support.

It may be noted that the inference that German leaders were uncertain of the sticking power of their ally was deduced indirectly from the propagandist's unwillingness to give the anxious German public any assurances on this point.

Inference 4. The FCC analyst continued to note Nazi concern over Italy's sticking power until the surrender of Italy took place on September 8. He then observed that, apart from long-range preparation, German propaganda had not specifically prepared its home audience for an immediate surrender.

Ever since the Mussolini "resignation," the German domestic radio has given little attention to the faltering ally, in the long-range expectation that the sticking power of the Italians was not overly strong. The term "Axis" almost disappeared from the Berlin radio, Italy was not given a tribute along with the other allies on the occasion of the anniversary of the war, and the will-to-fight of the partner was not glorified since the invasion of Italy. On the other hand, "German and Italian troops" were said to provide the resistance to the invasion and there was no immediate preparatory campaign for the surrender. The German people may have expected the fall of Italy sometime, but the domestic radio and press had not prepared them for a surrender now (*CEA* #35, September 9, 1943, p. A-1).

Goebbels' account makes it clear that the Nazi leadership itself had not received any advance inkling of the timing of Badoglio's move, though they had feared such a development ever since Mussolini's ouster.[76] The failure of the Nazis to prepare their own public in advance for an imminent Italian surrender, therefore, merely reflected their own unpreparedness.

CASE STUDY No. 12.4: GERMAN ESTIMATE OF OUTCOME OF EDEN'S TALKS WITH TURKISH FOREIGN MINISTER, NOVEMBER, 1943

This brief case history illustrates again the problem of inferring the expectations of an elite with regard to an opponent's diplomatic initiative. The talks between Eden and Menemencioglu, Turkish foreign minister, came immediately after the conclusion of the Moscow Conference of Foreign Ministers and aroused considerable speculation about the possibility of Turkey's dropping its neutrality to join the Allies.[77]

Did the Nazi leadership fear that Turkey would respond to possible Allied overtures at this time?

FCC	GOEBBELS
Apparently the Wilhelmstrasse did not feel that a change in Turkish foreign policy would immediately follow from the talks . . . (*CEA* #44, November 12, 1943, p. B-7).	The English make quite a theatrical show of this conference . . . and act as if Turkey were to enter the war tomorrow. I regard this as quite outside the realm of possibility (*Goebbels Diary*, November 8, 1943, p. 501).
	[Goebbels' comment on the Anglo-Turkish communiqué issued after the conclusion of the talks:] The Turkish newspapers are leaving no doubt that Turkey is not thinking of abandoning her position of neutrality. In other words, *developments at the Cairo Conference were exactly as we anticipated and as Papen predicted* (*ibid.*, November 9, 1943, p. 503; italics supplied).

Analyst's Reasoning. Since Goebbels and the German leadership had received explicit assurances from their ambassador to Turkey, von Papen, that Turkey would remain neutral, this case offers a nice opportunity to note precisely how the confidence of the German leaders concerning the outcome of the talks was reflected in Goebbels' propaganda.

The analyst noted that the primary purpose of domestic propaganda appeared to be the desire to shield Germans from the war-of-nerves aspect of these talks. The domestic audience heard only that the meeting was to take place, without any indication of the nature of the talks. No further information was given until November 8, when the domestic radio reported the conclusion of the talks and cited a Turkish press denial of the British suggestion that Turkish foreign policy would be changed.

In other words, Nazi confidence—i.e., the estimate that the outcome of the talks would be not unfavorable to Germany—could be deduced from the fact that *no effort was made to prepare the domestic public for a possible diplomatic setback*. This reasoning, it should be noted, is based exclusively upon the character of domestic propaganda, a more sensitive indicator than foreign propaganda for problems of inferring the elite's private estimates and expectations. (Nazi foreign propaganda at the time charged that pressure was being put upon the Turks to alter their neutrality.)

CASE STUDY NO. 12.5: GERMAN EFFORT TO FORESTALL AN EXPECTED ALLIED PSYCHOLOGICAL-WARFARE INITIATIVE

This case study illustrates how propaganda was employed by the Nazis to anticipate and forestall an expected initiative of the Allies in the psychological-warfare sphere. Beginning as early as November 12, 1943, German propaganda began to predict a Big Three (Churchill, Stalin, and Roosevelt) manifesto or ultimatum to the German people. These predictions mounted in volume and intensity during the Cairo and Teheran conferences of Allied leaders. In fact, this was practically the only thing told the German audience—that the purpose of the Big Three meeting at Teheran was to launch another Wilsonian Fourteen Points at the German people. Heavy sarcasm and ridicule were employed by German propaganda in commenting upon this possibility. The Teheran Conference ended, however, without the predicted manifesto. What had been the purpose of the Nazi propaganda campaign?

FCC	GOEBBELS
Evidently the Propaganda Ministry thought that by employing ridicule it could create the impression that the Nazis themselves were not worried about the forthcoming propaganda blow, and that Germans too should not regard it as worthy of serious attention. There is little doubt that the Nazis were considerably con-	It is claimed that an editorial committee has been appointed in Teheran to compose an appeal to the German people. But that appeal is not forthcoming! At any rate, we have already taken massive countermeasures in our propaganda against such an appeal. If it should actually come, it will find us by no means unprepared. The German people will surely

cerned over the propaganda effects of the conferences that have
just taken place. It is difficult to
establish to what extent they actually thought that a propaganda
manifesto to the German people
. . . was likely to emerge. . . . In
any event, the Propaganda Ministry might well have reasoned
that as long as such a manifesto
was even just possible, it would
be best to prepare the German
people for it (*CEA #*48, December 9, 1943, pp. A-2, 3).[78]

treat it as a scrap of paper that has
no political significance (*Goebbels
Diary*, December 6, 1943, p. 543).
[After the conclusion of the
Teheran Conference:] I believe
that the plan for an appeal to the
German people was dropped
mainly because of our anticipatory
propaganda (*ibid.*, December 7,
1943, p. 544).

Analyst's Reasoning. The analyst initially inferred that the aim of
Nazi anticipatory propaganda was to strengthen predispositions
among the German public to consider the possible Allied manifesto
as insignificant. Then, from the (inferred) fact that the Nazi propagandists were strongly pursuing this aim, the following additional
inferences were deduced: (*a*) that the possibility of an Allied manifesto was taken seriously by the Nazi elite and (*b*) that the Nazi
elite feared that such a manifesto might have a serious effect on
morale. These two inferences, of course, accounted nicely for the
fact that Nazi propagandists made a major effort to anticipate the
manifesto and to destroy any effect it might have had.

NOTES

1. In early discussions of content analysis as an intelligence tool this problem did not receive as much attention as was devoted to predicting enemy actions. This was probably due
in part to the fact that during the early part of World War II the initiative was held by the
Nazis. Later on, as Allied forces took the initiative, the FCC analysts became concerned with
Nazi propagandists' anticipation of Allied actions.

2. Instances of this type of inference are found in Case Study No. 12.1, Inferences 1, 2, 3,
5, 8, 9, 10, and 11 (pp. 177 ff.); Case Study No. 12.2, Inferences 1 and 2 (pp. 193 and 194);
and Case Study No. 12.5 (p. 216).

3. The case studies cited later in this chapter contain no instances of this type of inference.

4. Inferences of this type occur in Case Study No. 12.2, Inferences 4, 6, 8, and 9 (pp. 197,
201, 207, and 208).

5. Instances of this type of inference are cited in Case Study No. 12.1, Inference 4 (p.
181); Case Study No. 12.2, Inferences 3, 4, and 6 (pp. 196, 197, and 201); and Case Study
No. 12.3, Inference 4 (p. 214).

6. Inferences of this type are to be found in Case Study No. 12.1, Inferences 4 and 5
(pp. 181 and 182); Case Study No. 12.2, Inferences 1 and 4 (pp. 193 and 197); Case
Study No. 12.3, Inferences 2 and 3 (pp. 211 and 213); and Case Studies Nos. 12.4 and 12.5
(pp. 214 and 216).

7. An inference of this type occurs in Case Study No. 12.2, Inference 7 (p. 206).

8. An inference of this type is presented in Case Study No. 12.2, Inference 5 (p. 199).

9. No instances of this type of inference occur in the cases cited in this chapter.

10. An inference of this type is reported in Case Study No. 12.2, Inference 2 (p. 194).

11. See pp. 135–36 for remarks about the list of possible goals of preparatory propaganda which apply here as well.

12. The present list is predicated upon the assumption that all opponent actions are expected by the propagandist to have a *deprivational* effect, at least initially, upon his domestic audience and, conversely, an *indulgent* effect, at least initially, upon the opponent's own audience. The possible goals of anticipatory propaganda to unfriendly neutrals would correspond to those set forth for the opponent's audiences.

13. On this point see the relevant parts of R. E. Sherwood, *Roosevelt and Hopkins* (Harper & Bros., New York, 1948), and Dwight D. Eisenhower, *Crusade in Europe* (Doubleday & Co., Inc., Garden City, N.Y., 1948).

14. *Weekly Analysis* #28, dated June 13, 1942, but covering broadcasts for June 5–11, 1942, p. 7. (Note that each weekly FCC report covered the broadcasts of the immediately preceding week or ten days.)

15. Sherwood, *op. cit.*, pp. 563–77.

16. Winston S. Churchill, *The Hinge of Fate* (Vol. IV of *The Second World War;* Houghton Mifflin Co., Boston, 1950), pp. 341–42.

17. U.S. Army, A.G.O., Departmental Records Branch, T.A.G.O., *Führer Directives . . . German Armed Forces, 1942–1945* (Washington, D.C.), pp. 34–36.

18. *Weekly Analysis* #34, dated July 25, 1942, covering broadcasts of July 17–23.

19. Sherwood, *op. cit.*, p. 607.

20. *Weekly Analysis* #35, dated August 1, 1942, covering broadcasts of July 24–30, p. 6.

21. It was known to the FCC analysts that Goebbels' talks and much other material appearing in broadcasts to North America were taken from domestic materials. It was therefore safe for the analyst to assume in this instance that certain of the propaganda goals in Goebbels' talk were aimed at domestic and friendly neutral audiences.

22. *Weekly Review* #36, dated August 8, 1942, covering broadcasts of July 31–August 6.

23. This is purely a hypothetical consideration. The writer has no evidence that this was considered an important problem by Allied intelligence.

24. *Weekly Review* #39, dated August 29, 1942, covering broadcasts of August 21–27, p. 5.

25. *Weekly Review* #40, dated September 5, 1942, covering broadcasts of August 28–September 3, p. 14.

26. Quoted in Liddell Hart's account of his interrogations of Rundstedt and Blumentritt in *The German Generals Talk* (William Morrow & Co., New York, 1948), p. 229.

27. Part A, Vol. 36, August, 1942, pp. 362 ff. Though not immediately relevant, it is interesting that the German Naval Staff report then adds: "In order not to lessen the desired effect, it is self-evident that the Commands involved must adhere to the chosen course. This explains why the permanent representative of the Commander-in-Chief, Navy, at the Fuehrer's Headquarters stated that the study of the enemy's operations orders actually led to the published conclusions" (i.e., the Naval representative at Hitler's headquarters deliberately falsified the Navy's real views in order to give backing to the official interpretation of the Dieppe raid already decided upon). See also the account of Wehrmacht Chief-of-Staff Zeitzler's rejection of an intelligence estimate that the Dieppe raid was not a serious invasion attempt (in Milton Shulman, *Defeat in the West* [Secker & Warburg, London, 1947], p. 19), and his official report to Hitler representing the Dieppe raid as a major invasion attempt (in Chester Wilmot, *The Struggle for Europe* [William Collins Sons & Co., London, 1952], pp. 187–88).

28. *Weekly Review* #42, dated September 19, 1942, covering broadcasts of September 11–17.

29. *Weekly Review* #43, dated September 26, 1942, covering broadcasts of September 18–24.

30. *Weekly Review* #44, dated October 3, 1942, covering broadcasts of September 25–October 1.

31. *Weekly Review* #45, dated October 10, 1942, covering broadcasts of October 2–8, p. 1.

32. *Weekly Review* #46, dated October 17, 1942, covering broadcasts of October 9–15, pp. 19–20, and *Weekly Review* #47, dated October 24, 1942, covering broadcasts of October 16–22, pp. 3–4.

33. *Weekly Review* #47, p. 4.

34. *Weekly Review* #48, October 31, 1942, covering broadcasts of October 23–29, pp. 16, 25.

35. *Weekly Review* #49, November 7, 1942, covering broadcasts of October 30–November 5, p. 7.

36. Anthony Martienssen, *Hitler and His Admirals* (E. P. Dutton & Co., Inc., New York, 1949), p. 116.

37. *Ibid.,* pp. 133, 145.

38. Eisenhower, *op. cit.,* p. 98.

39. Curt Riess, *Joseph Goebbels* (Doubleday & Co., Garden City, N.Y., 1948), p. 233.

40. Shulman, *op. cit.,* p. 82. See also Albert Kesselring, *Kesselring: A Soldier's Record* (William Morrow & Co., New York, 1954), pp. 161–67.

41. Riess, *op. cit.,* p. 233; *Goebbels Diary,* p. 319 (entry for April 9, 1943).

42. Rudolf Semmler, *Goebbels: The Man Next to Hitler* (Westhouse, London, 1947), p. 70.

43. *Ibid.,* p. 71.

44. This list of intelligence targets is hypothetical in that it has been drawn up by the author without recourse to formal or informal official statements made at the time.

45. As remarked in the preceding chapter, each issue of the *CEA* covers the broadcasts for *the immediately preceding week*. This should be kept in mind in comparing the dates of the FCC analyses with the dates of the Goebbels diary entries.

46. *CEA* #11, March 26, 1943, p. C-8.

47. *CEA* #12, April 2, 1943, p. B-12.

48. *Ibid.*

49. However, the inference in question could be supported as well by a reconstruction of propaganda strategy and, in that event, the *indirect* method would have been used. Under the circumstances, the method used to make the present inference ought probably to be considered as ambiguous or borderline, since it is not certain whether the direct or indirect method was actually used.

50. *CEA* #15, April 23, 1943, p. C-6.

51. *Ibid.*

52. This account of Allied military planning is based upon Eisenhower, *op. cit.,* pp. 159 ff.

53. During Churchill's visit to Washington in May, 1943, the date for OVERLORD was set for May 1, 1944. This was reaffirmed at Quebec in August, 1943, and again at Teheran in November, 1943 (Sherwood, *op. cit.,* pp. 732, 746, 777 ff.).

54. *CEA* #18, May 14, 1943.

55. *CEA* #19, May 21, 1943.

56. Since the reasoning supporting this inference seems to bypass consideration of the propaganda strategy involved and links content indicators directly with an elite expectation, it may be considered an example of the *direct* method.

57. This hypothetical inference would have been made by the *direct* method.

58. The "Anglo-Saxon" order for an invasion of Sardinia and the Peloponnesus and the letter from the "English General Staff to General Alexander" refer to documents which British agents managed to pass into the hands of the German Abwehr shortly before the Allied invasion of Sicily. As the quotations from the Führer Conference of May 14, 1943, and *Goebbels Diary* (and other materials not cited) indicate, this was a highly successful effort at deception. The faked documents were planted on a dead body, ostensibly that of a British courier drowned in an airplane crash in the Mediterranean, which was allowed to drift ashore in Spain where it was considered likely that it would come to the immediate attention of German agents. The story of this deception has been told by Ewen Montagu, who was responsible for its conception and execution, in the book *The Man Who Never Was* (Evans Bros., London, 1953), which has recently been made into a movie. See also Samuel Eliot Morison, *Sicily-Salerno-Anzio, January 1943—June 1944* (Vol. IX of *History of United States Naval Operations in World War II;* Little, Brown & Co., Boston, 1954), pp. 44–47, 69–70; Wilmot, *op. cit.,* p. 188; and Ian Colvin, *The Unknown*

Courier (W. Kimber, London, 1953). In contrast to the effectiveness of the deception as far as German leaders were concerned, the plant was discounted by responsible Italian military leaders and intelligence officers, who thought that the Allies would invade Sicily.

59. *CEA* #20, May 28, 1943, p. C-10.

60. Eisenhower, *op. cit.*, pp. 169 ff.

61. From a personal interview between Student and M. Shulman, in Shulman, *op. cit.*, p. 84.

62. *CEA* #25, July 1, 1943, p. B-11.

63. *CEA* #33, August 26, 1943, p. B-4.

64. *CEA* #34, September 2, 1943, p. B-8.

65. *Goebbels Diary*, p. 408 (entry for July 27, 1943).

66. *CEA* #35, September 9, 1943, p. C-1.

67. It is quite likely that the Allied air and naval actions which attracted the attention of the German leaders were feints intended for this very purpose by the Allies. See the discussion of Operation STARKEY in Lt. Gen. Sir Frederick Morgan, K.C.B., *Overture to Overlord* (Doubleday & Co., Garden City, N.Y., 1950), Chap. IV.

68. *CEA* #18, May 14, 1943, p. A-2. This inference is discussed more fully in Chapter 13, p. 232, below.

69. According to Goebbels' account, Hitler said that Mussolini had been in low spirits when he arrived for conversations at Obersalzberg (April 7–10, 1943) but that Hitler had succeeded in perking him up. Goebbels added: "The Fuehrer is not at all convinced that the Italians will stay put when the heaviest strain comes" (*Goebbels Diary*, pp. 352, 370, entries for May 7 and 10, 1943).

70. *Goebbels Diary*, p. 383.

71. *Ibid.*, p. 395.

72. *Ibid.*, p. 403.

73. *Ibid.*, pp. 405–6, 407–8. See also Felix Gilbert, *Hitler Directs His War* (Oxford University Press, New York, 1950), pp. 43–44, 46–47, 52; Kesselring, *op. cit.*, pp. 202–3.

74. *CEA* #30, August 5, 1943, p. B-1.

75. See U.S. Navy Dept., *Führer Conferences on Matters Dealing with the German Navy, 1943* (Washington, D.C.), pp. 110 ff.

76. *Goebbels Diary*, p. 427 (entry for September 9, 1943).

77. For an account of the talks see Churchill, *Closing the Ring* (Vol. V of *The Second World War;* Houghton Mifflin Co., Boston, 1951), pp. 334–35.

78. This FCC report appeared just after the conclusion of the Teheran Conference, but the inferences therein contained had been formulated *beforehand*, during the height of the German propaganda of anticipation.

THIRTEEN

Inferences about Situational Changes Experienced as Favorable or Unfavorable by an Opponent

This chapter takes up the third of the general problem areas in making inferences mapped out in the Introduction. It attempts to show how propaganda analysis can be employed to throw light on situational changes—military, political, diplomatic, economic, or psychological—affecting the opponent's strength and power position.

Sometimes the propaganda analyst is interested primarily in whether the opponent is aware of certain events or changes in the situation which are already known to him (the propaganda analyst). In other cases the analyst is interested in inferring whether certain events or changes have taken place of which the opponent, but not the analyst's side, has direct knowledge.

Sometimes the analyst is interested primarily in assessing the *objective* character of events or changes in the opponent's situation, that is, whether they are favorable or unfavorable to the opponent's power position and potential. In other instances, the analyst is particularly concerned with inferring the subjective estimate made by the opposing elite, that is, whether the opposing elite considers certain events to have an indulgent or deprivational effect on its position, and with inferring the impact such estimates have on the opposing elite's expectations and intentions.

221

In the world of politics, especially when international relations are marked by a high degree of conflict, events are constantly taking place which have some bearing upon the power position of the actors and upon their ability to accomplish their major objectives. These events, which constitute changes in the situation, may or may not be clearly favorable to one side or the other. Every elite which takes a systematic approach to questions of world politics (and this is particularly characteristic of totalitarian elites) must decide which changes in the situation to discuss openly and how to interpret their significance for various publics.

Decisions on publicity are subject to a number of considerations, oftentimes of a complex nature. In some instances an elite has greater freedom of action than in others; some changes in the situation are not generally known and may not become so unless the elite decides to disclose them. In other cases the elite has little choice; knowledge of the events is already, or will soon become, widespread, and the opponent may already be talking about them. The significance of certain kinds of changes in the situation may be difficult to estimate, and the elite may be reluctant, therefore, to talk about such events or to commit itself as to their significance. Other types of events may be of a highly dramatic character, yet their real political worth may be rather trivial. In such cases, an elite may find itself in a dilemma. On the one hand, it can exploit the dramatic value of the event in order to give its followers a lift or to distract attention from more serious developments; on the other hand, such a strategy may be shortsighted in that members of the audience may perceive and resent the propagandist's manipulations. The elite is faced by a similar dilemma in deciding whether and to what extent to exploit events which have favorable consequences in the short run but perhaps less favorable implications in the long run.

The problem of whether and how to publicize day-to-day and week-to-week changes in the situation is further complicated by the need to fit current events into an over-all picture of political developments which the elite wishes various audiences to accept. Some events fit into an elite's over-all picture of political developments more easily than others. Some events lend themselves readily to use as confirmations of the general estimates and forecasts which the elite has been making. Events which appear to contradict the elite's general view, on the other hand, pose greater challenges to its communication policy.

A further problem arises from the need to fit treatment of current events into the middle-range propaganda and political strategies which the elite is pursuing. Changes in the situation often cannot be dealt with in terms of their objective significance or in terms of their relation to ultimate aspirations and long-range objectives. Rather, the public treatment of such events must be guided by the requirements of current policies, of both the relatively short-term and the middle-range objectives which the elite is pursuing at the moment.

The propaganda analyst, therefore, is faced with a formidable challenge in attempting to infer an elite's *private* view of the significance of situational changes from its public treatment of such events. Appraisal of the FCC's work in this general problem area indicates that the indirect method is especially useful for this purpose and that the direct method, too, shows some promise.

Prerequisites for the Indirect Method

The major prerequisite for using the *indirect* method in making inferences about situational changes is knowledge of the elite's general assessment of the importance of morale (in the broadest connotation of the term) and of the typical ways in which it deals with the implications of events for morale. Knowledge of this type is useful, because an inference about how the opposing propagandist manipulates morale can be the first step in an indirect inference about the elite's estimate of an event or about the character of the event itself. As the case studies cited later in this chapter will show, the FCC analysts frequently derived inferences about Nazi elite estimates and intentions from the Nazi propaganda handling of the implications of events for morale.

It must be emphasized that not all elites will be equally concerned about the consequences to morale of different types of events or will attempt to cope with them in the same fashion. The Nazi elite was minutely interested in the morale and opinions of its own domestic audiences and, to a lesser extent only, of groups in allied and enemy countries. Goebbels made discriminating, often rather subtle, use of propaganda communications for prophylactic and therapeutic purposes in dealing with morale problems. Some discussion at this point of these aspects of Goebbels' theory and practice of propaganda will be useful, since it reveals the value of information of this type to the propaganda analyst.

Goebbels was constantly alert to the potential consequences to morale of all types of actions and developments. His propaganda policies were geared to maximizing positive and minimizing negative impacts on morale of situational developments. He was not only concerned with current and past events but made it a point to anticipate developments, to foresee developing morale problems, and to shape his propaganda strategy accordingly. The positive impact on morale of an emerging favorable event could often be heightened and controlled, in Goebbels' calculation, by an intelligently conceived effort to mold his audience's predispositions and expectations. Similarly, the negative impact on morale of an emerging setback could be minimized by preparing the public for it in skillful fashion or by means of other propaganda devices. Since Goebbels himself needed to know the psychological characteristics of his public to do this job intelligently, the FCC analysts needed similar understanding of the German public in order to make the best sense possible out of Goebbels' propaganda.

As a result of systematic observation of Goebbels' efforts in this direction, the FCC analysts gradually gained insight into the techniques he employed. Some of their observations may be briefly noted.

1. Goebbels' first line of attack upon nascent negative attitudes among the German public which came to his attention, it was observed, was likely to be indirect. Without explicitly mentioning the negative attitude itself, Goebbels would provide arguments to the contrary in his propaganda.

2. A somewhat more direct attack upon negative attitudes was used at times by Goebbels. (When this followed an indirect attack, it therefore suggested that the indirect attack had been inadequate for its purpose.) The negative public attitude was ostensibly revealed in morale-building propaganda but was minimized by one or a number of devices: (a) the negative attitude was described only in part or in euphemistic terms, thus enabling the propagandist to discuss and counter it without fully admitting its seriousness; (b) the prevalence of the negative attitude among the public was denied by alleging that only a minority held the attitude or by describing these people in such a fashion as to isolate or discredit them.

3. Frequently Goebbels' propaganda would explicitly prescribe the *correct* attitude that Germans should take toward an issue or event. When the propaganda analyst learned to recognize this technique, the problem of making inferences was enormously simplified.

From the prescribed correct attitude, the analyst could infer the nature of the *incorrect* attitude.

4. An even more direct propaganda attack upon negative attitudes lay in an open and full admission of the existence of the attitudes. When such an attack followed 1, 2, or 3, the analyst could then infer that Goebbels was acting on information that an undesired public attitude had persisted or had become aggravated. This direct attack might also indicate that Goebbels now thought that the undesirable attitude was too widespread and keenly felt to be minimized in propaganda, or he might count upon his frank approach itself to gain a sympathetic ear for his arguments.

5. The propaganda approach to still graver problems of bad morale consisted of denunciations of those who held the wrong attitude, denunciations sometimes tinged with threats. In adopting this approach, Goebbels made the transition from a use of propaganda for prophylactic and therapeutic purposes to its use for purposes of inducing repression, or at least suppression, of overt manifestations of the undesired attitude.

6. This transition was carried further, finally, by public announcements of penalties inflicted upon persons guilty of wrong attitudes (e.g., rumor-mongering, defeatism, etc.) or wrong activities. This, of course, indicated an even more serious situation.

This catalogue, not necessarily a complete one, is intended to illustrate the range of Goebbels' methods for dealing with negative morale and to indicate a few of the inferential possibilities thereby accorded the propaganda analyst.[1]

The FCC analysts frequently made inferences about Nazi elite expectations and intentions indirectly on the basis of how Goebbels anticipated and manipulated the implications for morale of *future* developments. (This will be illustrated below.)

Every propagandist must face the problem of how best to handle an opponent's successes, which are intrinsically deprivational for the propagandist's side. This is part of a broader problem which may be stated in the form of a question: What, if anything, can propaganda do in the face of a patently unfavorable objective situation? The answer frequently made by students of propaganda is that, since propaganda is inherently dependent upon events, it cannot do much to change reality when reality is itself unfavorable. Although propaganda may help to exploit favorable events in order to hasten the demoralization of the opponent, the argument goes, it is practically impotent in the face of unfavorable developments. Admittedly, it may be able to hide certain negative developments and minimize others, but in the long run propaganda cannot change the course of developments or hide the truth indefinitely.

This propaganda problem is mentioned here chiefly in order to place in perspective two observations about Goebbels' attitude toward it, which departed from the stock answer to the problem in several important respects.

1. According to Goebbels, the theory of minimizing enemy successes, popular in World War I, fell into disrepute during World War II. Instead, pessimism was the favored tool in attempts to spur a nation to greater efforts. "Heretofore one had to subtract 50% of successes reported, now it is necessary to subtract 50% of all bad news."[2] The reporting of enemy successes as an incentive to greater efforts on the home front was a stand-by in Goebbels' repertory. He was influenced in this direction by an admiration of Churchill's "blood, sweat, and tears" appeal earlier in the war. Goebbels felt that the effectiveness of this appeal could not be demolished and that it made the English impervious to enemy claims of impending disasters.[3] Goebbels' own efforts to implement this theory came later in the war.[4] However, it is important to note that he applied this new approach of expediential pessimism only in situations of outstanding gravity in which a propaganda policy of attempted minimization would have been futile, if not dangerous. In other cases Goebbels (like all other propagandists in World War II) did not shrink from employing traditional techniques of minimization, evasion, compensation, etc. (See Case Study No. 13.8, p. 241, for an instance where the actual situation, at first minimized in Nazi propaganda, finally deteriorated to the point at which frankness became imperative.)

2. Goebbels conceded the general truth of the maxim that propaganda cannot transform or gild unfavorable situations (e.g., bombing attacks, ration cuts, etc.). But he felt that, even though military events placed him in a defensive position, it was still possible at times to wage offensive political warfare. The outstanding application of Goebbels' theory was the anti-Bolshevik campaign waged following the Stalingrad disaster. In Goebbels' words: "If cleverly conducted it [the anti-Bolshevik campaign] can achieve results even though the military situation does not look too promising. But one has to have some ingenuity and imagination."[5] According to Rudolf Semmler, Goebbels claimed at his March 14, 1943, conference of departmental heads of the Propaganda Ministry that the Russian advance on the

Eastern Front and his Red-menace propaganda had succeeded in frightening the Western Allies and the neutrals. Goebbels added, "I shall now try by every means to stimulate this fear, until at last there comes a breach between East and West. That is the great long-term object of my work, which I hope to attain by this summer." [6]

Mode of Reasoning (Using the Indirect Method)

In using the indirect method in this problem area, the propaganda analyst attempts to reconstruct the elite's estimate of an event or something about the situational change to which the elite is responding from its impact on any of the following components of the elite's calculations and behavior:

1. Its expectations.
2. The objectives and intentions of its policies.
3. Its assessment of the problems or opportunities created by the event.
4. Its assessment of changes in propaganda strategy made desirable by the event (related to changes in expectations, objectives and intentions).
5. Its assessment of changes in propaganda techniques for implementing standing propaganda goals made desirable by the event.

The first step in the analyst's procedure is to identify the propaganda goal being pursued by the opposing propagandist in attempting to control or influence the impact of a situational change upon the morale of one or more audiences. Additional inferences are then in the nature of a (partial) explanation for the adoption of that particular morale-manipulating goal. The general structure of the analyst's reasoning, in skeletal form, is as follows: "The enemy propagandist would not attempt to manipulate the morale of this audience in the manner he now does unless he knows of (or expects) a certain type of *situational change,* unless he is acting on the basis of a certain *estimate* of the significance of such a change, or unless he is acting on the basis of certain *expectations* created by a situational change."

Possible Goals of Morale-Manipulating Propaganda

A catalogue of all possible goals of morale-manipulating propaganda would be useful in helping the analyst to recognize the precise goal being pursued in any individual instance. An attempt to provide such a list is made at this point, subject to the same qualifying observations which were made in the two preceding chapters. This list is limited to propaganda directed to the domestic audience. It is also limited to propaganda responses to situational changes estimated by the propagandist to be *deprivational* to his side. Most propagandists may be assumed to be more actively concerned with negative than with positive impacts upon the morale of domestic and friendly foreign audiences. Of course, there are also techniques for controlling and minimizing positive impacts upon the morale of various audiences; many of these techniques have already been identified in the catalogues of propaganda goals listed in the preceding two chapters. All of the goals listed are variations of the basic objective of minimizing the unfavorable impact upon morale of adverse situational changes. That is, the specific goals listed concern different components of over-all morale. (A more systematic analysis of "morale," however, is not attempted.)

Possible Goals of Morale-Manipulating Propaganda [7]
(To Domestic and Friendly Neutral Audiences)

I. To reduce the negative impact upon morale of situational changes of a deprivational character by the technique of:
   A. Minimizing the magnitude and consequences of present or future adverse changes in the situation.
   B. Diverting (when practicable) public attention from the deprivational event in question to more favorable ones or to the adverse circumstances of the opponent.
   C. Broadening the time perspective within which the public should view the current deprivation by presenting it, for example, as an inevitable or unavoidable occurrence on the road to ultimate success.
   D. Shifting the public's attention to other values which may be indulged by depicting, for example, the adverse situation as offering an opportunity for moral compensation: "Good men will now show their mettle."

II. To control and channel into safe and useful directions the disappointment and hostility engendered in the public by the adverse change in the situation. More specifically:
   A. To strengthen hostility toward the opponent.
   B. To utilize the deprivational event to strengthen the public's willingness to make personal sacrifices and to accept new demands that the developing crisis may require the leadership to impose.

    C. To manipulate blame and responsibility for the setback in a direction favorable to the elite and to morale.

    D. To enlighten the public (and groups within the public) as to what is expected of them and what they can do (and should not try to do) in the face of the adverse situation.

III. To maintain and strengthen public confidence in leaders. More specifically:

    A. To strengthen confidence in the leadership's ability to master the difficult situation.

    B. To assure and/or enlighten the public as to the practicability of the leadership's plans for ultimate success.

    C. To assure the public of the leadership's concern with its welfare.

IV. To reduce the negative impact on morale of an expected setback by establishing realistic public expectations regarding the future and, specifically, by anticipating or preparing for the setback.

  V. To avoid giving the opponent useful information in propaganda communications designed to deal with the deprivational aspects of events.

The Direct Method

The major prerequisite for employing the *direct* method in this problem area is that content indicators be discovered which are independent of whatever propaganda strategy the opponent may be following in depicting situational events. As pointed out earlier, inferences under the direct method are made on the basis of noncausal empirical generalizations, or correlations. These generalizations can be reliably postulated only on the basis of a close observation of the way in which the propagandist under study has handled different types of situational changes in the past. Generalizations which characterize one elite's behavior in this respect will not necessarily apply also to another elite's communication behavior.

Only one case study in this chapter (No. 13.9, Inference 1, p. 243) qualifies as a possible example of the direct method. The implicit generalization, or correlation, upon which the inference in question rested can be formulated as follows: When an elite becomes dissatisfied with the level of success it is presently achieving in a certain area, its public communications will contain an increase in references to *future* successes in that area.

As is frequently the case with direct inferences, the noncausal correlation and the mode of reasoning employed in this inference could easily have been transformed into the pattern of causal imputation characteristic of the indirect method. That is, the analyst might have reasoned that the propagandist was adopting the goal of promising future success in the prescribed area in order to counter disappointment at the failure to achieve greater success there at present.

Content indicators derived from tentative noncausal correlations are often utilized by the analyst in a preliminary scanning of propaganda. In the course of a more precise definition of the inferential problem and a more intensive analysis of it, the analyst may transform initial noncausal correlations into generalizations about the propaganda behavior of the propagandist. In so doing, the direct approach initially applied in this scanning operation becomes transformed into the indirect method (see Part I, pp. 39, 42 ff.).

Even though this transformation often occurs, a list of content indicators which have been used in noncausal correlations is of some value. For it serves to alert the propaganda analyst to possible indicators of interest and to facilitate his initial inspection of a large body of propaganda materials. The following list of content indicators on which some of the noncausal correlations (implicit or explicit) in the FCC's work were based includes only those indicators which enter into two types of generalizations: (*a*) generalizations about *present* situational changes being experienced as deprivational by the (Nazi) elite and (*b*) generalizations about *future* situational changes expected to be deprivational by the (Nazi) elite. In each case the precise nature of the deprivational change in the situation has not been specified. It should be noted, too, that the "increase," "decrease," "emphasis," "de-emphasis" referred to may be quantitative and/or qualitative in nature.[8]

> I. *Content indicators possibly appropriate for inferring that deprivational changes in the situation are presently being experienced by the (Nazi) elite:*
> A. Increased attention to self.[9]
> B. Emphasis upon general-analysis-and-review statements about the area of deprivation as against present-action statements.
> C. Emphasis on future deprivations for the opponent.
> D. Emphasis on past indulgences.
> E. Emphasis on future indulgences.[10]
> F. Emphasis on the future, long-range advantages accruing to self from the present deprivation.
> G. Emphasis on the argument that the opponent suffers from a lack of control over events and available alternatives in the area of his advantage.

H. Emphasis upon the secondary, indirect disadvantages for the opponent accruing from his advantage.
I. Emphasis upon the unimportance of the present events that are deprivational.
J. Emphasis on the opponent's immorality.

II. *Content indicators possibly appropriate for inferring that the (Nazi) elite expects future deprivational changes:*

A. Decreased (or weakened) predictions of deprivations for the opponent.[11]
B. Decreased (or weakened) predictions of advantage, success, or indulgence for self.
C. Increased use of general, ambiguous claims of success as against specific claims of success.
D. Increased claims of secondary and indirect (as against primary) indulgences for self.
E. Increased predictions of future discord within opponent's camp (e.g., latent incompatibility of, and potential splitting of, opponent's coalition).
F. Increased predictions of future deprivations of the opponent by neutrals or by providential factors.
G. Less emphasis on predictions of future indulgence of self made on the authority of self as against those attributed to other sources.
H. Less emphasis on present success.
I. Emphasis on the opponent's immorality (including war-guilt allegations).
J. Emphasis on the opponent's strength.
K. Less emphasis on the defensive assets of self.
L. Decreased specificity of geographical references (to areas in which deprivation is expected).

A similar list of content indicators, derived from tentative generalizations about *indulgent* shifts in the environment, could be drawn up. These content indicators would frequently be the exact opposites of those listed above, which were selected for presentation here because they were more frequently encountered in the FCC work and seemed more interesting.

Case Studies

Most of the inferences in this general problem area which could be matched against relevant historical data are included in the nine cases presented here.

CASE STUDY NO. 13.1: INFERENCE ABOUT UNFAVORABLE GERMAN MORALE

The propaganda analyst may be able to infer the propagandist's private estimate of an unfavorable situational factor by identifying a propaganda strategy which is designed to counter that unfavorable situation indirectly without mentioning it explicitly.

Inference and Verification. The negative situational estimate in question concerned the widespread expectation among the German public that Italy would collapse and drop out of the war. The only available historical evidence for validating the inference is an entry in the Goebbels diary some months later; there seems to be no reason to question the accuracy of the inference, which was phrased in general terms only.

FCC	GOEBBELS
German domestic propaganda gives the impression that there is a nearly universal expectation among the Germans that the Italians will fold up soon (*CEA* #18, May 14, 1943, p. A-2).	[After Mussolini's resignation, Goebbels observed that] the common people [in Germany] have long anticipated and expected what is now happening in Rome (*Goebbels Diary,* July 27, 1943, p. 411).

Reasoning. From an examination of German propaganda, the analyst first inferred that the propagandist's goal was to bolster the German public's faith in the Italian ally. The propaganda content which inspired the identification of this propaganda goal was described by the FCC analyst as follows: "Both press and radio reiterate many times that the Italians are possessed of an unbreakable will to continue the war." The analyst then inferred that the decision to give such propaganda reassurances must have been based on an estimate that the German public doubted that Italy would remain in the war.

CASE STUDY NO. 13.2: INFERENCE ABOUT NEGATIVE CIVILIAN INFLUENCE UPON MORALE OF GERMAN SOLDIERS

Sometimes a negative factor is mentioned in the propaganda itself, albeit in a euphemistic fashion, in order to permit the propagandist to combat it more directly.

Inference and Verification.

FCC	GOEBBELS
As in the last war *gripers* [on the home front] are now threatening to infect the soldiers through letters they send to the front (*CEA* #14, April 16, 1943, p. A-6).	[Quoting from the report of the German Security Police (S.D.):] It is significant that all reports show that Germany is momentarily manifesting a worse attitude than the front. The better letters go from the front to Germany and not the other way (Microfilm Goebbels diary, April 11, 1943).

Reasoning. The inference was not difficult to make. The Nazi propagandist's goal—namely, to discourage civilian gripers from writing pessimistic letters to soldiers at the front—was easy to identify, since the negative factor was mentioned in the propaganda itself. (The content, as summarized by the FCC analyst: "A propaganda company reporter declares that soldiers do not want to hear petty complaints from people at home; people at home are told not to harass the front soldiers but to emulate the front in its ability to face difficulties without complaint.")

The mention of the negative factor in Nazi propaganda was phrased in somewhat guarded, euphemistic terms (that is, the propaganda assertion was that the "soldiers" did not want to hear "petty complaints," whereas, in fact, the Nazi elite was probably concerned about the transmission of serious complaints to the front). It remained, therefore, for the FCC analyst to draw upon his knowledge of the comparable history of World War I to appraise the full significance of the negative factor in the minds of the Nazi elite.

CASE STUDY NO. 13.3: INFERENCE ABOUT THE GERMAN PUBLIC'S CRITICISM OF THE NAZI LEADERSHIP'S INFORMATION POLICY

When propaganda displays concern over public criticism of information policies, it may be possible to infer some of the specific charges being made by the public.

Inference and Verification. Mussolini's unexpected resignation on July 25, 1943, placed German domestic propaganda in a difficult position. The public was concerned lest further unpleasant developments take place in Italy; the Nazi leadership, uncertain of future developments, could not give the public assurances to the contrary. Moreover, its reticence aggravated the concern of the public, which thereupon criticized the leadership for this reticence.

FCC	GOEBBELS
The Italian political situation and the fighting in Sicily have been the main preoccupations of the German people during the past week. The German people, at least in the *big* cities, are really agitated . . . by the changes in the Italian Government. The taciturnity of the radio about Mussolini's resignation has only aggravated the alarm as well as created a demand for further and more specific information (*CEA* #30, August 5, 1943, p. B-1).	From all over the country we receive reports reflecting the concern of the German people over the Italian crisis. Some sections of the population are almost in a state of panic. The people demand information, and wish the Fuehrer would speak. Naturally he can't do that at the moment. The people will have to wait exactly as we must wait for further developments in the crisis (*Goebbels Diary*, July 27, 1943, p. 412).

Reasoning. The first negative factor in the situation (the public's concern over past and future developments in Italy) was openly revealed in the propaganda itself and did not constitute a problem for inference. The second negative factor (the public's criticism of the Nazi leadership for its reticent information policy) was inferred by the FCC analyst indirectly after initially identifying the Nazi propaganda goal of meeting and dissipating the charge. The analyst noted a shift in the explanation given in the propaganda for taciturnity: "Previously Goebbels and Fritzsche [a high official in the Propaganda Ministry] merely justified governmental reticence in general, but [now] the . . . excuse of not wanting to give information to the enemy . . . is applied." From this shift in content the FCC analyst inferred first that the propaganda goal was now to *defend* the government's reticent information policy, and from this he deduced that such a propaganda goal must have been adopted because public criticism was being uttered and was of concern to the Nazi elite (at least to Goebbels).

CASE STUDY NO. 13.4: INFERENCE ABOUT THE NAZI ELITE'S SOBER ESTIMATE OF ITALY'S MILITARY POTENTIAL

The propagandist's effort to reorient public expectations in a more realistic direction may permit the analyst to draw inferences about a shift in the elite's own private expectations in the matter in question. **Inference and Verification.** After Italy's surrender to the Allies in September, 1943, it will be recalled, the Germans dramatically rescued Mussolini and announced the formation of a new Republican-Fascist Italian government. This event, together with other German countermeasures, gave German morale at home a tremendous boost. Shortly, however, the FCC analyst noted that German propaganda was taking a more sober view of Mussolini and of the prospects of his Republican-Fascist government.

FCC

There are evidences for the first time that the Nazis may feel that they have over-played the Republican-Fascist Government, its influence in Italy, and its support by Italians (*CEA* #39, October 8, 1943, p. D-1).

GOEBBELS

[Goebbels describes the change in Hitler's opinion of Mussolini after his first contacts with him following the rescue:]

I have never before seen the Fuehrer so disappointed in the Duce as this time. The Fuehrer now realizes that Italy never was a power, is no power today, and won't be a power in the future.

We may consider him [Hitler] absolutely disillusioned concerning the Duce's personality.

[In addition to the weight of Hitler's opinion, Goebbels was influenced by intelligence reports from Italy which reinforced the conclusion that the prospects of Mussolini's Republican-Fascist government were poor:]

The Duce intends to call a new Italian national army into being from the remnants of Fascism. I doubt whether he will succeed in this. The Italian people are not equal to grandly conceived revolutionary politics.

Pavolini [high-ranking collaborator in Mussolini's new government] is in Rome to build up the Fascist party and the Fascist militia. He isn't having much luck. In response to his first appeal . . .

> exactly fifteen men in the Italian
> capital reported! . . . One can
> see . . . to what depths Fascism
> has already sunk in public esteem.
> . . . *We must begin slowly to
> write off the Duce politically*
> (*Goebbels Diary,* September 23,
> 1943, pp. 469, 471, 479 and 481;
> italics supplied).

Reasoning. The identification of the new propaganda goal (toning down public expectations regarding a resurgence of Italian fascism) was made by the FCC analyst on the basis of his appraisal of a theme (of minor importance as far as number of appearances went) which several Nazi papers slipped into the otherwise favorable flood of publicity given to Mussolini and the Republican-Fascists. Thus, for example, the *Völkischer Beobachter* of September 29: "The battle is not yet won by the changes proclaimed by Mussolini, and the structural changes undertaken by him must not be regarded as a guarantee of future greatness." Similarly, the *Deutsche Allgemeine Zeitung* on the same day: "Powers on the other side [i.e., in Italy] are in no wise eradicated but have merely disappeared under the surface. Fascism is compelled strenuously and under hard fighting to reconquer its positions." [12]

To recapitulate: The FCC analyst first identified a new propaganda goal being implemented in Nazi domestic propaganda. He then reasoned that this propaganda goal must have been adopted as a result of a new Nazi elite estimate of the potential of its Italian Fascist ally.

CASE STUDY NO. 13.5: INFERENCE ABOUT NAZI ELITE PREPARATION OF GERMAN PUBLIC FOR A POLICY DEMANDING NEW SACRIFICES

When the propagandist attempts to prepare his own people for new sacrifices to be demanded shortly by the government, the analyst has an opportunity to predict the forthcoming governmental action. In this case the analyst was unable to analyze the significance of the preparatory propaganda until after the action took place.

Inference and Verification. During the winter of 1942–43 the battle for Stalingrad gradually developed into a disaster for Germany. At a relatively early stage in the prolonged battle Goebbels realized that a new mobilization of resources and manpower would be necessary to restore Germany's fighting strength. Even before defeat at Stalingrad was accepted as inevitable by other German leaders, Goebbels was urging behind the scenes the necessity for total mobilization. In his weekly *Das Reich* articles from mid-December, 1942, on, Goebbels supported his private policy recommendation with indirect public arguments to the effect that any possible hardship now could not be compared with that which would follow defeat and that the hardships endured by the soldiers ought to be an example to the civilian population. Only after several weeks, when the military crisis had developed to the point where the urgent requirements of further mobilization could no longer be neglected, did Hitler accept Goebbels' recommendation.[13] The Stalingrad disaster itself was solemnly but ceremoniously marked by a period of official national mourning, a daring but effective propaganda tour de force engineered by Goebbels. Concurrently with this glorification of defeat, a new national mobilization—"total mobilization"—was announced.

At this point, reflecting upon the meaning of the propaganda of the preceding weeks, the FCC analyst concluded:

> It appears now that Goebbels' talk about hardship and hero worship in recent weeks was not only a propagandistic *tour de force* possibly designed to dull the senses for future bad news by a shock therapy of bad-but-heroic news about Stalingrad, but also *served the function of preparing the German home audience for Sauckel's total mobilization* (FCC *Special Report No. 49*, "Toward a Global Munich?" February 1, 1943, p. 9; italics supplied).

CASE STUDY NO. 13.6: INFERENCES ABOUT THE NAZI PROPAGANDA EFFORT TO INFLUENCE DOMESTIC AND FOREIGN OPINION BY MANIPULATING THE PRESENTATION OF MILITARY DEVELOPMENTS

A number of inferences will now be presented to illustrate how propaganda analysis can provide insight into the elite estimates and policies which underlie the propagandist's ways of presenting favorable and unfavorable changes in the situation. From a military standpoint, the inferences that follow were of value in indicating that the Germans were deliberately underplaying their defensive successes and prospects on the Russian front. From the standpoint of psychological-warfare intelligence, the inferences provided insight into Goebbels' strategy.

Inferences and Verification. The Russian winter offensive of 1942–43 finally spent itself, and German forces rallied to achieve a stabilization of the front. In the meantime, however, Goebbels had been capitalizing upon the Russian advance (*a*) to preach total mobilization and (*b*) to implant the fear of Bolshevism among Germans, neutrals, and the Western Allies. The relative stabilization of the Russian front, including the retaking of Kharkov by German forces, and local German successes in North Africa took place while Goebbels' Bolshevik-bogey propaganda was in full swing. These German military successes were treated with such restraint by German propaganda that the FCC analyst, as well as the German public, drew certain conclusions regarding Goebbels' motives. Shortly thereafter the FCC analyst drew additional inferences from the manner in which Goebbels responded to the public's reaction to his treatment of the German military successes.

FCC	GOEBBELS
The Kharkov advance is treated soberly and succinctly in an apparent attempt to prevent an upsurge of popular enthusiasm. . . . The objective situation is still not regarded in Berlin as encouraging. The cessation of the Red drive is a wish and a hope, not yet a conviction. German military and civilian morale . . . might be shattered if present promises of new victories were followed by further defeats or retreats. Goebbels . . . is determined to avoid the propagandistic blunders of the Fuehrer in October, 1941, and in the summer and fall of 1942 (*CEA #9*, March 12, 1943, pp. A-2 and C-3).	The situation around Kharkov seems very favorable, and it is contemplated that in case of its fall [to German forces] a special bulletin ought to be issued. I am against it since such optimism might have to be taken down a few pegs very soon (Microfilm Goebbels diary, March 12, 1943). [Later:] The Fuehrer wants a special bulletin [to celebrate the taking of Kharkov], but I am against it and propose as an alternative a smaller ceremonial. . . . Otherwise it could leave the German people with the impression that now a big [German] offensive has begun which in no way corresponds to reality. The Fuehrer agreed to compromise (*ibid.,* March 15, 1943).
[Another reason for Berlin's failure to exploit recent successes more effectively:] The Red Menace Campaign is furthered by minimizing Axis successes and dramatizing Soviet strength (*ibid.,* p. C-4).	[With regard to the favorable military developments in the Kharkov area:] Altogether I don't find that the military situation fits into the propaganda line (*ibid.,* March 12, 1943). We are not really quite happy about this state of affairs [i.e.,

Russian reverses on the eastern front] for we were just gathering momentum in injecting a real fear of Bolshevism into the world. We can't do that now with as much success as we have in the past weeks (*ibid.*).

The Fuehrer fully endorses my anti-Bolshevik propaganda. That is the best horse we now have in our stable. He also approves of my tactics in letting the Bolshevik reports of victories go out into the world unchallenged. Let Europe get the creeps; all the sooner will it become sensible. Besides, our anti-Bolshevik propaganda is the apple of discord in the enemy camp (*Goebbels Diary*, March 9, 1943, p. 284).

Fear of the Red Army has been converted into a propaganda asset in the anti-Bolshevism and total mobilization campaign (*ibid.*, p. C-3).

[With reference to the improvement on the Russian front, which Goebbels regrets:] I would rather we held on to the rather darkly colored presentation . . . for it would be that much easier to push through total mobilization decrees (Microfilm Goebbels diary, March 1, 1943).

The Nazi elite apparently has reason to believe that Germans at home have assumed the official version of German set-backs in Russia and of the Bolshevik danger to be over-dramatized (*CEA* #10, March 19, 1943, p. A-3).

Goebbels clearly wishes to exploit further the morale-building effects of the recent heavy gloom campaign (he expressly denies that he painted the picture blacker than it was) (*ibid.*, p. C-4).

[Quoting the morale report of the German Security Police (*S.D.*), Goebbels comments:] Our present portrayal of the situation at the front is not really believed any more; it is assumed that an expediential pessimism lurks behind it . . . an assumption which is really not entirely erroneous (Microfilm Goebbels diary, March 2, 1943).

Reasoning. The FCC analyst was impressed by the failure of Nazi propaganda to adopt a certain goal (namely, to exploit present successes in order to compensate for past defeats) when the military successes achieved were sufficient to justify such a propaganda exploitation. His observation of the *non*implementation of this propaganda goal gave him insight into the propaganda strategy and the elite estimates which underlay the restrained reporting of German military successes.

CASE STUDY NO. 13.7: INFERENCE ABOUT THE NAZI INTENTION OF WITHDRAWING ON THE RUSSIAN FRONT

The fact that the propaganda analyst knows that military strategy and psychological-warfare policies are intimately co-ordinated by an elite may enable him to identify propaganda goals and thus indirectly arrive at inferences about military intentions. In this case the propaganda goal was that of preparing the domestic public for a military withdrawal.

Inference and Verification.

FCC	GERMAN LEADERS
Apparently to prepare for a [German] retreat from the Kuban bridgehead, there is detailed and comparatively large-volume reporting on the fighting in that sector. There is some reporting of [German] successes, especially in losses inflicted [on the Russians] but there is clear avoidance of any indications that the Germans intend to hold there indefinitely. Nor do the [German] propagandists . . . any longer inflate the importance of the bridgehead as a "potential springboard". . . as they formerly did in the apparent effort to get the Russians to divert as much as possible of their strength to that sector (*CEA* #36, September 16, 1943, p. C-1).	[At this time the following military order was transmitted from Hitler to the Army H.Q. involved in the action:] In order to free forces for other tasks, I have decided to evacuate the Kuban bridgehead and to withdraw the 17th Army across the Kerch Strait to the Crimea (U.S. Army, A.G.O., Departmental Records Branch, T.A.G.O., *op. cit.,* p. 89).[14]

Reasoning. The shifts in content themes, noted in the above quotation from the FCC report, suggested the inference. Previous familiarity with the manner in which German propaganda anticipated German military withdrawals and setbacks enabled the FCC analyst to spot and interpret these content shifts. The important shifts may be recapitulated:

1. Increased claims of success stressing largely (or exclusively) losses inflicted on the enemy (rather than, for example, the importance of the area itself).
2. Omission of an explicit or implicit commitment to hold the contested territory indefinitely.
3. Omission of the previous theme (the potential-springboard character of the territory) which had implied possible German offensive intentions in that area.

CASE STUDY NO. 13.8: PREDICTION OF CHANGE IN NAZI
PROPAGANDA PRESENTATIONS OF UNFAVORABLE MILITARY
DEVELOPMENTS ON THE RUSSIAN FRONT

In some cases the propaganda analyst's familiarity with the way in which the opposing propagandist operates enables him to anticipate a change in the propaganda strategy employed for depicting military developments.

Inference and Verification. Over a period of several months (August–September, 1943), German propaganda had adopted the aim of veiling and minimizing the continuing Russian advance by means of euphemistic stereotypes which made it appear that the German retreat was partly voluntary and under full control. (Some of the stereotypes were "disengaged according to plan," "shortening of the front," and "systematic evacuation without enemy pressure.") The FCC analyst observed that the situation on the eastern front was reaching the point where some change in the propaganda line must take place.

FCC	GOEBBELS
The Russian gains are so sweeping that German propaganda will have a hard time maintaining its propaganda strategy in the future. . . . If they continue to retreat [after reaching the Dnieper] they	These "successful evacuations" are getting the upper hand with the Axis. I don't believe we shall be able to use the expression much longer; it is making us more and more of a laughing stock. . . .

will have to find new and stronger justifications of their strategy, in order to maintain, with any chance of success, their claims that everything goes well, according to plan. Hitherto no intimations have been made that the Dnieper line will be the new defense line (*CEA* #37, September 24, 1943, pp. B-1 and B-5).

We must begin at last to give a clear picture to our peoples and the world about our situation. . . .

In the East, too, this question is now a burning one (*Goebbels Diary*, September 21, 1943, p. 461).

Shortly thereafter, the Russians pushed across the Dnieper, and the propaganda presentation of the Russian front changed. Euphemisms for German retreats and withdrawals dropped out. References to the fierceness of the fighting increased. Breakthroughs and dents were much more frequently admitted. Taking note of the new style of reporting, the FCC analyst concluded: "Apparently this [new] frankness was meant to restore German confidence in Nazi propaganda regarding the Russian front by making a clean sweep." [15]

Reasoning. The prediction of this change in propaganda strategy required that the analyst be sufficiently familiar with the operating code of the German propagandist to anticipate his reaction in the event that military developments continued for much longer to be unfavorable. The euphemistic treatment of German retreats, reasoned the analyst, could not be retained much longer without straining its plausibility and, therefore, undermining the German public's confidence in the propagandist. Knowing the importance which Goebbels attached to maintaining a reputation for credibility, the analyst inferred that Goebbels would soon have to change his line if the front were not stabilized.

CASE STUDY NO. 13.9: INFERENCES ABOUT NAZI ESTIMATES OF U-BOAT WARFARE

The series of inferences presented below will illustrate once again the manner in which propaganda analysis can decipher and go beyond an opponent's propaganda strategy to reconstruct the elite estimates and expectations which have shaped it.

Inference 1 and Verification. Although the full efficacy of the Allied anti-U-boat measures which had been introduced shortly before was not felt until the spring of 1943, an indication of Nazi apprehension on this score was provided by FCC propaganda analysis in early February.

FCC	German Leaders
There is no doubt as to Germany's confidence in ultimate victory through its successes in the war at sea. In recent weeks, however, this tone of confidence has been focussed upon long-range predictions rather than on present successes. . . . Such a tendency may well conceal some dissatisfaction with present conditions. . . . There are signs that the Nazis are still not quite satisfied with the alleged success of their U-boat campaign. . . . [The FCC analyst cites broadcast material referring to weather handicaps in extraordinary language:] Nazi propagandists are not in the habit of doing this when successes are easy and up to expectations (*CEA* #5, February 11, 1943, p. C-5).	[At a Führer Conference of February 8, 1943, Admiral Doenitz explained] that during this month the enemy, surprisingly enough, found out the locations of our submarines and, in some cases, even the exact number of ships. It was confirmed later on that his convoys evaded the known submarine formation (U.S. Navy Dept., *op. cit., 1943*, p. 6). [At a similar conference on February 26, 1943, Doenitz reported:] The month of February may be considered as typical for present submarine warfare. During 14 days at sea nothing was sighted. Three reasons may be advanced: bad weather and poor visibility, possibly the location of the submarines' position by the enemy, but above all, the complete absence of our own reconnaissance (*ibid.*, p. 13).

Reasoning. The strong, continuing Nazi propaganda optimism about U-boats, the FCC analyst noted, included several *new* content indicators which suggested some dissatisfaction and apprehension. These content indicators were:

1. Emphasis on long-range predictions as against claims of present successes.

(The assumption underlying the first FCC inference, based on this content shift, was the generalization previously mentioned, that increased references to future successes indicate a dissatisfaction with the level of present success.)

2. Unusual references to weather difficulties presented implicitly as an excuse for lack of greater successes by the U-boats.

(The unusual nature of such references caught the analyst's attention, a fact which emphasizes the importance of his familiarity with earlier Nazi propaganda on the U-boats.)

Inference 2 and Verification. Despite Doenitz' dissatisfaction with the conditions of U-boat warfare, a dissatisfaction tinged with apprehension, predictions of a great forthcoming U-boat offensive continued to be made during the spring. The official German claim of Allied merchant tonnage sunk during the month of March (926,000 gross registered tons) was one of the highest claims for any month of the war. For April, however, the German claim dropped to less than half the March total.

The FCC analyst made the useful, though relatively simple, inference that the drop in sinkings during April had not been anticipated by the Nazi leadership, nor had the German public been prepared for it. In fact, German propaganda had created just the contrary expectation among the public.

FCC	GOEBBELS
The German claim of sinkings for April is less than half of the claim for March and must be indeed disappointing in view of the expectations aroused with respect to Doenitz's all-out U-boat campaign (*CEA* #17, May 7, 1943, p. C-4).	Unfortunately submarine warfare did not come up to our expectations this month. April has been our most unfavorable month in two years, owing chiefly to the fact that our submarines did not succeed in engaging enemy convoys in major battles (*Goebbels Diary*, May 1, 1943, p. 350).

Inference 3 and Verification. What indications were available as to how long the Allied advantage over U-boats would continue? The propaganda analyst might find indirect indications of this in the Nazi elite's expectations, as reflected in their propaganda.

The first inference presented below suggests that the Nazi expectation of overcoming the Allied advantage was sober indeed, for Goebbels now ordered a major readjustment in the propaganda commitment as to the potential value of the U-boat arm. The FCC analyst reasoned that *such a readjustment would not have been undertaken unless the Nazi leaders expected the U-boats to remain at a disadvantage for some time.*

FCC	GOEBBELS
Slumps in shipping claims in the past have been acknowledged by Berlin, and excused on various grounds but have never involved a major propaganda adjustment as at present. . . . Of outstanding importance is the fact that in addition to these minor techniques [of evasion, compensation, and minimization], Berlin propagandists are beginning to make major adaptations in their shipping propaganda. It is highly significant that these adaptations are being introduced in Berlin's *domestic* propaganda. . . . Significantly, considerable restraint is now being exercised by Nazi propaganda not to relate U-boat warfare to a Second Front or to the outcome of the war at large (*CEA* #20, May 28, 1943, p. C-10).	[While Goebbels did not indicate specifically that he had changed his propaganda line, it can be reasonably assumed that the estimate he revealed in the following passage of the diary would have been followed by a suitable adjustment in his propaganda line:] The failure of our submarines to win victories is having regrettable consequences. The defense of the Anglo-American convoys is now so formidable that, if it continues, a new situation in submarine warfare will have arisen. . . . Our technical development both in the realm of submarines and of air war is far inferior to that of the English and the Americans. We are now getting our reward for our poor leadership on the scientific front (*Goebbels Diary*, May 14, 1943, p. 378).

The decline in U-boat effectiveness persisted through the summer of 1943, with the FCC analyst always watching for the first signs in German propaganda which would suggest that Nazi expectations were becoming more optimistic. In July, although the total sinkings claimed by German sources increased somewhat, the FCC analyst found no indication in propaganda that the Nazi expectation was any less sober than before. Rather, on the basis of his knowledge of the Nazi psychological-warfare patterns for celebrating real victories or for encouraging public expectations of future victories, the FCC analyst predicted:

When and if *special* communiqués appear once again [on U-boat successes], Berlin propagandists may be expected to claim that the race between offensive and defensive weapons has turned in favor of the U-boats.[16]

Inference 4 and Verification. In late September, 1943, German U-boats resumed activity in the North Atlantic after having withdrawn from that area for several months. Earlier in the year, new anti-U-boat defensive measures had given the Allies a definite technical advantage which brought the U-boat menace under control. During the summer of 1943, German leaders and propagandists spoke of efforts being made by German scientists to overcome Allied technical superiority in the war at sea. Finally, when U-boat packs returned to the North Atlantic in late September, the battle that then took place offered an opportunity to gauge whether the U-boats were again capable of challenging Allied supply lines. Allied naval intelligence on the battle would, of course, supply primary data on this point; the role of propaganda analysis was to furnish supplementary estimates.[17]

FCC

The description [in German propaganda] of this U-boat action indicates that the High Command is not ready yet to claim that the Allied defences against the subs have been licked. . . . If these [new U-boat weapons] were tried, they may not have received an adequate test . . . ; another conclusion . . . is that they did not succeed. It may be possible, of course, that the High Command does not want to commit itself as to the new weapons until it has gained several successes and confidence that they will continue. . . . The [German] High Command's *choice of words would seem to indicate that the U-boats "after weeks of pause" have found the conditions of battle no easier than before* (*CEA* #38, October 1, 1943, pp. B-5 and B-6).

GERMAN LEADERS

[Goebbels' summary of a private conversation with Hitler several weeks before the U-boat action took place:] Submarine warfare seemed somewhat more promising to him. The new gadget for neutralizing English radar has proven its worth. . . .

The Fuehrer expects more impressive submarine successes soon. . . . To me he seems even a bit too optimistic. . . . But in this case Doenitz, too, is hopeful, and Doenitz is a very cool and realistic calculator (*Goebbels Diary,* September 10, 1943, p. 436).

[After the attack, Goebbels wrote:] Unfortunately our concentrated submarine attack on a convoy in the northern Atlantic did not really get under way. . . . Nevertheless our submarines succeeded in sinking twelve destroyers and 15,000 tons [18] of shipping.

. . . It would be wonderful if submarine warfare took a new lease on life (*ibid.*, September 24, 1943, p. 483).

[Even before the U-boat action in question, Doenitz expressed his hopeful expectations in sober terms, as is indicated by his report at the Führer Conference on September 10, 1943:] Conditions for sending out submarines have definitely improved. Operations against convoys in the North Atlantic will begin again with the advent of the new moon in September. An attempt will be made to take the enemy by surprise. . . . It will be a hard fight despite our new weapons. . . . There is no doubt that enemy defense measures will rapidly be brought back to previous strength (U.S. Navy Dept., *op. cit., 1943,* p. 136).[19]

Reasoning. The main inference—that the German High Command was not confident that the Allied technical advantage was overcome and that its expectation of future U-boat successes remained modest or uncertain—was based upon several characteristics of the propaganda treatment of the action.

1. The *language* which Nazi propaganda employed in describing the most recent battle was compared by the FCC analyst with the language employed in describing past U-boat actions which had been relatively unsuccessful. The comparison permitted this conclusion: "It is significant that almost the same phrases as these have been used in the past four or five months by the [German] High Command in describing the small and infrequent successes achieved by the U-boats." Therefore, the conclusion seemed warranted that the High Command did not consider that the present action placed the U-boat in a more favorable light than the past actions.

2. All German propaganda descriptions of the U-boat action were carefully scrutinized by the FCC analyst to note whether any refer-

ences, explicit or implicit, to new German weapons had been made. The reason for this search was that German spokesmen and propagandists had reiterated for several months that German technicians were working on new methods for overcoming the technical superiority of Allied defense against the U-boat. The fact, therefore, that *no* reference was made to any new German U-boat weapons or tactics suggested to the FCC analyst two alternative hypotheses (quoted above) regarding the use of new weapons and the Nazi judgment of their efficacy.

3. Another inference was based upon this line of reasoning: References in German domestic propaganda to the use of new weapons or tactics in this action, *had they been made,* would have aroused immediate public hopes that a new period of U-boat successes was beginning. (Past statements by German leaders and propaganda on this topic had created such predispositions.) German propaganda, therefore, would not refer to new weapons and tactics in describing the present battle unless it were ready to encourage such public expectations. Therefore, the fact that no reference to new weapons was made permitted the inference that German propaganda did not want to arouse such hopes. (The FCC analyst noted that the success claimed in the present action by Nazi propaganda was attributed to "surprise," "unbending energy and skill," "courage and self-confidence," and "the unsparing use of all available strength"—that is, to anything and everything but new weapons and tactics.)

4. The inference that Nazi leaders were unwilling to conclude, on the basis of the present battle, that U-boats were again dominant or to raise expectations of a resumption of U-boat successes on the old scale was supported by the FCC analyst by other observations as well. Thus, he noted that two old compensatory propaganda themes, used previously to excuse the low sinkings achieved by the U-boats, were still used in Nazi propaganda after the new action in the North Atlantic. The continuation of these compensatory themes conflicted with the hypothesis that the Nazi elite's estimate and expectations regarding the U-boats were optimistic.

5. Finally, the FCC analyst inferred that Nazi propaganda was implementing the propaganda goal of *actively discouraging public hopes for a resumption of heavy sinkings by the U-boats.* This he inferred from Fritzsche's euphemistic effort to tone down expectations: "We are not naïve enough to indulge in speculation about the future on the basis of the fact of this victory."

The FCC analyst's inferences, be it noted, rested not upon a single line of reasoning but gained plausibility from the fact that several lines of reasoning supported each other.

NOTES

1. For several reasons a more thorough analysis has not been made here. Inferences about morale, for one thing, were particularly difficult to verify in the present investigation. Then, the morale reports of the German Security Police (*S.D.*), which would have served admirably for this purpose, were unfortunately not available to the writer for the period under scrutiny.

2. Microfilm Goebbels diary, March 3, 1943.

3. *Ibid.*

4. See, for example, Case Studies Nos. 13.5, 13.6, and 13.9 (pp. 236, 237, and 242), in this chapter, and the account of Goebbels' conscious effort to emulate the British handling of Dunkirk in staging his glorification of the Stalingrad disaster in Curt Riess, *Joseph Goebbels* (Doubleday & Co., Garden City, N.Y., 1948), pp. 244–48. Riess reports in part as follows: "Defeats, Goebbels stated, were only demoralizing when they became known to the public despite shrewd government measures to keep them secret; when, added to the original shock of defeat, the average citizen was shaken by the realization that his government was no longer telling him the truth. . . . History proved that a defeat must not be necessarily demoralizing" (p. 246).

5. Microfilm Goebbels diary, March 1, 1943. See also Case Study No. 13.6, p. 237.

6. Quoted in Rudolf Semmler, *Goebbels: The Man Next to Hitler* (Westhouse, London, 1947), pp. 76–77. For additional material on Goebbels' estimate of the necessary conditions for a splitting of the enemy coalition and a separate peace, see *Goebbels Diary*, pp. 435, 467–68 (entries for September 10 and 23, 1943).

7. It will be noted that the goals stated here resemble some of those listed in the two previous chapters. This is due to the partially overlapping subject matter of the three problem areas.

8. It should be emphasized, in order to correct past tendencies in content analysis to restrict attention to quantitative trends, that an increase, decrease, emphasis, or de-emphasis with respect to these content indicators may be conveyed by qualitative as well as by quantitative changes.

9. This leads to perhaps the simplest hypothesis, or noncausal correlation, in the group. Stated in the form of a complete sentence, it asserts: "When a situational change in present environment is experienced by an elite as deprivational, references to the self in relevant contexts of its propaganda increase in number and/or emphasis." Similarly, the complete form of the generalization can be formulated for the other content indicators listed.

10. Case Study No. 13.9, 1, p. 242, illustrates the successful use of this generalization.

11. Stated in its complete form, the generalization reads as follows: "When an elite expects a deprivational change in the situation to occur in the future, predictions of enemy deprivations in relevant contexts of its propaganda will diminish in number and/or in magnitude." Similarly, the complete form of the generalization can be formulated for the other content indicators listed.

12. *CEA* #39, October 8, 1943, p. D-1.

13. See Semmler, *op. cit.*, pp. 62–69, and Riess, *op. cit.*, pp. 244–52, which serve as an indirect verification for the inference in this case.

14. This order by Hitler is, of course, only an *indirect* verification, since it does not indicate whether the intention to evacuate was translated into a propaganda policy of preparing the German public in advance for the evacuation.

15. *CEA* #42, October 29, 1943, pp. B-1 ff.

16. *CEA* #29, July 29, 1943, p. C-14.

17. It is not known whether in this case the propaganda-analysis results were of any value, actual or hypothetical, to Naval intelligence.

18. The German High Command communiqué publicly claimed *45,000* gross tons of Allied merchant shipping. This discrepancy may reflect a propagandistic inflation by the High Command of the amount of tonnage thought to be sunk. Goebbels regularly received the private daily communiqué. His figure of 15,000 gross tons may have been taken from this, rather than from the public German communiqué; or perhaps Goebbels' figure is an erroneous transcription. For the purpose of this study, the important part of the above quotation from the diary is that Goebbels, on the basis of private information after the U-boat action, still expressed his hope for a revival of U-boat warfare in the conditional form.

19. For additional materials on the development of the U-boat situation from the German standpoint see Chester Wilmot, *The Struggle for Europe* (William Collins Sons & Co., London, 1952), pp. 123–27, 151–52, and Anthony Martienssen, *Hitler and His Admirals* (E. P. Dutton & Co., Inc., New York, 1949), pp. 173–80.

Part IV

Validation of Inferences

Introduction

One of the reasons for studying the wartime performance of the FCC propaganda analysts, as noted in the Preface, was to assess, if possible, the general utility of their technique as a means of making inferences about certain types of questions of interest to policy-makers. For this purpose, a sample of FCC analyses of German propaganda was selected, and an effort was made to verify each inference in this sample by matching it against relevant historical evidence concerning the Nazi conduct of the war. On the basis of rather exacting verification criteria, 85 per cent of the FCC inferences in this sample which could be scored (and 81 per cent of a larger sample) were noted as correct.

However, the fact that FCC analysts achieved such a high score of successes cannot be taken as conclusively demonstrating the utility of propaganda analysis as an intelligence technique. For, not unexpectedly, it proved difficult to make an adequate statistical analysis of the performance of the FCC analysts.

The conditions under which the FCC analysts operated were such that their performance probably does not constitute a satisfactory trial of the technique from the standpoint of the requirements for statistical analysis. It is not at all certain that several important prerequisites for statistical analysis were met. Thus, (*a*) propaganda analysis, as performed by the FCC, may not have constituted a well-defined method of inference; it may not have been sharply distinguished from other ways and methods of making inferences. (*b*) It is uncertain that the entire output of inferences made by the FCC analysts constituted a representative sample of the types of inferences which the propaganda-analysis method claimed to be capable of producing. In fact, there was no well-defined claim or theory regarding the utility of propaganda analysis as an intelligence method. And, in any case, the possibility cannot be excluded that in selecting problems on which to attempt inferences the FCC analysts tended to restrict the trial to an area in which they were more likely to be successful. (*c*) Since the verification of FCC inferences was fortuitous, depending upon the availability of relevant historical records, there can be no assurance that the group of verified inferences constitutes a representative sample of the entire output of FCC inferences. (*d*) Finally, the relative importance of individual inferences, which must be taken into account in any meaningful statistical analysis, cannot easily be determined.

Since it was not possible to test the general utility of propaganda analysis by means of a statistical analysis of the performance of the FCC, it is necessary to settle for a less rigorous and less conclusive appraisal. The evidence available for this purpose, summarized below (pp. 268–69), strongly suggests that propaganda analysis is capable of more than isolated, hit-or-miss successes on a variety of questions of interest to policy-makers and that its techniques, or methods, are capable of codification, refinement, and improvement.

FOURTEEN

Verification Procedures and Problems

Selection of Inferences

The Foreign Broadcast Intelligence Service (FBIS) was organized within the Federal Communications Commission in late 1941. Its propaganda-analysis operation was centered in the Analysis Division; monitoring and reporting of foreign broadcasts were the responsibilities of other divisions. The Analysis Division was divided into a number of geographical and political sections which produced propaganda analyses of Japanese, Italian, German, French, Russian, English, Spanish, Latin-American, and other materials. The sample of FCC inferences selected for evaluation was taken exclusively from analyses of Nazi propaganda [1] for the following reasons:

1. Historical materials to assess the accuracy of FCC inferences were relatively plentiful and readily accessible in the case of Nazi Germany, perhaps more so than in the case of Japan or Italy.

2. The background and experience of the present investigator, and that of colleagues immediately available for consultation, were more suited to an evaluation of the propaganda analyses of German materials than of other materials.

3. Evaluation of the propaganda analyses of German materials seemed likely to test the fullest potentialities achieved by U.S. propaganda analysis during World War II, for in all probability the techniques of analysis and inference developed in studying

Nazi propaganda were at least as far advanced as those applied in the analysis of the propaganda communications of other countries.

4. The experience gained in analyzing Nazi propaganda communications might be expected to have particular transfer value for analyses of other totalitarian propaganda.

A two-month sample period (March and April, 1943) of the work of the German Section was initially selected for intensive verification and appraisal because historical materials which might serve to verify the inferences were relatively plentiful for these two months.[2] Also, the German Section's output during this period seemed to reflect fairly accurately the problems encountered and the quality of work produced during the entire span of operations from late 1941 through early 1945. The two-month period chosen also recommended itself because, by March, 1943, the reorganization and expansion of the operations of the FCC's Analysis Division, initiated at the beginning of 1943, had been completed. A sample of the German Section's work taken from any period much later would not have been as useful, since in the latter part of 1944 and in 1945 a retrenchment in personnel and scope of operations was in effect.

Every propaganda inference in the nine weekly issues of the German Section's *CEA*,[3] as well as in special reports issued by the German Section during this two-month period, was systematically excerpted and transferred to a card-index file.

Each issue of the *CEA* contained approximately 80 inferences; the total number of inferences for the two-month sample period was 729.

Additional verifications were sought by spot-checking rather intensively, but not so systematically as in the case of the two-month sample period, all other reports produced by the German Section from June, 1942, to June, 1944.[4] The period thus spot-checked encompassed 23 months of the German Section's operations. It yielded a substantial additional number of verified inferences.

Scoring of Inferences

An effort was made to assess the accuracy of the 729 inferences in the two-month sample period, and of as many inferences falling outside this period as possible, by matching them against relevant information contained in official German war records, diaries, memoirs, captured documents, interrogation reports, etc. A large number of sources were examined for this purpose (see Appendix II). A small number of inferences which were in the nature of predictions of future events, perhaps 12 in all, were scored on the basis of subsequent developments.

In the scoring an attempt was made to approximate the ideal of direct empirical verification as closely as possible. That is, in order to make judgments as to the accuracy of inferences as conclusive as possible, it was initially required that they be based on historical evidence which was both quite reliable in character and directly relevant to the subject matter of the inference. This requirement of course reduced the number of FCC inferences which could be scored as either correct or incorrect and left a relatively large number for which no determination could be made. But it also served to minimize the subjectivity and uncertain validity which broader and more flexible scoring rules or criteria would have introduced.

The verification procedure was stringent and rigorous in another sense as well. A particularly determined effort was made to find historical evidence which might establish the *error* of each FCC inference. Moreover, the investigator remained alert to possibilities that the scoring procedure might inadvertently and indirectly favor the score of the FCC analysts in some way. As a matter of fact, this caution proved to be well justified. Midway in scoring the inferences, the investigator began to suspect that the initial decision to require direct historical evidence was making it easier to confirm accurate FCC inferences than to prove the error of inaccurate ones. The criteria for verification were then broadened somewhat, and all inferences were rescored. The result was a substantial increase in the relative number of inferences judged as incorrect (see Appendix I, pp. 276–77).

Difficult methodological problems are encountered in the use of historical records for verification of inferences. Although ideally explicit rules are desirable for deciding whether or not an inference is to be regarded as correct or incorrect on the basis of the available historical evidence, no effort was made to formulate a full set of such rules, for several reasons. First, the necessity for doing so was relieved to some extent by the initial decision to require strict and direct historical evidence—a requirement which was only somewhat moderated later in order to avoid a bias in the scoring procedure.

Then, too, it was perhaps less urgent that the scoring procedure be made fully objective for another reason. Many of the FCC inferences which were scored have been included in this report, together with an account of the historical evidence used in verifying them. These case materials provide readers with an opportunity for appraising the scoring decisions made by the investigator.

Finally, it was not deemed worth while to make the considerable research investment which would have been necessary in order to draw up explicit scoring rules because a detailed statistical appraisal of the FCC's score was in any case not possible, for reasons considered in detail in Appendix I.

The procedure for verifying inferences, however, was not entirely unsystematic. As has already been suggested, two distinctions or sets of criteria were employed by the investigator in assessing the accuracy or inaccuracy of inferences. It was recognized, first, that the *certainty* of any judgment as to the accuracy or inaccuracy of an inference depended upon the *appropriateness and reliability of the available historical evidence* for that particular inference. For example, to score an FCC inference about the official Nazi estimate on a given policy matter might ideally require the verbatim records of discussions among top Nazi leaders at the time. If this historical material were not available and it was necessary to rely, instead, upon the postwar recollections of a single leading Nazi for verifying the inference, these recollections would be regarded as less appropriate and less reliable for verification purposes. The scoring decision would accordingly have to be regarded as less certain. Considerations of this sort, familiar to historians, were taken into account in deciding whether the historical materials were adequate to permit any scoring decision and in weighing the degree of certainty of individual scoring decisions. The accuracy or inaccuracy of inferences was coded as very certain, certain, or not certain enough to be scored.

Another problem concerned the extent to which the *implication* of available historical material should be relied upon in scoring an inference as correct or incorrect. Ideally the contents of the historical material and of the FCC inference should coincide exactly, so that the accuracy or inaccuracy of the inference would be more or less self-evident. For example, as reported in Part III, British propaganda analysts inferred that the use of the V-1 (buzz bombs) had been postponed because something had happened as of a certain date to set back the German schedule for production and use of this weapon. This inference was rather directly verified on the basis of Goebbels' account, in his diary, of a talk with Hitler, in which Hitler admitted that a British air raid on the date in question had disrupted production of the V-1 and forced a delay of several weeks. In other cases, on the other hand, inferences could be scored as correct or incorrect only by relying to a greater extent upon the implication of the available historical evidence. Accordingly, a rough distinction was adopted in scoring inferences between those for which the historical material approximated the ideal of direct verification and those which rested upon an interpretation of the implications of the historical evidence. As was to be expected, it proved relatively easier to find direct historical evidence suitable for assessing inferences about important matters connected with the German conduct of the war (major events, instructions, decisions, etc.) than for inferences about detailed aspects of behavior and opinion.

While these two sets of distinctions do not encompass all of the criteria relevant for purposes of scoring inferences, they do constitute two of the more important ones. The fact that they at least were dealt with in a relatively systematic fashion may offer some assurance as to the adequacy of the scoring procedure. Moreover, the use of these distinctions did permit a check upon the possibility of a bias in the scoring procedure.

NOTES

1. The sample in this study was drawn from the analyses by the German Section in the Analysis Division's *Weekly Analysis* and (later) *Weekly Review* (up to 1943) and in the *Central European Analysis* (*CEA*) thereafter. Excluded from consideration were a series of weekly statements written by the German Section especially for the Office of War Information, which had as their purpose to point up German psychological-warfare vulnerabilities. Also excluded were the two- to four-page summaries of the *CEA* prepared for the over-all *Weekly Review*. These two reports largely duplicated for more specialized or general audiences inferences already presented in the *CEA*.

2. A continuous rather than a periodic sample of the FCC's work was desirable because of the continuity of the analysis from week to week.

3. The *CEA* reports included analyses of propaganda from German satellite radio stations and newspapers (e.g., Hungary, Rumania, Finland, etc.) as well as of official German propaganda. To focus the present evaluation more sharply, only analyses of official German materials have been considered.

4. The German Section's contributions to the *Weekly Analysis* prior to June, 1942, were not included in the spot-check because issues of this report prior to this date were not readily available.

FIFTEEN

Results

The main results of the effort to verify FCC inferences are presented in this chapter. The value of these results is largely descriptive, since, for the reasons discussed in Appendix I, the impressive score of successes achieved by the FCC propaganda analysts cannot be satisfactorily assessed by statistical means.

Number of Inferences Scored as Correct or Incorrect

Despite the substantial body of documentary material on the Nazi conduct of the war available for general research purposes, it proved difficult to find acceptable historical evidence for scoring most FCC inferences as correct or incorrect.

Of the entire output of 729 inferences made by the German Section in the two-month sample period (March and April, 1943), only 119 inferences (16 per cent) were verified in some way, i.e., scored as having been successful or unsuccessful. For the remaining 610 inferences, historical materials were either not available or deemed not adequate for purposes of making a scoring decision.

Scoring decisions could be made for but 118 inferences in the additional 23-month period that was spot-checked. The percentage of verifications in the spot-check period cannot be computed since the total number of inferences made during these 23 months was not counted. However, it is quite obvious that, as expected, the proportion of inferences that could be scored in the spot-check period was much lower than that in the two-month sample period, for which richer historical documentation was available.

Percentage of Correct Inferences

Inferences scored as being correct outnumbered those scored as incorrect by a large margin in both periods. In the two-month sample period 85 per cent of the 119 inferences for which some verification decision was made were scored as having been correct on the basis of available historical evidence. The proportion of success achieved in the spot-check period was somewhat lower (76 per cent). For the two periods combined, the percentage of successes was 81 per cent. (See Table 1.)

TABLE 1

PERCENTAGE OF FCC PROPAGANDA-ANALYSIS INFERENCES SCORED
AS CORRECT AND INCORRECT
(Verification on Basis of Historical Evidence)

	Correct	Incorrect	Other *	Total
Sample period (March–April, 1943)	101 (85%)	15 (13%)	3 (2%)	119 (100%)
Spot-check period (June, 1942–June, 1944, exclusive of sample period)	90 (76%)	18 (15%)	10 (9%)	118 (100%)
Sample and spot-check periods	191 (81%)	33 (14%)	13 (5%)	237 (100%)

* A small number of inferences were judged to be partly correct and partly incorrect. These comprise the "other" category; they are not to be confused with inferences for which no verification decision could be made for lack of historical evidence.

A chi-square test of significance was made of the difference in scores achieved in the sample and spot-check periods. The test indicated the high likelihood that the score of correct inferences achieved in the spot-check period (23 months) was significantly lower than that achieved in the two-month sample period.[1] This finding is not unexpected, since the spot-check period includes many inferences made in 1942, when propaganda analysis was in an early stage of development and the FCC analysts were acquiring appropriate skills.

The high percentage of successful inferences made by the FCC propaganda analysts, however impressive it seems, cannot be accepted as firm evidence of the utility of the technique in the absence of an adequate statistical test of its significance and reliability. Although the prerequisites for such a statistical analysis can hardly be met in the present instance, it can be argued that they are not totally lacking. A statistical analysis has therefore been made, and confidence intervals have been constructed for the true proportion of successful inferences in the two-month sample period. The results indicate that, were a statistical analysis justified in this case, the FCC's performance would constitute good evidence of the utility of the propaganda-analysis technique.[2]

Consideration was given to the possibility of testing the hypothesis that the method used by the FCC analysts in making their inferences was better than some random method, such as tossing a coin. Such a test was considered inapplicable for the following reason. For most of the problems to which the propaganda analysts addressed themselves neither the number of reasonable interpretations nor the number of alternatives actually considered by the FCC analysts could be reliably reconstructed from the FCC reports. Moreover, the number of alternatives undoubtedly varied from one inferential problem to another. The information essential for testing whether the performance achieved by the FCC analysts was better than that of some random method was therefore lacking.

Neither was an attempt made to test the hypothesis that, for the types of problems in question, the propaganda-analysis method of making inferences is better than educated guessing or research methods other than propaganda analysis. Such a test, had it been undertaken, might have taken the form of a retrospective comparison of the performance of the FCC analysts with that of wartime specialists who had employed other intelligence techniques. It would have been necessary to select a list of problems which could be said to provide a fair test of the relative worth of the methods being compared. Apart from the difficulty of making such a selection, it would not have been possible to guarantee that the performance of the methods on these problems could be systematically compared, since verification, which depended upon the availability of relevant historical evidence, was necessarily incomplete and fortuitous. Unless the selection of problems took it into account, it is quite possible that not all of the methods for which a comparison was desired would have produced inferences on each of the problems included on the preselected list. These latter two difficulties might be overcome by discarding the idea of a preselected list and relying instead for the comparison between propaganda analysis and any other method solely upon that group of problems for which (*a*) both methods attempted inferences and (*b*) adequate verification was possible. The fortuitous nature of such a sample, however, would in turn raise new and difficult questions concerning the possibility of a statistical analysis (see Appendix I).

Still another obstacle to a comparative analysis of this type was the very real possibility that some of the methods being compared (including propaganda analysis itself) were not well-defined techniques which provided independent estimates on the problems comprising the test (see Appendix I, pp. 273–74).

Since a systematic and useful comparison did not seem feasible on the basis of a retrospective appraisal of past performances, this type of assessment was not attempted. The present study can offer no conclusions, therefore, regarding the relative merits of propaganda analysis and other, perhaps alternative, methods of research on similar problems.

Other Results

There were a number of more specific questions concerning the utility of propaganda analysis to which firm answers would have been desirable. Is the technique able to infer *certain* types of antecedent conditions more successfully than others? Are *certain* subject matters, or topics, more readily inferred than others by the propaganda-analysis technique? Of the two methods of inference (direct and indirect) found in the FCC's work, was one appreciably better than the other as a means of making accurate inferences? Was there any appreciable difference in the utility of the two types of content indicators (frequency and nonfrequency) used by the FCC analysts? Finally, does making inferences in a formal, explicit, and systematic fashion increase the likelihood of success over that achieved by a more intuitive style of making inferences?

Because of the various limitations upon statistical analysis, conclusive answers to these questions were not possible in the present study. Accordingly, only a brief summary and interpretation of the descriptive results on these questions are presented.

1. Approximately the same percentage of successes was achieved by the FCC analysts for inferences about Nazi propaganda matters (82 per cent), Nazi elite behavior (89 per cent), and situational factors (86 per cent) (see Table 2). However, these results do not dem-

onstrate conclusively that propaganda analysis is as good a method for inferring elite behavior and situational factors as it is for inferring propaganda behavior. That is, the possibility cannot be excluded that the percentage of successes achieved by the FCC in inferring Nazi elite behavior and situational factors is an inflated measure. For the FCC analysts may have ventured to state inferences on elite behavior and situational factors only on those occasions on which they felt rel-

TABLE 2

Verification Results by Antecedent Condition of Inference
(Two-Month Sample Period, March–April, 1943)

Antecedent Condition Inferred	Total (in Two-Month Sample Period)	Number for Which Verification Was Obtained	Number of Inferences Scored as Correct	Percentage of Inferences Scored as Correct
1. Propaganda directives	19	7	6	
2. Propaganda techniques	47	3	3	
3. Propaganda goals	380	51	41	
(Total: Propaganda matters)	(446)	(61)	(50)	(82%)
4. Elite policies and intentions	85	18	15	
5. Elite expectations	35	10	10	
6. Elite estimates	41	8	7	
(Total: Elite behavior)	(161)	(36)	(32)	(89%)
7. Situational events	122	22	19	(86%)
	729	119	101	(85%)

atively confident of the plausibility and correctness of their inferences. They seem to have been aware that inferences about elite behavior and situational factors brought them into more direct competition with research specialists in other agencies and were therefore slower to make inferences on these subjects. And there seems to have been some feeling among the FCC analysts that the utility of propaganda analysis was largely limited to analysis of propaganda strategy, which again tended to limit their eagerness to make inferences on elite behavior and situational factors except where they were quite sure of their grounds.

What these results do suggest, perhaps, is that if propaganda analysts are permitted to exercise their own *ad hoc* judgment as to the specific occasions on which to try for inferences about elite behavior and situational factors, they are likely to achieve as good a score of successes in this broader area as when they try only for inferences about propaganda strategy.

2. The FCC inferences were also classified according to nine topics, or subject matters. The percentage of successful inferences in these nine categories varied but was relatively high for almost all of them. The data suggest that propaganda analysis did better on various domestic matters related directly or indirectly to internal morale than on problems of diplomacy, relations with Axis partners, and

TABLE 3

VERIFICATION RESULTS BY TOPIC OF INFERENCE
(Two-Month Sample Period, March–April, 1943)

Topic of Inference	Total Number of Inferences Attempted	Number of Inferences for Which Verification Was Obtained	Number of Inferences Scored as Correct	Percentage of Inferences Scored as Correct
1. Nazi domestic propaganda	369	39	35	90%
2. Nazi foreign psychological warfare	239	39	30	77%
3. German morale	192	21	21	100%
4. Military events	185	41	36	88%
5. Diplomacy and foreign relations	69	15	10	67%
6. German domestic economic policies	26	3	3	100%
7. German domestic political policies	18	1	1	100%
8. Relations between Axis partners	15	3	2	67%
9. Intra-elite conflicts among Nazis	7	2	1	50%
	1120 *			

* The total exceeds the actual total number of inferences in the sample period—729—because of numerous instances of double and triple coding of the topic of inference under which a single inference could be subsumed.

psychological warfare to foreign audiences, but because of the small frequencies under several categories and other limitations upon statistical analysis, they do no more than suggest this (see Table 3).

3. The FCC analysts appear to have relied primarily on the indirect method in attempting inferences about Nazi elite behavior and situational events. At least, traces of the indirect method could be seen more clearly and in many more inferences than was the case for the direct method. Of 133 inferences on elite behavior and situational factors [3] for which historical materials permitted a scoring decision, well over half (80) utilized the indirect method. This is a minimum figure since it includes only indirect inferences which could be definitely established as such. In contrast, only 3 of the 133 inferences could clearly be established as having been derived by means of the direct method. For the remaining 50 inferences in this group, no clear determination was possible of the use of any method of inference.

Eighty-one per cent of the indirect inferences in this group were scored as correct. There were too few clear-cut cases of the direct method to permit any comparison of successes achieved by the two methods.

4. In over half of the inferences which could be scored (129 out of 248) it was not possible to determine conclusively whether a frequency or nonfrequency content indicator had been employed by the FCC analysts. The results do not show any appreciable difference in the level of success achieved by these two types of content indicators (82 per cent for nonfrequency inferences; 79 per cent for frequency inferences; see Table 4).

5. Several results were unexpected and of interest, though their sig-

TABLE 4

VERIFICATION RESULTS BY TYPE OF CONTENT INDICATOR EMPLOYED
(Two-Month Sample Period and Twenty-Three-Month Spot-Check Period)

Type of Content Indicator	Scored as Correct	Scored as Incorrect	Other *	Total
Frequency	33 (79%)	7	2	42
Nonfrequency	63 (82%)	10	4	77
Indeterminate	104 (81%)	18	7	129
				248 †

* A small number of inferences were judged to be partly correct and partly incorrect, or were so structured as to make a clear-cut determination impossible.

† The total is slightly higher than the total number of verified inferences (237) because of double-coding in a few instances.

nificance is far from clear. The percentage of successes for inferences in which *no clear method of inference* (either direct or indirect) could be discerned was about as high as that for inferences in which use of one or the other was evident. Again, the level of success achieved in inferences in which *neither a frequency nor a nonfrequency content indicator* could be discerned was as high (81 per cent) as that for inferences in which use of one or the other type of indicator was evident.

At first glance, these two results seem to indicate that making one's inferences in a formal, explicit, and systematic fashion does not increase the likelihood of success, and that a more intuitive form of educated guessing is equally successful. While this may be true in fact, the present results should be viewed with considerable caution as evidence for this important conclusion. In the first place, the ostensibly intuitive inferences which turned out so well in this case were made by analysts who were also making relatively systematic inferences on closely related subjects. It is possible that the more explicit methods of inference being developed and applied by the FCC analysts throughout this period contributed indirectly to the quality of the less formalized inferences which they also ventured to make. In other words, it cannot be assumed that propaganda analysts who confined themselves *exclusively* to an intuitive approach to inference would do as well as the FCC analysts did when they attempted intuitive inferences.

Second, the conditions of the wartime trial under which the FCC analysts made their inferences and wrote their reports offer several grounds for caution in interpreting the data summarized above concerning the relative merits of explicit *vs.* intuitive styles of inference. It cannot be assumed that the FCC reports faithfully reflect in all cases the explicitness and detail of the reasoning on which inferences were actually based. Rather, the only accounts of inferences available today in these FCC reports are often edited, revised, and abbreviated versions of earlier, more detailed drafts prepared by the propaganda analysts. Several operational and administrative considerations could and did affect the amount of detailed reasoning which was reproduced in the published FCC reports. Space and time pressures did not always permit a full and explicit written presentation of the analyst's reasoning on behalf of his inferences. Not every inference could very well be written up in equal detail if deadlines were to be met and the length of the report kept to manageable proportions.

When circumstances permitted, the FCC analyst probably gave a fuller account in writing for those inferences that were complicated in structure and had been relatively difficult to make. He was also likely to document more fully inferences on important matters, those which provided findings of an unexpected character, and those which were likely to be challenged by clients of the FCC analyses. For these reasons, it would be hazardous to regard the contents of the FCC reports as providing reliable and adequate material for assessing the comparative worth of systematic *vs.* intuitive approaches to making inferences.

Summary and Evaluation

The object of the effort to score FCC inferences was not to pass judgment on the performance of the FCC analysts. Rather, it was to utilize data on the successes and failures of the FCC analysts to arrive at a general conclusion regarding the utility of the propaganda-analysis method which they had employed. In practice, as pointed out in detail in Appendix I, it was not possible to make the types of statistical analyses that would have been desirable for this purpose because the prerequisites for such analyses could not be satisfied. Therefore, in the present study, a conclusive, statistical demonstration of the utility of propaganda analysis in this area of research for policy-making purposes is not and cannot be provided.

However, the fact that approximately 80 per cent of the FCC inferences turned out to be accurate on the basis of an exacting validation procedure can hardly be dismissed or ignored in attempting a less rigorous appraisal of the merits of propaganda analysis. Nor does the case for the worth of propaganda analysis rest exclusively upon a favorable interpretation of this score. A variety of other considerations, to which reference has been made at various points throughout this report, are also relevant. Briefly recapitulated, they are:

1. The fact that the FCC analysts succeeded in making correct inferences on a wide variety of questions, many of them of undoubted interest and importance to policy-makers at the time.

2. The fact that accurate inferences were made not only on matters of Nazi propaganda strategy but also on Nazi intentions, the calculations and estimates which underlay Nazi policies, and the situational factors influencing Nazi choices of policy and action.

3. The fact that the FCC analysts were able to give a consistently reliable analysis on a given intelligence problem over a period of

time, which strongly sugge'sts that propaganda analysis is capable of more than isolated, hit-or-miss successes (see Part III, pp. 191–209).

4. The fact that the successes achieved by the FCC analysts were not lucky guesses or the result solely of gifted intuition but, as this study indicates, were also based on *methods* of inference which can be, and have been, articulated and codified to an appreciable degree.

5. The fact that, as we have seen, the methods and procedures of the FCC propaganda analysis could be made more explicit and partially codified provides both the analysts themselves and their clients with the basis for a much-needed internal check on the plausibility of inferences.

6. The fact that the different types of generalizations and knowledge utilized in making and supporting propaganda-analysis inferences can be, and have been, identified, thus paving the way for the development of a science of propaganda analysis.

NOTES

1. The chi-square test was based only on those cases for which the verification decision was definitely positive or negative. (Thus, the 3 inferences in the sample period and the 10 inferences from the spot-check period which were scored neither as correct or incorrect were omitted.) The tabulation was as follows:

	Correct (+)	Incorrect (−)	Total
Sample period	101	15	116
Spot-check	90	18	108
Total	191	33	224

The test yields a chi-square value of 17.64 with one degree of freedom. The probability of achieving or exceeding such a value is in the order of .001. Assuming that the conditions of the trial remained the same in both periods, the test therefore indicates the high likelihood of a significant difference in scores achieved.

2. If the prerequisites listed in Appendix I were satisfied, the sample proportion $\hat{P} = .85$ would be an unbiased estimate of the true proportion P of valid inferences made by the propaganda-analysis method, etc. Being a sample estimate, however, $\hat{P}$ would vary from sample to sample, and it would be desirable to know within what limits it is probable (to a certain degree) that the true proportion lies. This statement may be made: With a confidence of .95 the true proportion of valid inferences lies within the interval

$$\hat{P} \pm 1.96 \sqrt{\frac{\hat{P}\,(1-\hat{P})}{N}}$$

or, in this case,

$$.85 \pm 1.96 \sqrt{\frac{(.85)\,(.15)}{119}}$$

The confidence interval is then (.786, .914). Or, if a higher level of confidence is required, say at .99, then 1.96 is replaced by 2.57 and the interval is (.766, .934). The results follow from the fact that for sample sizes this large $\hat{P}$ is essentially normally distributed with mean P and variance $P(1-P)/N$. The factors 1.96 and 2.57 are obtained from a table of the normal distribution. These intervals give one an idea of how good an estimate of the true proportion P has been obtained with the present verification score (85 per cent) and the number of validated inferences (119).

3. It should be remembered that a choice between the direct or indirect method exists only when inferences are being made about elite behavior or situational events. Inferences about propaganda behavior (propaganda directives, techniques, or goals) are by definition based on the indirect method.

Appendixes

Note on Problems of Statistical Analysis

As is usually the case in applying statistical analysis to the results of some experiment, the main problems in assessing the worth of the propaganda-analysis technique were not statistical. A definite assessment could not be made from the data available from the historical trial given propaganda analysis during World War II by the FCC. A number of prerequisites or conditions would have had to be met in order to subject the performance of the FCC analysts to statistical analysis. This appendix comments at some length on what these prerequisites are and why they could not be met in the present case.

Was the FCC Propaganda-Analysis Method of Inference a Well-Defined One?

A statistical test of the FCC's performance presupposes that its propaganda analysis constitutes a *well-defined method of inference.* Only if this were true would one be justified for purposes of statistical analysis in regarding the FCC experience as an occasion on which the propaganda-analysis method was given a historical trial. In fact, however, propaganda analysis was in the process of development during the course of the FCC operation. Before proceeding to a statistical analysis of performance, therefore, it would be necessary to establish first whether the work of the FCC indeed reflects any well-defined, systematic method (or methods). Second, it would be necessary to differentiate FCC inferences which clearly exemplify a given method of inference from those which merely reflect efforts to develop one.

As was noted in Parts I and III, it was possible by means of rational reconstruction to identify two methods of inference implicit in much of the work of the FCC analysts. But reasoning patterns were often so diffuse and blurred that many inferences could not be regarded as exemplifying either of the two methods of inference in question (see Part IV, p. 266). Accordingly, the character of the FCC's performance does not justify the sharp contrast, which the research questions posed for statistical analysis assume, between a well-defined, systematic method and no method at all.

Of somewhat uncertain tenability, also, is the assumption of a sharp distinction between a unique propaganda-analysis method and other methods. Since the methods of inference employed by the FCC analysts were not explicitly defined and systematized, it is likely that their inferences were not solely based upon, and exclusively supported by, propaganda-analysis evidence. Thus, it is possible that at times (although probably not very often) the FCC analysts based their inferential hunches upon sources other than Nazi propaganda and, consciously or unwittingly, superimposed them upon a propaganda analysis which did not really test their plausibility in any logical sense. When this occurs, propaganda analysis does not constitute an *independent* technique for evaluating inferences. The support it lends to an inference is in a sense spurious, and it follows that the fact that such an inference turns out to be correct does not constitute probative evidence of the value of the propaganda-analysis technique.

The shortcoming in question is not that inferential hypotheses are obtained outside of the propaganda analysis itself, but rather that the propaganda analysis does not really contribute to assessing the plausibility of such hunches but only seems to. In other words, the position taken here is that the origin of the inferential hypothesis is irrelevant as long as its plausibility can be independently assessed by means of a systematic propaganda-analysis method. Spurious propaganda-analysis support for an inference is likely to occur in the absence of a clear-cut method of inference which is explicitly applied.

Did the FCC Inferences Constitute a Representative Sample of Propaganda-Analysis Inferences?

Another prerequisite for a statistical analysis is that the entire output of inferences by the FCC should constitute a representative sample of the types of inferences which the propaganda-analysis method claims to be capable of producing in the area of policy research in question.

The necessity for having a representative sample in this case can be illustrated by a hypothetical example. Assume that the claim is advanced that propaganda analysis is able to make inferences within a certain area of policy research. Assume also that the propaganda analysts know that this is not, strictly speaking, the case but that one can do quite well with the method within a more restricted field of investigation. They may therefore confine their inferences to this smaller area. In this event the results they achieve are likely to give an overly favorable impression of the more general claims made for the method if the restriction which took place when they were actually applying the method is overlooked. The actual work performed, in the event such restriction takes place, is obviously not an adequate sample for testing the general claim made.

Whether the work of the FCC was indeed representative in this sense can only be conjectured, because the FCC inferences available as data are the result of a historical trial of propaganda analysis which was more or less freely *explorative rather than systematic*. In the first place, there was no well-defined claim or theory advanced regarding the utility of propaganda analysis as an intelligence method which might have determined the structure of the trial undertaken by the FCC.[1] There is therefore no pre-existing basis against which to judge the representativeness of the FCC's work as a sample for statistical analysis of its performance.

Second, it is difficult retrospectively to define the FCC's work as being a specific representative sample of anything in particular. The FCC analysts did indeed cover a broad range of questions of policy interest, and various types of inferential problems were successfully undertaken. But information as to how they selected and rejected problems for propaganda analysis—that is, as to the decisions which determined the output now available for statistical analysis—is not adequate to reconstruct reliably the principles of selection and rejection that were presumably operative at the time. It is clear that a variety of considerations influenced such decisions, but precisely what some of the complex and subtle operational and personal factors were which influenced such decisions is not so clear.

If the FCC had selected problems for propaganda analysis from a list of specific requests or requirements put to it by other agencies, it might be possible to clarify some of these questions. But this was not the case. The FCC analysts were left largely free to explore the potentialities of their new method without any systematic controls over their selection of problems.[2] Accordingly, it is difficult to describe the FCC's work as a sample suitable for statistical analysis.

Did the Verified Inferences Constitute a Representative Sample of All FCC Inferences?

Another prerequisite for a statistical analysis is that the group of *verified* inferences (that is, inferences whose accuracy can be assessed) be a representative sample of the entire output of FCC inferences. Two possibilities of distortion were considered. First, since whether or not inferences were verified depended upon the availability of relevant historical records, the sample of verified inferences is a *fortuitous* one. If the sample were also to be considered a representative one, the probability of finding verification for a correct inference would have to be the same as the probability of finding verification for a false inference. A rough indirect check was made upon the representative character of the fortuitous sample. While this check could not be conclusive, it did serve to strengthen confidence in the assumption that the fortuitous sample of verified inferences was representative of the entire body of FCC inferences in certain relevant respects.[3]

Second, there was the additional possibility of a bias in the verification procedure itself, which was referred to in Part IV. The largely implicit rules employed by the investigator for deciding whether available historical materials were sufficiently appropriate and reliable, and directly enough related to the content of the inference, may inadvertently have favored either confirmation of correct inferences or proof of error of false inferences. In either case, a bias of this sort derived from the scoring *rules* themselves would have distorted the representative character of the sample of verified inferences. This possibility was indeed present, and steps were taken to minimize it.

The initial decision to require very strict, direct evidence in historical materials in order to score inferences as accurate or inaccurate was found to have inflated the score of successful inferences achieved by the FCC analysts. Even on a priori grounds there is reason to believe that verification results will be distorted by the requirement that historical evidence *explicitly and directly* confirm or establish the error of an inference. This expectation was strengthened by an examination of the character of the *Goebbels Diary*,[4] which turned out to be the main source for verifications in this study. The diary is more likely to *affirm* Goebbels' propaganda policies than to list policies which he did not pursue, though of course this is not invariably the case. Therefore, it is not possible to establish all the errors in inference made by the FCC analysts with a scoring rule which requires that *explicit proof* of error of an inference be found in the *Goebbels Diary* or in other Nazi records.

Accordingly, in order to avoid a technical bias in the scoring procedure, it was decided to redefine the verification rules to permit inferences to be established as correct or incorrect on the basis of the *implication* of the available historical evidence. That is, FCC inferences could be scored as incorrect when they were merely implicitly ruled out by statements about Nazi policies and calculations appearing in the *Goebbels Diary* and in other historical sources. All FCC inferences were reassessed on the basis of this somewhat more flexible scoring procedure. Not only was the result a larger number of inferences whose accuracy could be assessed, but, as expected, there was a relative increase in the proportion of incorrect inferences. Thus, whereas the total number of inferences scored as correct increased from 82 to 191, the total of incorrect inferences increased from 6 to 33. The dependence of the results of any statistical appraisal upon the scoring rules is nicely illustrated. The crucial methodological decision becomes at what point to draw the line between verification (either positive or negative) and nonverification. In the present study it was felt that any additional broadening of the scoring rules would have so increased the subjectivity of the procedure as to endanger altogether the attempt at a relatively systematic empirical verification of inferences.

Was the Relative Importance of Individual Inferences Taken into Account?

A satisfactory statistical analysis of the FCC's performance would also require that the *relative importance* of individual inferences be taken into account. In policy-research operations of this kind, some types of estimates (or inferences) are more important than others to intelligence clients and policy-makers. Similarly, from the standpoint of these clients, it is more serious if the estimates provided by propaganda analysts are wrong on certain problems than on others. It is precisely such considerations (known as "decision functions" and "risk functions") which are of central interest in current statistical theory.

It suffices here to note that only if the relative importance of individual FCC successes and failures were taken into account would a meaningful statistical analysis of the utility of the propaganda-analysis method be possible. Since other prerequisites for statistical analysis were lacking, the difficult task of grading the relative importance of different types of FCC inferences was not undertaken.

NOTES

1. Some FCC analysts may have leaned toward the theory that the utility of propaganda analysis was limited largely to inferences about propaganda strategy. Such a theory is suggested, for example, in Ernst Kris and Hans Speier, *German Radio Propaganda* (Oxford University Press, London, 1944), pp. 291 ff., 457–58. Nonetheless, in practice many inferences about elite behavior and situational factors were also made. It may well be, therefore, that it this theory existed at all, it consisted of nothing more precise than a general reluctance to claim too much for the new method of propaganda analysis.

2. This discussion should *not* be understood as implying a preference for greater control over those who are engaged in an initial operational trial of a new analytical method. While a relatively unrestricted situation such as that in which the FCC analysts worked limits the possibility of a later statistical audit of results, precisely the looseness and freedom of the situation may have been highly instrumental in enabling the FCC analysts to develop propaganda-analysis methodology for purposes of inference. It must be remembered that propaganda analysis was *not* a well-defined method. The purpose of the historical trial in this case was not primarily to *test* the utility of a method but to *develop* a method. The controls over operational use of propaganda analysis that are necessary to permit subsequent statistical analysis of results, therefore, should perhaps be considered as being more appropriately added *after* a well-defined method is available for testing.

3. The check employed, not reported here in full, made use of the sevenfold classification of inferences according to antecedent condition inferred (see Part I, Chapter 1). The fortuitous character of the verification procedure could bias the *over-all* score of successes if the possibility of finding adequate historical evidence for verification were greater for types of antecedent conditions on which propaganda analysis was in fact more successful. Accordingly, the percentage of successes for each of the seven groups of inferences was computed. Then this percentage, or score, was applied to the *total number* of inferences of that type attempted by the FCC (that is, those for which no scoring decision could be made for lack of historical evidence as well as those scored as accurate or inaccurate). This gave the *estimated* absolute number of accurate inferences for each of the seven types of inferences. This number was based on the important assumption that, had it been possible to assess the accuracy of all inferences, the *proportion* of correct inferences in each category would have remained the same as when only a smaller number of inferences were verified fortuitously. Then the estimated absolute number of accurate inferences for all seven types of inferences was added up, and a hypothetical over-all percentage or score of correct inferences was computed. This hypothetical percentage, it turned out, closely approximated the over-all percentage of successes for the fortuitous sample, thus lending some support to the belief that the latter score was not biased simply because more inferences of one type rather than another happened to be verified on the basis of available historical evidence.

4. This is the term used in this study to refer to Louis P. Lochner (ed.), *The Goebbels Diaries, 1942–1943* (Doubleday & Co., Inc., Garden City, N.Y., 1948).

Sources Consulted for Verification of FCC Inferences*

Sources Yielding Verification

CHURCHILL, WINSTON S. *The Hinge of Fate;* Vol. IV of *The Second World War.* Houghton Mifflin Co., Boston, 1950.

CRAVEN, W. F., and CATE, J. L. (eds.). *Europe: Argument to V-E Day, January 1944 to May 1945;* Vol. 3 of *The Army Air Forces in World War II.* University of Chicago Press, Chicago, 1951.

GERMAN NAVAL STAFF, OPERATIONS DIVISION. *Records,* Part A, Vol. 36, August, 1942.

GILBERT, FELIX. *Hitler Directs His War.* Oxford University Press, New York, 1950.

GOEBBELS, JOSEPH. *Tagebuch.* (Microfilm of the original German manuscript of Goebbels' diary, made available through the courtesy of the Hoover War Library, Stanford University, Stanford, Calif.)

INTERNATIONAL MILITARY TRIBUNAL. *Trial of the Major War Criminals before the International Military Tribunal,* Nuremberg, Germany, 1948.

KESSELRING, ALBERT. *Kesselring: A Soldier's Record.* William Morrow & Co., New York, 1954.

LIDDELL HART, B. H. *The German Generals Talk.* William Morrow & Co., New York, 1948.

LOCHNER, LOUIS P. (ed.). *The Goebbels Diaries, 1942–1943.* Doubleday & Co., Inc., Garden City, N.Y., 1948.

MARTIENSSEN, ANTHONY. *Hitler and His Admirals.* E. P. Dutton & Co., Inc., New York, 1949.

* See the Case Studies in Part III.

OFFICE OF U.S. CHIEF OF COUNSEL FOR PROSECUTION OF AXIS CRIMINALITY. *Nazi Conspiracy and Aggression.* U.S. Government Printing Office, Washington, 1946.

RIESS, CURT. *Joseph Goebbels.* Doubleday & Co., Inc., Garden City, N.Y., 1948.

SEMMLER, RUDOLF. *Goebbels: The Man Next to Hitler.* Westhouse, London, 1947.

SHERWOOD, R. E. *Roosevelt and Hopkins.* Harper & Bros., New York, 1948.

SHULMAN, MILTON. *Defeat in the West.* Secker and Warburg, London, 1947.

U.S. DEPARTMENT OF THE ARMY, A.G.O., DEPARTMENTAL RECORDS BRANCH, T.A.G.O. *Führer Directives . . . German Armed Forces, 1942–1945.*

U.S. NAVY DEPARTMENT, WASHINGTON, D.C. *Führer Conferences on Matters Dealing with the German Navy, 1942.*

———. *Führer Conferences on Matters Dealing with the German Navy, 1943.*

WILMOT, CHESTER. *The Struggle for Europe.* William Collins Sons & Co., London, 1952.

Zeitschriftendienst No. 8681, April 16, 1943.

Additional Sources Which Did Not Yield Verification

ALLEN, W. E. D., and MURATOFF, PAUL. *The Russian Campaigns of 1941–1943.* Penguin Books, 1944.

ANDERS, LT. GEN. WLADYSLAW. *An Army in Exile.* Macmillan & Co., Ltd., London, 1949.

BRADLEY, OMAR N. *A Soldier's Story.* Henry Holt & Co., Inc., New York, 1951.

BUCKLEY, CHRISTOPHER. *Norway, The Commandos, Dieppe;* Vol. 4 of *The Second World War, 1939–1945.* H.M.S.O., London, 1951.

BULLOCK, ALAN. *Hitler: A Study in Tyranny.* Odhams Press, Ltd., London, 1952.

CLIFFORD, ALEXANDER. *Three against Rommel.* George C. Harrap & Co., Ltd., London, 1943.

COLVIN, IAN. *Chief of Intelligence.* Victor Gollancz, Ltd., London, 1951.

CRAVEN, W. F., and CATE, J. L. (eds.). *Plans and Early Operations, January 1939 to August 1942;* Vol. 1 of *The Army Air Forces in World War II.* University of Chicago Press, Chicago, 1948.

———. *Europe: Torch to Pointblank, August 1942 to December 1943;* Vol. 2 of *The Army Air Forces in World War II.* University of Chicago Press, Chicago, 1949.

CUNNINGHAM, A. B. *A Sailor's Odyssey*. Hutchinson & Co., Ltd., London, 1951.

D'ARCY-DAWSON, JOHN. *European Victory*. MacDonald & Co., Ltd., London, n.d.

FRISCHAUER, WILLI. *Himmler: The Evil Genius of the Third Reich*. Odhams Press, Ltd., London, 1953.

GREINER, HELMUTH. *Die Oberste Wehrmachtführung, 1939–1943*. Limes Verlag, Wiesbaden, 1951.

HALDER, FRANZ. *Hitler als Feldherr*. Münchener Dom-Verlag, München, 1949.

HARRISON, GORDON A. *Cross-Channel Attack; United States Army in World War II: European Theater of Operations*. Office of the Chief of Military History, Department of the Army, Washington, 1951.

Hitler Minutes, Führerhauptquartier (Führer's Headquarters), Introduction and Fragment, Nos. 1a–5, 7–8, 11–50, September, 1942–April, 1945.

KING, ERNEST J., and WHITEHILL, WALTER MUIR. *Fleet Admiral King: A Naval Record*. W. W. Norton & Co., Inc., New York, 1952.

KLEIST, PETER. *Zwischen Hitler und Stalin, 1939–1945*. Athenäum-Verlag, Bonn, 1950.

LIDDELL HART, B. H. (ed.). *The Rommel Papers*. Harcourt, Brace & Co., Inc., New York, 1953.

LINKLATER, ERIC. *The Campaign in Italy;* Vol. 2 of *The Second World War, 1939–1945.* H.M.S.O., London, 1951.

MONTGOMERY, FIELD MARSHAL BERNARD LAW. *El Alamein to the River Sangro*. E. P. Dutton & Co., Inc., New York, 1949.

OVEN, WILFRED VON. *Mit Goebbels bis zum Ende,* Vols. I and II. Dürer-Verlag, Buenos Aires, 1949 and 1950.

PAGET, R. T. *Manstein: His Campaigns and His Trial*. William Collins Sons & Co., Ltd., London, 1951.

PATTON, GEORGE S., JR. *War As I Knew It*. Houghton Mifflin Co., Boston, 1947.

PICKER, DR. HENRY. *Hitlers Tischgespräche in Führerhauptquartier, 1941–42*. Athenaum-Verlag, Bonn, 1951.

SCHMIDT, DR. PAUL. *Hitler's Interpreter*. The Macmillan Co., New York, 1951.

SPEIDEL, LT. GEN. HANS. *We Defended Normandy* (trans. IAN COLVIN). Herbert Jenkins, Ltd., London, 1951.

WESTPHAL, GEN. SIEGFRIED. *The German Army in the West*. Cassell & Co., Ltd., London, 1952.

WILSON, FIELD MARSHAL HENRY MAITLAND. *Eight Years Overseas, 1939–1947.* Hutchinson & Co., Ltd., London, 1950.

Name Index

Name Index

The Library of Congress has catalogued this book as follows:

George, Alexander L

   Propaganda analysis; a study of inferences made from
Nazi propaganda in World War II. Evanston, Ill., Row,
Peterson [1959]

   287 p.   25 cm.

   1. Propaganda analysis. 2. World War, 1939–1945—Propaganda.
3. Propaganda, German.

HM263.G43   301.154   59–8462 ‡

Library of Congress

OTHER VOLUMES OF RAND RESEARCH

COLUMBIA UNIVERSITY PRESS, NEW YORK,
NEW YORK:

Soviet National Income and Product, 1940–48, by Abram Bergson
and Hans Heymann, Jr., 1954
Soviet National Income and Product in 1928, by Oleg Hoeffding,
1954
Labor Productivity in Soviet and American Industry, by Walter
Galenson, 1955

THE FREE PRESS, GLENCOE, ILLINOIS:

Psychosis and Civilization, by Herbert Goldhamer and Andrew
W. Marshall, 1949
Soviet Military Doctrine, by Raymond L. Garthoff, 1953
A Study of Bolshevism, by Nathan Leites, 1953
Ritual of Liquidation: The Case of the Moscow Trials, by Nathan
Leites and Elsa Bernaut, 1954
*Two Studies in Soviet Controls: Communism and the Russian
Peasant, and Moscow in Crisis,* by Herbert S. Dinerstein and
Leon Gouré, 1955
A Million Random Digits with 100,000 Normal Deviates, by The
RAND Corporation, 1955

HARVARD UNIVERSITY PRESS, CAMBRIDGE,
MASSACHUSETTS:

Smolensk Under Soviet Rule, by Merle Fainsod, 1958

McGRAW-HILL BOOK COMPANY, INC., NEW YORK,
NEW YORK:

The Operational Code of the Politburo, by Nathan Leites, 1951
*Air War and Emotional Stress: Psychological Studies of Bombing
and Civilian Defense,* by Irving L. Janis, 1951

Soviet Attitudes toward Authority: An Interdisciplinary Approach to Problems of Soviet Character, by Margaret Mead, 1951

Mobilizing Resources for War: The Economic Alternatives, by Tibor Scitovsky, Edward Shaw, and Lorie Tarshis, 1951

The Organizational Weapon: A Study of Bolshevik Strategy and Tactics, by Philip Selznick, 1952

Introduction to the Theory of Games, by J. C. C. McKinsey, 1952

Weight-Strength Analysis of Aircraft Structures, by F. R. Shanley, 1952

The Compleat Strategyst: Being a Primer on the Theory of Games of Strategy, by J. D. Williams, 1954

Linear Programming and Economic Analysis, by Robert Dorfman, Paul A. Samuelson, and Robert M. Solow, 1958

PRINCETON UNIVERSITY PRESS, PRINCETON, NEW JERSEY:

Approximations for Digital Computers, by Cecil Hastings, Jr., 1955

International Communication and Political Opinion: A Guide to the Literature, by Bruce Lannes Smith and Chitra M. Smith, 1956

Dynamic Programming, by Richard Bellman, 1957

The Berlin Blockade: A Study in Cold War Politics, by W. Phillips Davison, 1958

The French Economy and the State, by Warren C. Baum, 1958

PUBLIC AFFAIRS PRESS, WASHINGTON, D.C.:

The Rise of Khrushchev, by Myron Rush, 1958

Behind the Sputniks: A Survey of Soviet Space Science, by F. J. Krieger, 1958

ROW, PETERSON AND COMPANY, EVANSTON, ILLINOIS:

German Rearmament and Atomic War: The Views of German Military and Political Leaders, by Hans Speier, 1957

West German Leadership and Foreign Policy, edited by Hans Speier and W. Phillips Davison, 1957

The House without Windows: France Selects a President, by Constantin Melnik and Nathan Leites, 1958

STANFORD UNIVERSITY PRESS, STANFORD, CALIFORNIA:

Strategic Surrender: The Politics of Victory and Defeat, by Paul Kecskemeti, 1958

JOHN WILEY AND SONS, INC., NEW YORK, NEW YORK:

Efficiency in Government through Systems Analysis: With Emphasis on Water Resource Development, by Roland N. McKean, 1958

MAY 9 1990
SEP 19 1990

MAR 1 4 2001

OCT 2 6 2002